One Rule to Live By
BE GOOD

*An Unbelievable
True Story*

Orest Stocco

One Rule to Live By

Copyright © 2019 by Orest Stocco

All rights reserved. No part of this book may be reproduced or transmitted in any form or by any means without written permission of the author.

ISBN 978-1-926442-22-8

Edited by Penny Lynn Cates

Cover Design by Penny Lynn Cates

*I dedicate this book to Penny Lynn Cates,
without whom I would never have realized my life's mission;
thank you, my love.*

"He labors good on good to fix, and owes
To virtue every triumph that he knows."

Character of the Happy Warrior
William Wordsworth

A Note for the Reader

In his first book *Maps of Meaning: The Architecture of Belief*, Dr. Jordan B. Peterson, University of Toronto Professor of Psychology and Clinical Psychologist, defines a paradigm as "a complete cognitive tool, whose use presupposes acceptance of a limited number of axioms (*or definitions of what constitutes reality, for the purpose of argument and action*), whose interactions produce an internally consistent explanatory and predictive structure. Paradigmatic thinking," he continues, "might be described as thinking whose domain has been formally limited; thinking that acts "as if" some questions have been answered in the final manner," which, in simple terms, means that **we are only as free as our beliefs allow us to be; and to grow in personal and cultural freedom, we have to expand the paradigm of our belief systems.**

In his second book *12 Rules for Life: An Antidote to Chaos*, which has become a global bestseller slated to be translated into fifty languages, professor Peterson introduces the world to a responsible way of living that defines a paradigm of cognitive thinking that brings direction and purpose to one's life, especially to the younger generation that seems to have lost its way in this postmodern world of moral relativism, nihilism and confusion; but then what?

"Vanity of vanities, sayeth the Preacher, vanity of vanities, all is vanity. What profit hath a man of all his labor which he taketh under the sun?" we are told in *Ecclesiastes*; and after all is said and done (no one knows how the Preacher came upon his wisdom), he came to this resolution: *"...of making many books there is no end; and much study is a weariness of the flesh. Let us hear the conclusion of the whole matter: Fear God, and keep his commandments: for this is the whole duty of man. For God shall bring every work into judgment, with every secret thing, whether it be good, or whether it be evil,"* which is the imperative of professor Peterson's message; but still, why?

He cannot tell us what profit we have of all our labor; the most that he can tell us is that we can find some measure of meaning and purpose by taking responsibility for our life, both moral and practical (*Rule 8: Tell the truth—or, at least, don't lie*, is his favorite rule), which goes a long way to satisfying the longing in our soul for wholeness and completeness. But, yet again; where does one go from here? Or, to put it in the words of his critics, "What lies at the top of the mountain?" Peterson tells us how to get there, but not why.

And this—*pardon the presumption*—is why I was called by my oracle to write *One Rule to Live By: Be Good*, to bring the imperative of professor Peterson's message to happy resolution, and to answer the Preacher's terrifying question.

Orest Stocco
Georgian Bay, Ontario
February 14, 2019

Table of Contents

1. Ask the Question, and the Answer Will Come 1
2. The Imponderable Myth of My Life 12
3. Why Rules to Live By, Anyway? 25
4. The Horror of Human Suffering 31
5. The Self that Isn't a Self 41
6. The Paradox of Our Shadow Self 50
7. The Mystery of Personal Identity 58
8. The Unbearable Anguish of Being Called 70
9. The View from Where I Am 80
10. The Jordan Peterson Phenomenon 89
11. On the Effect of Jordan Peterson's Message 101
12. The Mystique of Jordan B. Peterson 110
13. There Are No Right or Wrong Paths in Life 117
14. The Existential Conundrum 128
15. The Sacred Individual 135
16. Live Your Own Path and be Cool 144
17. Outside the Box, or Cloud-cuckoo-land? 150
18. The Crossroad of Jordan Peterson's Life 160
19. All Paths Lead to the Sacred Self 168
20. The Dilemma of Evolution 174
21. Expanding the Existential Paradigm 180
22. The Hope of Jordan Peterson's Message 185

23. The Curse of Our Modern World 192
24. If J. Peterson is Dangerous, God Help Us! 200
25. Integrating the Sacred Back into Society 208
26. A New Paradigm for Our Crazy World 215
27. Jordan Peterson's Most Important Rule 222
28. Jordan Peterson and the Authentic Life.....................................229
29. No Ordinary Psychologist 235
30. A Little Corner of Joyful Plenitude 244
31. Nietzsche, Dostoevsky, and Solzhenitsyn 251
32. Dr. Peterson's Jungian Gift to the World..................................261
33. Message from the Woodpecker 271
34. Taking a Hiatus from Writing this Summer 285
35. The Great Choreographer of Life 290
36. The Brilliance of Friedrich Nietzsche 302
37. The Call to the Inner Life 311
38. My Mandala, My Mandate 319
39. Not a Prophet or Reformer, Just a Writer 329
40. My Call to the Final Surrender 343

1. Ask the Question, and the Answer Will Come

I finished writing my book of poetry last year, *Not My Circus, Not My Monkeys*, which I published on Lulu first and is now available on Amazon, and I introduced my collection of *"100 poems for today's crazy world"* with the following *daemonically* inspired poem:

What the Hell
Is Going on Out There?

Hierophants of the world,
what the hell is going on out there?
Your antennae are out of whack,
and all you report is madness,
madness, and more madness, or
am I too blind to see?

Hierophants of the world,
tell me the truth, has the world
gone mad or is this some new sanity
beyond my ability to process
and understand?

Hierophants of the world,
I've lost all faith in religion, science,
and politics, but not in the better nature
of my fellow man, so please tell me,
what the hell is going on out there?

My poem came to me unbidden and word perfect, but I wasn't angry at the world when I wrote it; I was angry at myself for my inability to process and understand what the hell was going on out there. But the Universe heard my plea, and time went by...

Little did I expect however that the answer would offer itself in the better nature of a fellow countryman, a budding hierophant that I saw coming three years before he stepped onto the world stage with his overnight bestseller *12 Rules for Life: An Antidote to Chaos*, a transplanted western boy from small-town Alberta by the name of Jordan B. Peterson, a clinical psychologist and U of T professor of psychology who began posting his lectures online five years before where I "chanced" upon him while doing research for a book I was working on, which, strangely enough, was titled *A Sign of Things to Come;* but because I don't believe in chance, I put the word in quotations. It was just my oracle speaking to me, as it always does whenever I'm called to write a new book.

    I watched one of professor Peterson's lectures on C. G. Jung *(Jung: Personality and its Transformations),* and he made such a strong impression upon me that over the next few days I watched half a dozen or more of his lectures; that's when I *knew that he was going to make his mark on the world one day— because I heard life calling him to his destiny!*

    In fact, I was so moved by his passion, intelligence and authenticity that I sent him copies of my own books to read, *The Lion that Swallowed Hemingway* and *The Pearl of Great Price*, because I *knew* that his own remarkable journey to "wholeness and singleness of self," as Carl Jung described the goal of the individuation process, was leading him to the mysteries of the **secret way** just as Jung's own journey had led him, as he tells us in his commentary to Richard Wilhelm's translation of the ancient Taoist text, *The Secret of the Golden Flower*:

    "I was completely ignorant of Chinese philosophy, and only later did my professional experience show me that in my technique I had been unconsciously led along the **secret way** which has been the preoccupation of the best minds in the East for Centuries" (*The Secret of the Golden Flower,* Richard Wilhelm translation, p. 86).

    Like Jung, I also found the **secret way**; and my heart went out to professor Peterson. That's why I sent him my books to read, in the hope that he might glean some insights from my own journey of self-discovery that would lead him to the **secret way** also.

That was three years ago. Last year I was working on a new spiritual musing *(this is a personal genre that I created; a platypus blend of journaling, free-flow thinking, and Socratic reasoning)*, which I normally post online on my Spiritual Musings blog before publishing them in book form, but I hit a blank wall and did not know how to bring my spiritual musing to closure.

Though I'm always surprised when it happens, whenever I hit a wall in my writing *the merciful law of divine synchronicity* kicks in and offers me a way out of my predicament; that's why I was strongly "nudged" to watch professor Peterson's lectures on C. G. Jung again, and something Peterson said was exactly what I needed to bring my spiritual musing to resolution, and it behooves me to quote it here to illustrate how the **secret way** works in my life:

The Purpose of Art is Art's Purpose

> "The truth must dazzle gradually
> Or every man be blind—"
> —*Emily Dickinson*

I don't know why I was called to write this spiritual musing, but while working on another book this morning (*A Sign of Things to Come*) I wrote something that jumped out at me like a news bulletin from tomorrow, a hierophantic insight that was a remarkable confirmation of the theme of my new book on a sign of things to come but which called out to be explored in today's spiritual musing, an insight that falls squarely into that dreaded category of dangerous spiritual musings that always scare me.

A dangerous spiritual musing can hit so close to home that it can nick the sacred bone of my life and come back to play nasty with me; but that, essentially, is the theme of today's spiritual musing— daring to take the risk and cross the line into the unknown territory of the creative unconscious where the objective will of the creative principle of life and the subjective will of the author become one willful purpose, which brings to mind those famous words by the celebrated poet of *The Wasteland*: "We shall not cease from exploration /And the end of all our exploring /Will be to arrive where we started."

From the earliest age, I wanted to be a writer like my high school hero and literary mentor Ernest Hemingway; but in grade twelve I read Somerset Maugham's novel *The Razor's Edge* and was called to become a seeker like Maugham's intrepid hero Larry Darrell, and I spent many years exploring the sacred teachings of the world to find an answer to the haunting question of my life, *who am I?*

Happily, I found the answer to my question, and my explorations brought me right back to where I started, which was my desire to become a writer; and I wrote indefatigably to make up for all the years I had spent looking for my true self. And the more I wrote, the more I learned about the art of creative writing, until one day I discovered the secret that all great writers eventually find, like the inscrutable poet Emily Dickinson, and that's the dangerous subject of today's spiritual musing—

Tell all the truth but tell it slant,
Success in circuit lies,
Too bright for our infirm delight
The truth's superb surprise;

As lightning to the children eased
With explanation kind,
The truth must dazzle gradually
Or every man be blind.

My life partner Penny Lynn Cates joins me in my writing room for coffee every morning, and we talk about our dreams and other things, and always about the book she brings in with her to read. It's surprising how quickly she can read a book in such a short time each morning before going to work for the day, like *The Selected*

One Rule to Live By

Stories of Mavis Gallant, 887 pages long; Alice Munro's *The Love of a Good Woman*; and the book she's currently reading, John Updike's *Pigeon Feathers and Other Stories,* and we talk about her impressions of the stories and the authors.

That's how I gauge the quality of the books she reads, because I trust Penny Lynn's judgment implicitly; and her impressions of John Updike's writing confirmed professor Harold Bloom's indictment that John Updike was "a minor novelist with a major style, hovering always near a greatness he is too shrewd or diffident to risk." Penny loved Mavis Gallant, and even more Alice Munro's stories; but John Updike she could take or leave, because his stories, though masterfully crafted and brilliantly written, did not leave a lasting impression. "They fade away as soon as I read them. It's like he never gets to the soul of his story," Penny said to me, and I had to wonder why, because as much as I loved John Updike for his brilliant style and uncanny mastery of *le mot juste,* his stories faded away on me also, unlike Hemingway's stories which always left a lasting impression; but when I was given the insight for today's spiritual musing, I knew why—which is why I felt compelled to explore it in today's musing; and so, once again into the breach...

Creative writing is a mystical experience. Norman Mailer called it "spooky," but he didn't' know why, and neither does any other writer that I'm aware of (except perhaps Emily Dickinson); but I resolved this mystery in my spiritual musings, because writing my musings brought to the fore the mystical element of creative writing, which proved to be *the intelligent guiding principle of life* that guides our creative unconscious but which has also been called "God within" by Emerson and "Spirit" by Wordsworth and other poets; and herein lies the danger of today's spiritual musing, because it dares to bring God into the dynamic of the creative writing process which will be sure to raise a few eyebrows, literary and otherwise.

Without mincing words, then; I've come to see that **'the generous Spirit that makes the path before us always bright'** as Wordsworth tells us in his poem *Character of the Happy Warrior,* which I made the ideal of my life, is the Logos, the *élan vital* of life, and writers have the gift of tapping into the creative force of life with their writing. And herein lies the dilemma of the creative writer's art, because tapping into the creative force of life incurs an inexplicable moral responsibility that can intimidate the most gifted writer, as it seems to have done the prodigiously talented John Updike.

Literary critic and Sterling Professor of the Humanities at Yale University, professor Harold Bloom felt that John Updike was too shrewd or diffident to risk the greatness of his art, but he never explained why, which is what I feel I was called upon to explore in today's spiritual musing; but to do so, I have to explain that the writer who does not work in willful harmony with *the intelligent guiding principle of life* will impede the flow of the creative Logos and damage the integrity of his art—like the novelist who controls his characters instead of letting his creative unconscious give them a life of their own so they can bring to light the archetypal truth of their story. "Art is the truth above the facts of life," said the author of *Out of Africa* Karen Blixen, which our own Nobel Laureate Alice Munroe brought much closer to home with aphoristic genius in her comment, "Memoir is the facts of life. Fiction is the truth of life."

I quote these eminent writers to make the point that **the inherent purpose of art is to explore the truth of life.** That's why Hemingway began every story that he wrote with the truest sentence that he knew, upon which he built the rest of his story to satisfy his literary credo to "tell it the way it was." But that's not the whole secret of Hemingway's art, because being true to "the way it was" does not always satisfy the creative process, as Hemingway learned when he experimented with his novel *The Green Hills of Africa,* a strait biographical account of his African safari with his second wife Pauline Pfeiffer which proved to be an artistic failure that taught Hemingway the lesson of his life that every great writer must learn: **it takes the miraculous power of imagination to lift one's writing to the lofty heights of art**.

Hemingway revealed his "secret" in his memoir *A Moveable Feast,* the final book of his life that he was working on just before taking his own life with his favorite shotgun at his home in Ketchum, Idaho: "I was learning something from the paintings of Cezanne that made writing simple sentences far from enough to make the stories have the dimension that I was trying to put into them. I was learning very much from him, but I was not articulate enough to explain it to anyone. Besides it was a secret."

That "secret" made Hemingway a great writer. After licking his wounds for the artistic failure of *The Green Hills of Africa*, the resourceful writer used the same African safari experience to write two of his best short stories, "The Short Happy Life of Francis Macomber," and my favorite Hemingway story "The Snows of Kilimanjaro," which proved to Hemingway that the miraculous power of imagination was necessary to make art, thereby confirming what Adrienne Rich said about creative writing: **"Poetry is an act of the imagination that transforms reality into a deeper perception of what is."** Hemingway gave his African safari experience to the guiding principle of his creative unconscious, and the deeper perception of his experience was revealed in his two remarkable stories that bared the wretched soul of his protagonists.

That's how art is made. But as much as I understood how art is made, I could not quite give my understanding of the secret of art the clarity it deserved; and then synchronicity kicked in to assist me, which was proof yet again of *the intelligent guiding principle of life* that I had learned to trust implicitly…

I started writing this spiritual musing yesterday morning, but I had to stop because I could not take it any further; it needed "something" to bring it to resolution, and as serendipity would have it, this "something" came to me when I was nudged later in the evening to go on YouTube and watch professor Jordan Peterson's lectures on Jung again, and something the professor said about art jumped out at me, because it was *exactly* what I needed to bring resolution to my spiritual musing.

As he gave a Jungian interpretation of the movie *The Lion King* to his students, professor Peterson inadvertently revealed that certain "something" about the creative process that I needed to bring resolution to my spiritual musing. **"Art cannot be designed for a purpose. The purpose of art is art's purpose,"** he said, which is the secret of all great writing that I intuited to be *the intelligent guiding principle of life.*

Ironically, this is the mystical nature of the creative process that has been called spooky by Norman Mailer (and other writers, like Martin Amis), because no one understands how it works. But the psychologist Carl Jung intuited this secret in his essay "Psychology and Literature" in his book *Modern Man in Search of a Soul*: "**The artist is not a person endowed with free will who seeks his own ends, but one who will allow art to realize its purpose through him.** As a human being he may have moods and a will and personal aims, but as an artist he is a 'man' in a higher sense—he is 'collective man'—one who carries and shapes the unconscious, psychic life of mankind" (*Modern Man in Search of Soul*, C. G. Jung, p. 169; bold italics mine).

Which implies that the creative process is *the intelligent guiding principle of life* that brings the truth of life into existence through the medium of the artist but which, as Hemingway and all great artists come to learn, can only be done when the artist engages the transcendent function of his imagination and transforms the reality of his experience into a deeper perception of that experience, as Hemingway did with his African safari experience when he wrote his two famous short stories, "The Short Happy Life of Francis Macomber" and "The Snows of Kilimanjaro."

Being aware of the mystical nature of the creative process, I engaged my own imagination to transform one of the most private experiences of my own life: *I flipped a coin to make up my mind for me*. I did this for six months with every major decision of my life for the experimental purpose of "letting go and letting God." I did this to learn to trust my gut instincts, which proved to be very effective; and twenty years later I gave this experience to my creative unconscious to work into a story, and with the power of my imagination I transformed my experience of "letting go and letting God" into a deeper perception of my experience, and the truth of my experience became my novel *The Golden Seed*; so, I know how this mystical process works. But what does it mean to say that the purpose of art is art's purpose? *What is art's purpose?*

I could explore this until the end of time, but the short answer is that **art's purpose is to bring to light the archetypal truth of man's existence;** and when an artist imposes his will upon the will of the intelligent guiding principle of the creative process he impedes the archetypal truth that the Logos seeks to bring to light; and this separates the great artist from all the rest, regardless how gifted an artist may be, like John Updike who hovered near a greatness that he was too shrewd or diffident to risk.

Which means, if the logic of art holds true as I believe it does, that the greater the truth the intelligent guiding principle of the creative process seeks to bring to light, the greater the risk the artist will have to take; and, as the history of art tells us, only the very few dare to risk their all for the greater truth of their art, as Ernest Hemingway did when he bared his wretched soul in "The Short Happy Life of Francis Macomber" and "The Snows of Kilimanjaro," and as Emily Dickinson did in her poetry that continues to haunt the world with the ineffable mystique of her "secret."

I continued watching professor Peterson's lectures with growing fascination, because he was answering my poem's angry question and satisfying my need to know what the hell was going on out there; and then the good professor was pushed to the edge by the pernicious forces of identity politics and radical political correctness gone loony, and he took a courageous stand for free speech by refuting an amendment to the Canadian Human Rights Act in Bill C-16

After carefully parsing the legislation, Citizen Peterson did not view Bill C-16 as an egalitarian coda that would merely expand the list of prohibited grounds of discrimination to include gender identity and gender expression. In his view, being forced to use "preferred pronouns" amounted to "compelled speech," and he flat out refused to use invented pronouns under government fiat; and he made several videos explaining his position and posted them on You Tube, and they went viral and catapulted him onto the world stage. And then he published *12 Rules for Life; An Antidote to Chaos,* his well-reasoned response to the nefarious forces of postmodern nihilism, identity politics, and political correctness gone loony, and that launched him onto the global stage; and to everyone's surprise, including himself, he became the heroic hierophant that the world was calling for.

More time passed; and then I read an interview of Jordan Peterson by Christie Blatchford in the *National Post (January 20, 2018)*, and I was once again strongly "nudged" to send him a copy of *My Writing Life*, the sequel to my literary memoir *The Lion that Swallowed Hemingway* that I had sent him three years earlier when I *heard* life calling him to his destiny, plus a copy of my twin soul book *The Merciful Law of Divine Synchronicity* (twin soul to my book *Death, the Final Frontier*), which I deeply "felt" would help to satisfy the good professor's Jungian longing for the guiding principle of the **secret way**—a terrible presumption, I know; but, like my hero Socrates, I always listened to my oracle, and I sent the following personal note along with my two books:

> Professor Peterson. Pardon my presumption. Please accept a courtesy copy of *My Writing Life*, a sequel to *The Lion that Swallowed Hemingway* that I was nudged to send you three years ago, and a copy of my twin soul book *The Merciful Law of Divine Synchronicity* which may excite your interest, given your passion and admiration for C. G. Jung.
>
> Once again, I was nudged to send you these books upon reading your interview with Christie Blatchford in the *National Post (Saturday, January 20, 2018)*, after reading Conrad Black's column first, of course (I just love that man's metanoic change of heart after his public humiliation and prison sentence), and I read the excerpt of your new book *12 Rules for Life: An Antidote to Chaos* as well, because the thought occurred to me that being as Jungian as you seem to be you might be intrigued by someone who actually experienced what Jung called "wholeness and singleness of self," it being that rare fruit of the individuation process. Incredible as it may seem, this was my experience; and I was nudged to send you these books to give you a literary insight into the life of an individual who actually satisfied the longing of his soul for wholeness and completeness.
>
> Again, pardon my presumption. But if you can find the time in your busy life to read them, I'm sure you'll understand my reason for sending them; and I hope they give you inspiration for your own courageous individuation process.

Respectfully,
Orest Stocco

One Rule to Live By

More time passed; and on *March 17, 2018* I read a three page feature article in the *Toronto Star* headlined, "Who's Afraid of Jordan Peterson," by the insightful Vinay Menon, and so moved was I by the good professor who had thrust his articulate sword into the heart of the nefarious beast of postmodern nihilism and its odious offspring political correctness with his Amazon bestseller *12 Rules for Life: An Antidote to Chao* and sold-out public talks which drew thousands of young people hungering for the Logos and all the interviews that he gave across North America, Europe, and Australia that I heard a call from my muse (*much louder than most calls*) to write a book that would cut to the quick on the natural process of individuation and help resolve soul's longing for wholeness and completeness, and the title that came to me by providential decree was: *One Rule to Live By: Be Good;* and being a servant of my muse, I went to my computer and began writing this story...

2. The Imponderable Myth of My Life

Of course, I ordered *12 Rules for Life: An Antidote to Chaos* from Amazon (and several books on Alzheimer's for research I'm doing for a novel I'm working on modeled on my relationship with one of my readers who fears getting Alzheimer's like her mother, a novel called *Sundays with Sharon* inspired by Mitch Albom's *Tuesdays with Morrie),* and I also put Peterson's *Maps of Meaning* on my Amazon wish list because I have to read it to fully appreciate the brilliant hierophant who's answering the angry question of my poem; and when Peterson's *12 Rules* came in, I immediately read the Forward by Dr. Norman Doidge, MD, author of *The Brain that Changes Itself* (whom, curiously enough, I had quoted in my book *The Merciful Law of Divine Synchronicity*), as well as the first chapter, *"Rule 1: Stand Up Straight with Your Shoulders Back,"* and this gave me the entry I needed to work my way into *One Rule to Live By: Be Good;* and I couldn't wait to finish *12 Rules for Life*.

In the meantime, I kept watching the good professor on YouTube, because the more I listened to what he had to say, the more he satisfied my need to know what the hell was going on out there, and his interview with philosophy professor Stephen Hicks (*Postmodernism: History and Diagnosis)* brought to mind my spiritual musing *"BEWEL 262,"* a personal experience of how *the omniscient guiding principle of life* brings one's outer and inner life into alignment (or, as professor Peterson would say, restores order out of chaos), and I *knew* that my oracle wanted me to tell the story of the imponderable myth of my life to lay the biographical foundation for *One Rule to Live By: Be Good,* which is the only rule that one needs when one has evolved far enough to take evolution into their own hands to complete what Nature cannot finish and realize wholeness and singleness of self.

One Rule to Live By

"Man must complete what Nature cannot finish," said the old alchemists, which spoke to Jung's psychology of individuation that he drew from ancient Alchemist and Gnostic texts and his own life experience as a pioneering psychoanalyst who saw up to eight clients a day most of his life and who analyzed over eighty thousand dreams in the course of his life; but that's what brought Gurdjieff's teaching into my life, because he also said that Nature can only evolve man so far and no further, and to complete what Nature cannot finish man must take evolution into his own hands to realize his true nature, which is why Gurdjieff called his teaching "work on oneself." This is why I was called to write *One Rule to Live By: Be Good*, to illustrate with the imponderable myth of my life the three stages of soul's evolution through life, with biographical emphasis upon the third and final stage of evolution where I found professor Jordan B. Peterson chomping at the bit to enter:

BEWEL 262

"Watch the synchronicities, the coincidences,
because they will bring you goodness."

Padre Pio, from my novel
HEALING WITH PADRE PIO

When I left my philosophy studies at university in my third year, I left for one reason only: philosophy was casting me adrift into a sea of endless speculation, and I had to get back to *"terra firma"* or risk drowning; so I made a vow to build my life upon the truth of my own experiences and not on what other people thought, however brilliant and sophisticated, and year by year my worldview grew out of the gnostic truth of my daily life; that's how I came to believe that our life is choreographed by an *omniscient guiding principle*. I didn't want to believe it, but it was forced upon me by my own daily life experiences.

True, we have free will, and we choose the life we live; but as free as we may be, our life is still choreographed by an unseen agency. It took most of my life to work my way through the dilemma of this conundrum, but I caught my first glimpse of this paradox in my teens when I read *Hymn to Zeus,* by the Stoic philosopher/poet Cleanthes:

> Lead me, Zeus, and you too, Destiny,
> To wherever your decrees have assigned me.
> I follow readily, but if I choose not,
> Wretched though I am, I must follow still.
> Fate guides the willing, but drags the unwilling.

This is the paradox, then: **we are free to live our destiny, or be dragged by it**. But how can we be sure that we even have a destiny, let alone be free to live or be dragged by it? This is the subject of today's spiritual musing…

I've explored this question in my novel *Healing with Padre Pio,* so I need not elaborate here; but I do have to explain how I came to my belief that we are all destined for a purpose, which the poet John Keats caught a glimpse of in a letter to his brother that he titled "The Vale of Soul Making."
"There may be intelligences or sparks of divinity in millions, but they are not Souls till they acquire identities, till each one is personally itself," he wrote in his letter; and then with poetic genius, he answers his own question and solves the riddle of our destined purpose*: "How then are these sparks which are God to have identity given them? How but by the medium of a world like this?"* Which is why Carl Jung said in *The Red Book*, the chronicle of his quest for his lost soul: **"This life is the way, the long sought-after way to the unfathomable, which we call divine. There is no other way, all other ways are false paths."** In short, our own life is the way to our true self. Just as Padre Pio said to me: "Life is a journey of the self."
The gifted Romantic poet and prescient Swiss psychoanalyst came to the same conclusion, that we are all sparks of divine consciousness destined to realize our own identity through life; and whether we like it or not, like the acorn seed that has to become an oak tree, so too are we destined to become what we are meant to be.

One Rule to Live By

But this was John Keats's truth, and Carl Jung's; how in the world did it become mine?

As one would expect, it's a long and very complicated story, which I worked out in my novel *Cathedral of my Past Lives* first and then in *The Summoning of Noman*; but for brevity's sake, let me just say that this truth came to me by way of an incredible personal experience when *the merciful law of divine synchronicity* introduced me to a past-life regressionist in Orillia, not too far from our new home in Georgian Bay, who unexpectedly brought me back to the Body of God where all souls come from, and which became the inspiration for *Cathedral of My Past Lives* that was based upon my seven past-life regressions.

It was my fourth past-life regression, and to my astonishment I was brought back to the Body of God where all souls come from; but what shocked me was that I did not have reflective self-consciousness. I was an un-self-realized atom of God in an unfathomable sea of embryonic souls that constituted the un-self-realized nature of God, and in the same regression I was sent to Earth to acquire my own identity for the purpose of individuating the consciousness of God through the evolution of my *essential* nature.

There I was, in my first primordial human lifetime, the alpha male of a group of ten or twelve cave-dwelling early hominids, and I *actually* experienced the dawning of my own reflective self-consciousness—the birth of a new "I" of God, if you will; and from that moment on, I was separated from the un-self-consciousness of life and initiated into the divine mystery of my pre-destined purpose, which was to realize my *essential* nature through the natural evolution of my newborn reflective self-consciousness—*"a bliss peculiar to each one by individual existence,"* as John Keats presciently expressed it in his letter "The Vale of Soul Making."

Now that I had given birth to my own dawning sense of reflective self-consciousness, I became the author of my personal karmic destiny which was initiated by my newborn self-conscious will, however rudimentary; and from lifetime to lifetime, I grew and evolved through the natural process of karmic individuation until I was conscious enough in self-reflection to realize that there had to be more to life than what I experienced with my five senses; and I became a seeker of life's purpose and meaning.

In one of my regressions, I was brought back to ancient Greece where I began my quest for my true self as a student of Pythagoras, who taught the **secret way**; and in another regression, I was brought back to my Sufi lifetime in ancient Persia, where I tried again to achieve my destined purpose of realizing my true identity (what Jung called "wholeness and singleness of self" and Jesus called our "eternal life"), but I failed miserably by going out of my mind trying to live the ascetic teachings of a secret Sufi sect called The Order of the White Tiger, and I had to live a few more lifetimes before I had evolved enough to take up the **secret way** again, which I did in my current lifetime with Gurdjieff's teaching of "work on oneself." And this brings me to the point of today's spiritual musing—the paradox of free will and our destined purpose.

However questionable it may be *(and there will certainly be those who will question my sanity),* through personal experience I came to see that we all come from God as un-self-realized souls divinely encoded to become fully self-realized souls through natural evolution, and from the moment we give birth to a new "I" of God we become the author of our own karmic destiny and grow and evolve through karma and reincarnation until we have evolved enough to take evolution into our own hands and complete what Nature cannot finish; only then can we fulfill our destined purpose and realize wholeness and completeness.

But it took years of living the **secret way** to reconcile my personal karmic destiny with my encoded spiritual purpose, which I could not have done without divine guidance; hence the belief that was forced upon me by all the perfectly timed coincidences throughout my life that our life is choreographed by a divine imperative that I came to call *the omniscient guiding principle of life*, like the way I was introduced to the **secret way** with Gurdjieff's transformative teaching of "work on oneself."

In my second year at university, I asked a fellow philosophy student who was going home to Toronto for the Christmas break to bring me back a book *of his own choosing* from his favorite little book store, and for reasons which he could not explain, he brought me a book that he felt I had to read. The book meant nothing to him, but it changed the course of my life. It was *In Search of the Miraculous*, by P. D. Ouspensky, who was a student of the enigmatic mystic/philosopher George Ivanovich Gurdjieff.

I've written about my relationship with Gurdjieff's teaching in my books *Gurdjieff Was Wrong, But His Teaching Works* and *The Lion that Swallowed Hemingway*, so I needn't bother here; suffice to say that I have experienced the guiding principle of life many times in my quest for my true self *(though I often didn't recognize it until many years later)*, and to confirm my conviction that our life is choreographed by divine agency, I'd like to share the latest miracle in today's spiritual musing, the astonishing little saga of how we came to purchase our new 2015 Honda Civic LX; but before I do, let me explain what I mean by the **secret way** in light of my own incredible journey of self-discovery…

Only now, late in my life, have I come to see how "Old Whore Life" (my metaphor for the shadow side of karma that I explored in my second volume of spiritual musings, *Old Whore Life: Exploring the Shadow Side of Karma*) continues to seduce the world with exclusive claims to spiritual teachings that lull believers into mental stupors that inhibit their divinely encoded purpose of waking up to their true self, and I know this from personal experience because I was seduced by more than one of these teachings, starting in my youth with my Roman Catholic faith which contends that our soul is created at the moment of human conception, that we only live one lifetime, and that Jesus died on the cross to save us from eternal damnation; and then with Gurdjieff's colossal misperception that not everyone is born with an immortal soul but can create one if they know how, which Gurdjieff did; and with the Buddhist teaching, which contends that we do not have an individual and autonomous self; and with an offshoot Christian solar cult teaching that claimed secret knowledge of how to nourish our soul with rays from the sun believed to be imbued with the sacred energy of the Logos but which did irreparable damage to my eyesight; and finally, with a teaching that I lived for more than thirty years which claims to be "the most direct path to God" by virtue of what it proudly calls the "Mahanta," the Inner and Outer Master of this fabricated teaching that the original founder purloined from ancient spiritual traditions and marketed to the modern world as the New Age Religion of the Light and Sound of God. Difficult if not impossible to believe, but true; and I have the scars to prove it.

In their own ironic way though, all of these teachings are true insomuch that life is an *enantiodromiac* process of evolution through the natural individuation of *being* and *non-being* (our inner and outer self), and every teaching will over time give birth to its own opposite, just as sure as the day becomes night as the light begins to fade away; but that's far too abstruse for today's spiritual musing. Suffice to say that it took a long time for me to see that there is only one way to our true self, and that way is inherent to all paths in life, as Carl Jung came to realize in *The Red Book*; and I hope to illustrate the omniscient guiding principle of the **secret way** with the dramatic little saga of how we came to purchase our new 2015 Honda Civic LX.

But how the guiding principle of the **secret way** led us to our purchase cannot be appreciated without explaining the divine logic of *the omniscient guiding principle of life*, which I would never have been able to grasp without the unbelievable experience of my seven past-life regressions.

I explained this in my essay "On the Evolutionary Impulse to Individuate" in my third volume of spiritual musings, *Stupidity Is Not a Gift of God;* so, suffice to say that the Logos, the creative force of life that nurtures, sustains, and guides souls back to God, *is* the **secret way** that I came to call *the omniscient guiding principle of life,* and its divine imperative is to resolve the paradox of our personal karmic destiny and our encoded spiritual purpose so we can continue on our journey to wholeness and completeness. And one way that the **secret way** speaks to us is with remarkable coincidences, like the kind Robert. H. Hopcke explored in *There Are No Accidents, Synchronicity and the Stories of Our Lives.* "Our lives have a narrative structure, like that of novels," says Hopcke, "and at those moments we call synchronistic this structure is brought to our awareness in a way that has a significant impact upon our lives."

Whether we are conscious of it or not, the choices we make in life create karma that has to be resolved; and whether we resolve it in our current lifetime or a future life does not matter—it *has* to be resolved, because it is an immutable law of life. This is our personal karmic destiny that we forge with every choice we make; but our karmic destiny can only evolve us so far through the natural process of evolution, which is why *the merciful law of divine synchronicity* has to kick in to bring our karmic destiny back into alignment with our divinely encoded purpose to wholeness and completeness.

This is where the **secret way** comes into play to assist us on our journey to our true self, like it did in marine zoologist David Whyte's life when he was called by the omniscient guiding principle of life to take up the path of writing poetry to realize his own identity, which he explored in his memoir *Crossing the Unknown Sea: Work as a Pilgrimage of Identity,* and which I also wrote about in my own memoir *Do We Have an Immortal Soul?* And more dramatic still, how it came into play in the incomparable jazz musician Herbie Hancock's life while playing with the legendary Miles Davis.

When experienced, the redemptive grace that synchronicity bestows upon one's life can change the course of one's karmic destiny, and young Herbie Hancock had gone as far as his karmic destiny could take him on his musical journey through life, and providence mercifully intervened with one of the most remarkable quirks of fate that one could ever experience on one's journey to wholeness and completeness—*a wrong chord that transformed young Herbie Hancock's musical career!*

Herbie Hancock was in his early twenties, on stage playing the piano with the Miles Davis Quintet in a concert hall in Stockholm, Sweden in the mid-1960s, and "the band is tight—we're all in sync," he writes in his autobiography *Possibilities,* and they were playing one of Miles's classics, "So What?" Herbie continues: "Miles starts playing, building up to his solo, and just as he's about to really let loose, he takes a breath. And right then I play a chord that is just *so* wrong. *I don't even know where it came from*—it's the wrong chord, in the wrong place, and now it's hanging out there like a piece of rotten fruit."

And many years later, the seasoned Herbie Hancock reveals in his autobiography how Miles Davis, who was himself an initiate of the **secret way** through music, took that "rotten piece of fruit" and built on it with the creative genius of his talent: "Miles pauses for a fraction of a second, and then he plays some notes that somehow, miraculously, make my chord sound right. In that moment, I believe my mouth actually fell open. What kind of alchemy was this? And then Miles just took off from there, unleashing a solo that took the song in a new direction. The crowd went absolutely crazy."

It took Herbie Hancock many years to understand what happened that moment onstage, which illustrates the spiritual alchemy of the **secret way**. In his mind, the young musician judged his chord to be wrong; but Miles Davis never judged it— "he just heard it as a sound that had happened, and he instantly took it on as a challenge, a question of *How can I integrate that chord into everything else we're doing?* And because he didn't judge it, he was able to run with it, and turn it into something amazing. Miles trusted the band, and he trusted himself, and he always encouraged us to do the same. This was one of the many lessons I learned from Miles."

This is how an initiate of the **secret way** mentored a young musician to initiate himself into the mysterious alchemy of music so he could continue on his own path to his true self, not as dramatic as what happened to the legendary bassist Victor L. Wooten, who tells the story of his own initiation into the **secret way** in his book *The Music Lesson: A Spiritual Search for Growth Through Music*; but Herbie Hancock's story speaks to the synchronous power of goodness that came from a "wrong" note that shifted his personal paradigm and initiated him into the **secret way** that woke him up to his own path so he could fulfill his life through music; and this leaves me with one final point to clear up, and then I can relate the story of how we came to purchase our 2015 Honda Civic LX and bring my spiritual musing to resolution…

I've gone to great lengths to show that our own life *is* the way to our true self, and whatever religion, teaching, or career path that we embrace can be a gateway to the **secret way**; but what I didn't make clear is that it's in *how* we live our life that initiates us into the **secret way**.

This is what Gurdjieff taught me how to do. By "working" on myself with his transformative teaching of *conscious effort* and

One Rule to Live By

*intentional suffering (*and *non-identifying* and *self-remembering)*, I learned *how* to live my life and wake up to the **secret way** that is inherent to all ways in life; which is how I came to see that our own life is the way to what we are destined to be, our true self whole and complete.

Herbie Hancock's life was music, and Miles Davis taught him how to *live* his life as a musician to fulfill his life and destined purpose; that's how Herbie Hancock initiated himself into the **secret way** through music, just as David Whyte learned how to *live* his life as a poet to initiate himself into the **secret way** through poetry; so it does not matter which path one takes in life, as long as one knows *how* to live their life they will initiate themselves into the **secret way** and grow in their destined purpose.

The mystery lies in *how* we live our life, which took me many years to work out; and when all is said and done, this mysterious *how* depends upon our ability to bring our karmic destiny into agreement with our encoded spiritual purpose, making one destiny out of our two destinies.

That's the **secret way** of every path in life, then; the wisdom, courage and commitment to keep our karmic destiny in co-operative agreement with our encoded spiritual purpose, which is the imperative of this unfolding story *One Rule to Live By: Be Good,* and which, curiously enough, speaks to what my Penny Lynn and I experienced with the dramatic little saga of our 2015 Honda Civic LX, a practical life lesson that was forced upon us by the divine choreographer of life…

Penny and I did not choose to purchase our new 2015 Honda Civic LX, it chose us in that strange way that *the omniscient guiding principle of life* choreographs one's life to assist us in our journey through life. A Hallmark rep for the past twelve years, Penny was working at the Real Canadian Superstore in Wasaga Beach; and having made an appointment to service our 2005 Honda Civic for the winter at the Canadian Tire service center nearby, she was going to drop the car off and walk to the Superstore and pick it up later.

I asked her to have new winter tires installed also, but when the mechanic put the car on the hoist to do an oil change, he noticed that the fuel lines were rusted and corroded, and the brake lines as well, and he told Penny to be careful braking because the brakes could fail at any time. In fact, he even cautioned her to not drive the car like that; so, Penny asked him for an estimate on new brake and fuel lines.

The mechanic came back from the office with an estimate of four thousand dollars, including service and new tires, which took Penny by surprise. The mileage on our car was just under 262000 kilometers, and the mechanic asked Penny if we had the timing chain replaced because at that mileage that would be the next thing to go. And then he said to her, "If it was my car, I wouldn't pour that kind of money into it. It's not worth it." But he would fix it if that's what she wanted. Penny called me and asked if I was sitting down, and after she gave me the news we decided to wait on the service and discuss it when she came home.

It wasn't a difficult decision, given that we had already just poured a thousand dollars into the car when we serviced it to go up north to tend to our triplex in my hometown of Nipigon and visit Penny's family in the Lakehead, and we decided to look at some used Hondas on the weekend; but a good pre-owned was almost as expensive as a new one, so we decided to bite the bullet and buy a new Honda Civic instead.

The new 2015 models were already on the dealer's lot, but we decided to purchase a new 2014 model instead, because it would be a little cheaper; so, we arranged financing with Honda and made the deal. But we wanted a specific color, which they didn't have on the lot, and the salesperson, a pleasant young woman who gave us one-thousand-dollar trade-in value for our old Civic, was going to bring one in from an out-of-town dealer, but while waiting for our new vehicle to be brought in from a dealer in southern Ontario, our car broke down on her way to work in Wasaga Beach the following week, and Penny barely managed to pull into the Beer Store parking lot and park it because it was unsafe to drive.

She called me and I drove to the Beach with my work van, and then we called a tow truck and had the car towed to our Honda dealer in Midland; but because Penny needed a car for work, we decided then and there to purchase a new 2015 model off the lot, which turned out to be only a few dollars more for the monthly payments we would be making for the 2014 model; and, despite the breakdown of our car, the sales lady still honored the thousand-dollar trade-in value for our old Honda.

We waited while they serviced our new car, and when it was ready to be driven off the lot the sales lady went over the details and set the Blue Tooth for Penny's cell phone; but when I walked around our new Honda Civic LX, I noticed our new license plate: BEWEL 262.

I loved the symbolic implications of BEWEL (the symbolic language of life was telling us that everything was going to **BE WELL** for us now); but when I shared this "message" with Penny, she looked at our new licence plate and the number 262 jumped out at her, and she said, "The mileage on our car was 262000 when it died on me. Our new plate is BEWEL 262. What do you make of that?"

I broke into laughter. "That's even better yet. 262 is short for the mileage on our car when it gave up the ghost in the Beach, and the secret language of life is telling us that the spirit of our old Honda has incarnated into our new Honda Civic LX and everything's going to be well for us now. I know it sounds foolish, Penny Lynn; but good God, it feels good to get this kind of symbolic confirmation!"

I didn't have to finish reading *12 Rules for Life: An Antidote to Chaos* to know where it was going. It was artfully designed to reconcile one's *existential* outer life with one's *essential* inner life, just as the divinely choreographed experience of how we came to purchase our new 2015 Honda Civic LX that brought our outer life into greater alignment with our inner life and symbolically confirmed it by telling us that all was going to **BE WELL** for us (*until the next crisis*); but I was looking forward to finishing *12 Rules for Life: An Antidote to Chaos,* because I loved watching how the good professor Jordan Peterson connected the dots to the perplexing riddle of the human predicament, and by human predicament I mean the existential dilemma of our outer and inner life.

But try as he might, I also *knew* that professor Peterson was stuck in the second stage of soul's evolution through life; that's why I was "nudged" once more by the inner guiding principle of my life to send him copies of *My Writing Life* and *The Merciful Law of Divine Synchronicity* when he stepped onto the world stage with his message of self-reconciliation that he articulated in his overnight bestseller *12 Rules for Life: An Antidote to Chaos*, because my books spoke to my own individuation process through the third and final stage of evolution, and I *felt* they might open him up a little more to the **secret way** that reconciles our inner and outer self.

This was my experience, as incredible as it may seem, and I honestly don't expect anyone to believe me, least of all a critically minded, academically trained and research oriented professor of evolutionary psychology with twenty years of experience as a practicing clinical therapist whose own remarkable journey of self-discovery, which he studiously chronicled in *Maps of Meaning: The Architecture of Belief* and shared on his online lectures, had taken him to the precipice of the mesoteric second stage of soul's evolution through life but who was desperate to enter the third and final stage where the paradoxical nature of man's existential predicament can finally be resolved but who was still too timid to enter *(for personal reasons, or to safeguard his professional reputation, I cannot say; but I do know that his hero C. G. Jung made the commitment and bravely integrated his personal gnosis of the* **secret way** *into his psychology of individuation)*; but, as Jesus said in his cryptic teachings of the **secret way**, the eye of the needle is difficult to pass through, and not many souls do—however rich, or otherwise. This is why my heart genuinely went out to the good professor, and why I was called by my oracle to write *One Rule to Live By: Be Good...*

3. Why Rules to Live By, Anyway?

Rules are organizing principles, and they put one's life in order; and unless we put our own life in order, life can be very, very difficult. As Dr. Jordan Peterson painfully learned through his twenty years of clinical practice, life can break a person down; that's why rules to live by are necessary, they make one stronger for life.

"To stand up straight with your shoulders back is to accept the terrible responsibility of life, with eyes wide open," he writes in *12 Rules for Life*. "It means deciding to voluntarily transform the chaos of potential into the realities of habitual order. It means adopting the burden of self-conscious vulnerability, and accepting the end of the unconscious paradise of childhood, where finitude and mortality are only dimly comprehended. **It means willingly undertaking the sacrifices necessary to generate a productive and meaningful reality.** (It means acting to please God, in the ancient language)" (*12 Rules for Life: An Antidote to Chaos,* by Jordan B. Peterson, p. 27, bold italics mine).

One would not believe the rules that I chose to live by when I lived Gurdjieff's transformative teaching of "work on oneself." I even had to create one rule in my *Royal Dictum* (my edict of self-denial, inspired by Sophocles' tragic play *Oedipus Rex* and the Preacher's opening words in *Ecclesiastes*) that was so insufferably difficult to live by that it bore a hole through the impenetrable wall of the mesoteric second stage of evolution and gained me entry into the esoteric third and final stage of growth and understanding where life finally gave up the **secret way** to me; so, believe me, I know what it means to live by rules. It was this experience that gave birth to the meanest saying of my entire life: *"The shortest way to God is through hell."*

That's why I look forward to reading the rest of Peterson's book, because I know that every one of his twelve rules for life was born of his own journey of self-discovery, and his individuation process fascinates me for its honesty, integrity, and desperation; like a lone voice crying in the wilderness that has finally been heard like a clarion bell around the world.

But as St. Padre Pio said to me when the gifted psychic medium channelled him for my novel *Healing with Padre Pio*, "Life is a journey of the self," which was amplified by what Jesus said in Glenda Green's book *The Keys of Jeshua* (which followed her first book *Love without End, Jesus Speaks* that St. Padre Pio suggested I read), "There is nothing but the self and God." However, long before I wrote *Healing with Padre Pio* and read Glenda Green's books, I had already painfully learned that life was an individual journey, and it all added up to the same thing: **all paths in life lead to the self, and not until one takes responsibility for their own evolution will life give up its secret.**

This is why Gurdjieff said that there was only self-initiation into the mysteries of life, and I knew that professor Jordan Peterson's valiant perspective in *12 Rules for Life* would open one up to life's mysteries; because taking responsibility for one's life makes one more conscious, and consciousness is the key that opens the door to the final third stage of evolution where one can complete what Nature cannot finish and be one's true self.

But opening the door to the third and final stage of evolution is not easy. Not because one is not intelligent enough, many exceptionally brilliant people have tried and failed and will continue to fail to open this door to wholeness and completeness, because intelligence is not sufficient for entry—brilliant little Friedrich Nietzsche, Sartre, Camus, Kierkegaard, Bertrand Russell, Ayn Rand, Richard Dawkins, Christopher Hitchens, Salman Rushdie, Sam Harris & company, including big brain Ken Wilber (*A Brief History of Everything*), all exceptionally brilliant in mind but tragically arrogant in spiritual obtuseness; it takes a special kind of wisdom to open this door— **"Strait is the gate, and narrow is the way, which leadeth unto life, and few there be that find it,"** said Jesus (Matthew, 7: 14); and that's the real mystery of the human predicament.

But I would never have known this had not my oracle spoken to me (by way of inspired thought, in this case) when Gurdjieff's teaching could do no more for me and I created my *Royal Dictum*, which bore a hole through the mental impasse that Gurdjieff's teaching had brought me to because my edict of self-denial resolved the consciousness of my paradoxical nature (my *being* and *non-being*, which constitute one's inner and outer self), a hole large enough for me to pass through the eye of the needle and realize my true, eternal self as Jesus promised.

"He that loveth his life shall lose it; and he that hateth his life in this world shall keep it unto life eternal," said Jesus (John 12: 25); but who is willing to "die" to the false consciousness of their outer self to realize the eternal consciousness of their inner self? Not very many. Only those who have gone as far as life can take them and have nowhere else to go; that's why my heart goes out to anyone whose path has taken them as far as it possibly can, like the good professor Jordan Peterson. And this is not an arrogant presumption; it's a cruel, hard fact of the teleological imperative of soul's natural individuation process which, if I had any practical sense whatsoever, I would keep to myself but cannot because, like the mystic poet Jalaluddin Rumi, my oracle has also shouted into my ear, *"Tell it unveiled, the naked truth! The declaration's better than the secret."*

My truth then, in all of its vulnerable nakedness, arrogance, and humility declares that we are all sparks of divine consciousness that come from the infinite Body of God, that karma and reincarnation are an incontrovertible fact of life, and that the purpose of life is to individuate the un-self-realized *I Am* consciousness of God, a personal gnosis that would tax anyone's credulity, including inveterate truth-seeking professor Jordan B. Peterson.

But when all is said and done, the only truth that really matters in the end is the truth of one's own life experience, and mine has brought me to this astonishing perspective outside the limited paradigm of cognitive thinking. As my hero C. G. Jung *(who privately believed in reincarnation but could never admit to it openly to safeguard the scientific credibility of his psychology)* would say, this is what I was meant to be; this is who I am; this is my personality, and I have to be true to who I am no less than professor Peterson had to be true to who he was when he was called by life to stand up for free speech. He couldn't help himself. The *way* called him, and his soul depended on it.

As I experienced in my fourth past-life regression, we come from the Body of God as embryonic souls, seeds of divine consciousness encoded with God's DNA, to realize our own identity through the evolution of our karmic imperative, and the only way we can do that is to align our karmic destiny with our encoded spiritual purpose; and this is the mystery that baffles the world, because we have to do the impossible and square the circle to resolve the paradoxical consciousness of our dual nature, our inner and outer self that Jesus spoke to when he was asked in the Gospel of Thomas when his kingdom would come and he replied: **"When the two will be one, the outer like the inner, and the male with the female neither male or female,"** to which Thomas added: "Now the two are one when we speak truth to each other and there is one soul in two bodies with no hypocrisy"—one self, whole and complete; the divine fruit of evolution that Jesus called the pearl of great price...

God is merciful, then; and this is not a cliché with me. My journey of self-discovery awakened me to the **secret way** that finally revealed itself to me as the *omniscient guiding principle of life*, which throughout history has been called God, Holy Spirit, Providence, the Logos, the Word, Baraka, Chi, Tao, vital life force, and simply the way (Hemingway called it "juice"); and it is the same spark of divine consciousness that we are all born with.

This is why Jesus said that the kingdom of God was within, and which Jung caught a glimpse of in his own remarkable journey of self-discovery, as he points to in his essay "The Development of the Individual": "The undiscovered vein within us is a living part of the psyche; classical Chinese philosophy names this interior way 'Tao,' and likens it to a flow of water that moves irresistibly towards its goal. The rest in Tao means fulfillment, wholeness, one's destination reached, one's mission done; **the beginning, end, and perfect realization of the meaning of existence innate in all things.** Personality is Tao" (*The Essential Jung*, by Anthony Storr. p. 210; bold italics mine).

Just as the acorn seed is an oak tree in *potentia*, so are we the potential realization of the seed of our essential nature (the *I Am* consciousness of God); which is why I look forward to reading the rest of professor Peterson's *12 Rules for Life: An Antidote to Chaos*, because his book is an organizing principle that will harness the special energy of gnostic meaning that one needs to awaken to the **secret way** that will take one through the mesoteric second stage of evolution and to the hidden door of the esoteric third and final stage of growth and self-fulfillment where one can complete what Nature cannot finish and realize their destined purpose of wholeness and completeness.

The good professor is frantically knocking on the door of inner growth and evolution with his *12 Rules for Life: An antidote to Chaos,* and our crazy modern world, which is suffering from a demoralizing crisis of meaning, has heard him loud and clear; and that's the perplexing mystery of his sudden popularity and irresistible appeal, especially to wayward young men looking for direction and purpose; which brings to mind Christ's saying: **"Ask, and it shall be given you; seek, and ye shall find; knock, and it will be opened unto you. For every one that** *asketh, receiveth; and he that seeketh findeth; and to him that knocketh, it shall be opened"* (Matthew, 7: 7-8).

When my muse asked, *"What the hell is going on out there?"* the Universe heard my plea, and out of the halls of academia a brilliant hierophant by the name of Jordan B. Peterson stepped out of shadows into the light of common day with his maps of meaning and began answering the angry question of my poem with his valiant defense of free speech, and then his overnight bestseller *12 Rules for Life: An Antidote to Chaos* knocked on the door of the **secret way** so loud and clear that my oracle summoned me to write *One Rule to Live By: Be Good*, which, hopefully, will crack open the door to one's soul for the light within to shine and make the path before them always bright, as Wordsworth intuited with poetic genius in *Character of the Happy Warrior,* the light of one's own divine nature that professor Peterson's hierophantic message calls one to...

4. The Horror of Human Suffering

All three stages of human evolution have their own perspective. The *exoteric* first stage is primordial and all about existential survival, the stage where soul begins the individuation of its reflective self-consciousness, and it grows and evolves in self-conscious awareness from one lifetime to the next until it has evolved enough to gravitate to the *mesoteric* second stage of evolution where it begins to sense its divine nature, and the more it grows in its divine nature, the more it is driven by its encoded imperative to satisfy its longing for wholeness and completeness; but the natural process of evolution through karma and reincarnation cannot satisfy soul's longing for wholeness and completeness, and soul gets stuck in the second stage of evolution.

"*As each plant grows from a seed and becomes in the end an oak tree, so man must become what he is meant to be. He ought to get there, but most get stuck,*" said Carl Jung in an interview; and soul gets stuck because it cannot resolve the paradoxical nature of its inner and outer self, just as Jung himself got stuck in his own remarkable journey through life: "*At that time, in the fortieth year of my life, I had achieved everything that I had wished for myself. I had achieved honor, power, wealth, knowledge, and every human happiness. Then my desire for the increase in these trappings ceased, the desire ebbed from me and horror came over me...My soul, where are you? Do you hear me? I speak, I call you—are you there? I have returned, I am here again. I have shaken the dust of all the lands from my feet, and I have come to you. I am with you. After long years of long wandering, I have come to you again...*" (*The Red Book*, A Reader's Edition, by C. G. Jung, p. 127, italics mine).

Jung was called to his destiny, as every soul will be called when life has made them ready for the *esoteric* third and final stage of evolution (*regardless of what path one is on*), and with absolute resolve he went in search of his lost soul, which I also had to do; but I've told this story in *The Pearl of Great Price* and need not repeat it here. Carl Jung also told the remarkable story of finding his lost soul in his "confrontation with the unconscious" that he recorded in six black notebooks that he reworked with brilliant illustrations in *Liber Novus*, now known simply as *The Red Book*.

And it was here, banging on the door of the third and final stage of evolution that I came upon professor Jordan Peterson online; and it was not an accident. His silent cry was so loud and desperate that it pierced my heart center; that's why I felt *compelled* to send him *The Lion that Swallowed Hemingway* and *The Pearl of Great Price,* a terrible presumption if not a damn impertinence that must have left him wondering, probably throwing my books onto a shelf and leaving them there to gather dust; and I'm sure he was no less baffled by *My Writing Life* and *The Merciful Law of Divine Synchronicity* that I sent him three years later; but my oracle spoke to me, and I *listened*...

It's a lonely journey to one's true self, the loneliest journey in the world; which is why so many souls fell by the wayside in the Sufi poet Farid u-Din Attar's allegory *Conference of the Birds*. Out of the thousands of souls (symbolized as birds in this allegory of soul's quest for God, led by the wisest of birds, the hoopoe bird, which in this story I've identified as Jordan B. Peterson), *only thirty birds completed their quest for God in whose face they saw their own image, thus fulfilling soul's longing for wholeness and completeness;* so, it takes as much wisdom as it does courage to step outside the paradigm of conventional thinking and into the third and final stage of evolution.

"And do you now believe in God?" the canny interviewer John Freeman asked the eighty-four-year-old Carl Gustav Jung in the now famous 1959 *Face to Face* BBC interview at Jung's home on the shore of Lake Zurich in Kusnacht, Switzerland.

One Rule to Live By

Surprised by the question, the venerable octogenarian replied, with a glint in his eye and the sweetest smile on his wizened face: *"Now? Difficult to answer. I know. I don't need to believe, I know."* By this time in his life, and the distance he had travelled in his lonely journey to wholeness and singleness of self, Carl Gustav Jung did not have to apologize for what he had discovered about God and man and the divine self, and he told John Freeman that God was a matter of experience with him and not belief, which only convinced his detractors that he had been a Gnostic all along—*as if that was a bloody fault!*

But that only spoke to the willful malevolence that Jung had to endure from his resentful detractors who felt threatened by his enlightened perspective, just as Jordan Peterson *(who was strongly advised by his professors while pursuing his doctorate in psychology to steer clear of that heretic Jung)* began to experience when he was catapulted onto the world stage with his own enlightened perspective. To the Indian novelist and essayist Pankaj Mishra, who not only skewered his book *12 Rules for Life* but took a pathetic cheap shot at the author as well in his review in *The New York Review of Books* ("*Jordan Peterson & Fascist Mysticism*"), Peterson tweeted back: "And you call me a fascist? You sanctimonious prick. If you were in my room at the moment, I'd slap you happily."

Bravo, Jordan! That's why in Australia later in the year when he was asked if he believed in God he wisely deflected his answer by talking about various belief systems, having sadly learned how a straight answer would only ensnare him; but he had also learned from the "Shaman of Zurich," as Carl Jung was called by the locals, to hide himself in plain sight as Jung did in his gnostic psychology of individuation; and the good professor now deals with ironic brilliance the malevolent forces of life that he has become wise to and want to take him down, and the world loves him for his fearless common sense and uncanny scholarly wisdom—"*I act as if God exists,*" he replies today to the question that wants to pigeonhole him, *"and I'm terrified that he might..."*

The perspective from the third and final stage of evolution is so radically different from the viewpoint of the first and second stages that one would be wise not to share it, because the world will only turn on them for fear of being seen for its shallowness and hypocrisy; like it did with my intrepid pug-faced hero Socrates who was tried and condemned for corrupting the youth of Athens with his "seditious" philosophy of virtue. This is the sage wisdom behind Lao Tzu's puzzling saying, *"Those who speak, do not know; and those who know, do not speak."*

But last month I was called to write a spiritual musing that offers such a radical perspective on human suffering that it may just help to ease the pain of man's anger at God for all the senseless pain and suffering in the world; and the only reason I'm going to quote it here is because professor Jordan Peterson's emotional sincerity while delivering his lecture *"Existentialism: Nazi Germany and the USSR"* devastated me, and my heart bled much too profusely for me not to respond.

I was so moved by his nightmarish terror of man's willful malevolence responsible for most of the world's suffering, like the unspeakable horrors of the Nazi concentration camps and Stalin's gulags that wiped out millions of innocent people *(which haunted young Peterson for years)*, that I have to share my insight on human suffering to ease the unbearable anguish of unknowing:

The Paradox of Human Suffering

Stephen Fry annoyed me. He always did. Many people do, usually people that we're exposed to all the time in the media, movie actors, singers, comedians, public figures whose life is revealed through their thoughts, beliefs, opinions, betrayals and self-betrayals, whatever constitutes their ego/shadow personality; and Stephen Fry, an openly gay comedic actor, writer, and public persona annoyed me.

It wasn't because he was gay, that didn't matter a wit to me; it was because of his whole demeanor, his ego/shadow personality that was so thick with Stephen Fry that there was no room for anyone else, including and especially God; that's what annoyed me.

"Quantity kills quality," goes the old saying; and there was so much Stephen Fry in Steven Fry that he killed Stephen Fry; that's the tragic irony of Stephen Fry.

Of course, this is just my perception; but it's not a perception born of bias, malice, a warped sense of righteous belief, or metaphysical speculation for that matter. This is just the way I see Stephen Fry from outside the existential paradigm of conventional thinking, from that place of personal resolution where one can see both sides of the human predicament; like the side of God that Stephen Fry was annoyingly blind to in "Stephen Fry Annihilates God," the YouTube interview that I chanced upon the other evening.

The interviewer says to Stephen Fry: "Suppose that what Oscar (the celebrated social wit Oscar Wilde who wrote *The Importance of Being Ernest* whom Fry admired from the age of fifteen and tried to emulate his whole life) believed in as he died, in spite of your protestations; suppose it's all true, and you walk up to the pearly gates and you are confronted by God. What will Stephen Fry say to Him, Her, or It?"

And Stephen Fry, who played the infamous gay writer in the movie *Wilde*, replies: "I will basically, this is theodicy I think; I'll say, bone cancer in children? What's that about? How dare you? How dare you create a world in which there is such misery that is not our fault? It's not right. It's utterly, utterly evil. Why should I respect a capricious, mean-minded, stupid God who creates a world which is so full of injustice and pain? That's what I would say."

"And you think you're going to get in?" asks the interviewer, with a wry smile.

"No. But I wouldn't want to. I wouldn't want to get in on His terms. They're wrong," Fry replies, and herein lies the crux of today's spiritual musing…

Ironically, the creative impulse that impelled me to offer my perspective on human suffering that puzzles celebrated atheists like Stephen Fry and countless believers alike who are no less bewildered by the human predicament that they also fall prey to spiritual paralysis, did not come to me from the Fry interview; it was set free while reading something about Mitch Albom's healing journey in my new novel *Sundays with Sharon* that was inspired by the book *Tuesdays with Morrie* by Mitch Albom, the former student of sociology professor Morrie Schwartz who was dying of ALS, also known as Lou Gehrig's disease.

In a sudden flash of insight, I caught the bittersweet irony of Morrie's suffering, and I *knew* that I had to write a spiritual musing on his dying experience that Mitch Albom recorded in his heart-wrenching little book *Tuesdays with Morrie*. This is the sentence in *Sundays with Sharon* (Chapter 7, "Thank You for Being My Friend") that set my idea free: **"Through Morrie's friendship, Mitch got linked to his inner self and began his own healing journey to wholeness and completeness like his old coach Morrie Schwartz."** In one flash of insight, I saw the paradoxical nature of human suffering.

For whatever reason, which I can only attribute to the creative principle of my life that I call my oracle and my muse, this sentence lifted me up above the physical, mental, and emotional agony of Morrie Schwartz's suffering as his body wasted away with ALS, and I was allowed to see the spiritual healing that came with his suffering; and the moment I saw the miraculous power of human suffering, I was given the title of today's spiritual musing: "The Paradox of Human Suffering," which automatically triggered my memory of the Stephen Fry interview that annoyed me so much when I saw it the other evening.

Fry continues his annoying answer to the loaded question: "Now, if I died and it was Pluto, Hades, and if it was the twelve Greek gods, then I would have more truck with it; because the Greeks were, they didn't pretend not to be human in their appetites, and in their capriciousness, and in their unreasonableness. They didn't present themselves as being all-seeing, all-wise, all-kind or beneficent, because the God who created this universe, if it was created by God, is quite clearly a maniac. Utter maniac. We have to spend our life on bended knees thanking Him? What kind of God would do that? Yes, the world is very splendid; but it also has in it insects whose whole life cycle is to burrow into the eyes of children and make them blind. They eat outwards from the eyes. Why? Why did you do that to us? You could easily have made a creation in which that did not exist. It is simply not acceptable. So, you know, atheism is not just about not believing there is a God; but on the assumption that there is one, what kind of God is He? It's perfectly apparent that He is monstrous, utterly monstrous, and deserves no respect whatsoever. The moment you banish Him, life becomes simpler, purer, clearer, and more worth living, in my opinion—"

To which the bemused interviewer Gay Byrne responded, "That sure is the longest answer to that question that I ever got to this entire series," which caused Fry to burst into laughter, thus bringing to a close the short clip of Stephen Fry's annihilation of God; but did Fry annihilate God, or simply display a tendentious and supercilious ignorance of the creative life principle? Must give me pause…

Writers bring to light what we already know, so they say; but sometimes the creative unconscious surprises us with new insights, as mine did with what was revealed in that sentence that set free the idea for today's spiritual musing: **"Through Morrie's friendship, Mitch got linked to his inner self and began his own healing journey to wholeness and completeness like his old coach Morrie Schwartz."**

When I wrote this sentence, I did not see it; neither did I see it when I read and edited the chapter for the fourth or fifth time. But for some reason known only to my muse, I *saw* what my creative unconscious was telling me in the phrase **healing journey**. In a flash, it came back to me that all of Morrie's suffering was healing his soul, which I did not discern when I first wrote it; and that's when the title of today's spiritual musing popped into my mind, "The Paradox of Human Suffering," because no one—*and especially the incorrigible Stephen Fry*—can see the miracle beyond the pain and agony of human suffering; but I did in Morrie Schwartz's journey to the final frontier of his life as he was dying of ALS. And that's what reminded me of the Fry interview that I was compelled to watch again to affirm my insight.

As the pre-Socratic philosopher Heraclitus tells us, life is always in a state of flux, forever changing from one state into another, one continuous flow of being and becoming forever in the process of uniting the opposites and becoming one with the Logos; a mystifying philosophy that has intrigued the world ever since Heraclitus propounded it, a philosophy that implies an inherent guiding principle to the human condition that Heraclitus called the Logos—which is what I caught a glimpse of in all the pain and agony of Morrie Schwartz's suffering in that remarkably revealing sentence, "**Mitch got linked to his inner self and began his own healing journey to wholeness and completeness like his old coach Morrie Schwartz.**" By the miracle of creative writing, I *saw* that all of Morrie's suffering was healing his weary soul and making him whole. That's what called fifteen million people in forty-five countries to read *Tuesdays with Morrie*—because it spoke to their own weary soul crying to become whole…

Stephen Fry can moan and groan and whine and complain and shout in vitriolic anger at a creative principle of life that he cannot fathom, but he too will grow and resolve through the natural process of individuation through karma and reincarnation into one self whole and complete and see that all of this suffering in the world serves a higher purpose than we can see, as it did with Mitch Albom's old sociology professor dying of ALS, because the closer Morrie Schwartz came to the end of his life's journey the more his suffering healed his soul and helped make him whole.

As the former atheist/agnostic professor revealed to his former student, who began recording their Tuesday talks with his big Sony tape recorder, the closer he came to dying the more he came to see that his body was a mere shell, a container for the soul and that death was not cold and final as he once believed. But this isn't a mystery that one can explain; one can only experience it, as Mitch Albom began to do when his old professor's journey to the final frontier of his life reconnected him with his inner self and destined purpose to wholeness and completeness, and Mitch began serving life instead of always taking from life like he used to, unlike the incorrigible Stephen Fry whose whole self-serving demeanor affronted me deeply.

Mitch Albom learned from his old professor that it was better to give than to receive, and with the monetary success of *Tuesdays with Morrie,* and the books that followed, he funded a number of charitable organizations, his orphanage with over forty children in poverty-stricken Haiti being his favorite; that's how the former student honored his old professor, by giving back to life like he taught him in the final class of his life on life's greatest lesson that **only through goodness can we realize our true self.**

After watching the Stephen Fry interview for the second time, I watched two more videos on Stephen Fry: "Who Do You Think You Are?" in which he traces his English and Jewish family roots, and "Stephen Fry: The Secret Life of the Manic Depressive," in which he reveals his troubled youth (expelled from two schools when he was 15 and at 17 absconded with a friend's credit card and was charged with theft that got him three months in prison) and his life-long battle with bipolar disorder, formerly known as manic depression, a mental condition that causes periods of dark depression and elevated moods known as mania. And after watching these videos, I deeply empathized with Stephen Fry's conflicted journey through life; but as much as I tried to get over my annoyance, he was still too much Stephen Fry for me.

"Life is a hierarchy of devouring," said Charles Templeton, the former evangelist who helped launch the evangelical movement with Billy Graham, but who, by some *enantiodromiac* twist of fate, lost his Christian faith and became a believer in Darwinian determinism; and he was half right, because our existential life is all about evolution and survival of the fittest.

But as so often happens when people lose their faith in God, he went to the extreme end of the spectrum. "I believe that there is no supreme being with human attributes—no God in the biblical sense—but that all life is the result of timeless evolutionary forces, over millions of years. I believe that, in common with all living creatures, we die and cease to exist as an entity," declared Charles Templeton in his memoir *Farewell to God: My Reasons for Rejecting Christianity*.

But like my hero C. G. Jung, I *know* that God *is,* and I *know* that we are more than our physical body; and that's the mystery that professor Peterson explored in his deeply researched *Maps of Meaning: The Architecture of Belief* that I cannot wait to read. In the meantime, I'm assiduously watching his online lectures; and I just love following his logic as he explores the narrative of soul's evolution though life in the ancient stories and myths of the world *(especially his mythic perspective on the Christian Bible)* and evolutionary biology that help him reason his way through his wall of unknowing. And listening to his book tour talks and interviews is spell-binding— *a real life allegory of a flocking of the birds to the wise counsel of an exceptionally gifted hoopoe bird...*

5. The Self that Isn't a Self

"I am what I am not, and I am not what I am," concluded the French existentialist Jean-Paul Sartre, reflecting the dual nature of our self-consciousness, the *being* and *non-being* of our evolving *enantiodromiac* nature; but how can this be? How can we possibly be what we are not? What is this impenetrable mystery?

This was my call to destiny, my mission in life—to resolve the mystery of the self that wasn't me, that aspect of my personality that wasn't who I thought myself to be; and how did I know that it wasn't me? How could I possibly be a false me and a real me at one and the same time? That's what I set out to resolve in the twenty-third year of my life when I dropped my comfortable life in Canada and fled to Annecy, France to begin my long and insufferable quest for my true self.

I've explored this story over and over in my writing (two dozen books to date), but most succinctly in my most intimate memoir *The Pearl of Great Price,* and I need not restate my story here *(readers keep telling me that I repeat myself, but my life is what it is, and I explore my life with a deeper and more nuanced perspective with each new book that I write, as I'm presently doing in this exciting new context of professor Jordan Peterson's hierophantic message, and I keep getting surprised with how dots get re-connected with the ever-expanding eye of creative insight);* suffice to say that my knowledge of the dual consciousness of our reflective self did not come to me without sacrifice, and the price that I was called to pay would make one shudder. But there was no other way to pass through the eye of the needle and work my way through the third and final stage of evolution to complete what Nature could not finish; and that's the bloody irony—*because we have no choice!*

We are all teleologically driven by our divine nature to become our true self, and not until we find the way to our true self will we satisfy the longing in our soul for wholeness and completeness. Here we are then, standing at the gateway of the inner circle of life, as far as the process of natural evolution through karma and reincarnation can take us, but we have no idea where to go next, where to look, how to enter; and we despair. *Oh God, how we despair!*

This is the existential predicament that has blighted the world with a paralyzing crisis of meaning. The divine imperative of our inner nature has driven us against the impenetrable wall of our desperate unknowing, crushing our spirits or making us stronger; but either way, not until we dare to risk it all will we find the answer to the haunting question of our inevitable individuation.

And it's here that we find all the broken souls, all the wretched and miserable people who cannot make sense of life, some shaking their fist at God and others falling into such despair that they cast a pall upon everyone around them. *"All we have is hope, but what hope is there?"* said Margaret Atwood, author of the dystopian novel *The Handmaid's Tale* that was made into a TV series last year and continues in season two with a much bleaker picture, casting a cloud of spiritual darkness on social consciousness; and what does this say about postmodern neo-Marxist nihilism that drives the good Dr. Jordan Peterson with a *daemonic* zeal to heal the world?

He's right to see the world as order and chaos, because this is the *enantiodromiac* nature of the human condition; and this is the clue to the mystery of the *being* and *non-being* of our evolving self-consciousness. But how can we possibly see this if we relegate the individuating reflective self of man to the neurobiology of our brain? Is the self an epiphenomenon of our brain, or is it independent of our brain? Is it a product of our neurobiology, or is it "something" that we are born with?

In all honesty, it boggles my mind whenever I read the literature and listen to all the naysayers like the talented Margaret Atwood; and it's beginning to bore the hell out of me when people—*and the more brilliant, the more annoying!*—argue from the perspective that our reflective and autonomous self is a byproduct of our brain. But knowing that there is only self-initiation into the mysteries of life, I have to make allowances for this horrifying spiritual obtuseness.

But this is professor Jordan Peterson's dilemma, standing on the razor's edge of this haunting question—which reminds me of the epigram that Somerset Maugham quoted to introduce the story of his hero's spiritual quest in his novel *The Razor's Edge* that inflicted me in high school with what professor Harold Bloom called an "immortal wound" (a wound that pierces one's soul with wonder) and called me to become a seeker like Maugham's hero Larry Darrell, a quote from the Katha-Upanishad, one of the holy scriptures of the East: *"The sharp edge of the razor is difficult to pass over; thus the wise say that the path to Salvation is hard."*

I was called to walk the razor's edge, as every soul must when they have come to the limits of personal evolution; and though I got cut and bled many times, I managed to survive and find my true self. And it's from this deeply esoteric outside-the-box perspective that I wrote the spiritual musing that I was called to write by the movie *Still Alice* that Penny and I saw last summer:

Personal Identity and Alzheimer's

"We are more than the memory of who we are," I said to Penny on our drive home from the Uptown Theatre and early dinner at Wimpy's Diner in Barrie yesterday afternoon, and I knew instantly that this was my entry point into the spiritual musing that the movie *Still Alice* had inspired; and this morning I called upon my muse to help me explore the haunting question of personal identity and

Alzheimer's that the remarkable movie *Still Alice* inevitably gave rise to...

    I didn't really want to see *Still Alice,* starring Julianne Moore who won an Oscar for her moving performance as the fifty-year old Alice Howland, professor of linguistics at Columbia University afflicted with early-onset Alzheimer's, because I knew it would be a tear jerker; but we went anyway, and it proved to be no less than a three-tissue movie.

    But it wasn't so much the emotional impact that Alice had upon me as Alzheimer's ravages her memory, even though that in itself easily moved me to tears; it was the unbearable irony of her tragic predicament: Alice is an exceptionally bright high-achiever whose personal identity is inextricably linked with her intellect, and when she loses her memory she loses her sense of self-identity and slowly sinks into an abyss of blank-faced dumbness from which she won't recover.

    This bothered me more than her disease, not because I didn't empathize with Alice's rapid deterioration and the effect it had upon her loving family, but because this beautiful and gracious wife and mother of three responsible adult children was hopelessly trapped by the spiritually suffocating scientific constraints of her medical condition; and with each passing day and hour and minute her comfortable middle-class world slowly shrank into memory-fading oblivion.

    "You know, sweetheart," I said to Penny as we drove through Minesing on our way home to Bluewater in Georgian Bay after the heartbreaking movie and simple hot hamburger dinner at Wimpy's Diner; "what a person believes in makes a difference in how they feel when they're faced with their own mortality, or facing a tragic disease like Alice's in the movie. Do you remember me telling you about my buddy Michael Ignatieff's novel *Scar Tissue* that dealt with this same issue of Alzheimer's and personal identity?"

    "Vaguely," Penny said. "But you're going to remind me, aren't you?"

    I was being sarcastic when I called the disgraced former leader of the Liberal Party of Canada Michael Ignatieff my buddy, because I had lost respect for him when he forced a totally unnecessary election that decimated the Liberal Party and reduced it to third party status. "Those who can't, teach," I responded to his catastrophic and personally humiliating defeat (he even lost his own Toronto's Etobicoke-Lakeshore riding) when he resigned as leader of the Official Opposition and ignominiously shrunk away with his bushy academic tail between his legs to teach at the University of Toronto and then back to Harvard's ivory tower from where he had been plucked by the Liberal Party establishment to be the next Pierre Trudeau to save Canada from Premier Stephen Harper and the Conservative Party.

I respected the former professor/journalist/author Michael Ignatieff, whose TV show *Ignatieff* I watched with avid interest (I distinctly remember his interview with Hemingway's third wife Martha Gellhorn, whose life with Hemingway inspired the movie *Hemingway and Gellhorn,* which in turn inspired my literary memoir *The Lion that Swallowed Hemingway*), and I read with fascination Ignatieff's autobiographical novel *Scar Tissue* that was shortlisted for the Booker Prize, because the core of his story was about Alzheimer's and personal identity, just as the movie *Still Alice* that was based on the *New York Times* bestselling eponymous novel by neuroscientist Lisa Genova.

I didn't lose respect for Ignatieff because he aspired to become Prime Minister of Canada, which is a noble if not impossible ambition for even the most astute politician; but because it was an arrogant presumption to think that he could squirm his way to the top position of the Liberal Party and become Prime Minister of Canada without paying his political dues, which was why he was branded by the Conservative Party attack adds during the ill-timed election as "arrogant and elitist," and it wasn't by any stretch of imagination that I connected the dots of his massive ego with his novel *Scar Tissue* whose theme was so intimate and personal that it caused a rift with his family, especially with his brother Andrew who was primary caregiver for his mother and not his fictional self as he wrote in his novel *Scar Tissue.*

Michael Ignatieff's mother fell prey to Alzheimer's, and he watched her lose her sense of self as her memory faded from week to week until she mercifully passed away in a nursing home; and his novel explored the theme of loss of memory and self-identity, because the narrator of *Scar Tissue* is a philosophy professor not unlike the author who is haunted by his fear of inheriting his mother's Alzheimer's, and what better way for the professor-turned-politician, who when campaigning for the leadership of the Liberal Party of Canada cleverly called himself "neither atheist nor believer," to immortalize his name than to become Prime Minster of Canada just in case Alzheimer's erased his memory? What better confirmation could one have to validate their insecure egoic need to *be*?

I have no doubt that in his mind the Harvard professor's motives for entering Canadian politics were pure and altruistic (despite the fact that he lived outside Canada for thirty years, he professed to a philosophy of *engagement* to justify his commitment to the Liberal Party), but novels based on one's personal life have a tendency to reveal much more than the author realizes, as many writers have learned after a critical study of their work; and Michael Ignatieff's intensely personal novel *Scar Tissue* reflected the tremulous shadow side of the author's scholarly trained ego that goes straight to the issue of consciousness and individual identity: **is our reflective self-consciousness an epiphenomenon of our biology, which disappears when our body dies; or does our reflective self co-exist with our physical body and continues to exist non-biologically after our body dies?**

This is the core issue of *Scar Tissue* that Michael Ignatieff tried to come to terms with creatively through narrative inquiry, and it is the same issue in the movie *Still Alice* that is left hanging in the air as Alice fades away into herself, and it also happens to be the issue that I devoted my whole life to resolving and writing about in my novels, poetry, and memoirs and which is the premise of today's spiritual musing. Having said this, I can now proceed to the heart of the issue of being and not being who we are…

Alzheimer's is like a magnifying glass, focusing our attention on the individual self; because as one loses one's memory with the ravages of this disease, one's self-identity disappears. But where does it go? That's the heart of the issue.

One Rule to Live By

Science would have us believe that when we die, the matrix of consciousness that makes up our self-identity dies with us; or, generously speaking, science may allow the possibility that, like energy which can neither be created nor destroyed but simply changes form, the matrix of our reflective self-consciousness may simply go back into the cosmic stream of life, which is what the Buddhist philosophy contends.

Ignatieff's inquiry into the issue of Alzheimer's and self-identity appears to hold this point of view; and bringing his narrative to closure, the author/narrator says: "But I know that there is a life beyond this death, a time beyond this time. I know that at the very last moment, when everything I ever knew has been effaced from my mind, when pure vacancy has taken possession of me, then light of the purest whiteness will stream in through my eyes into the radiant and empty plane of my mind."

But this is the non-self of the Buddhist philosophy; not the individuated consciousness of our autonomous self that pre-exists our physical body and continues to exist when our body dies.

I've already explored this issue in my book *Stupidity Is Not a Gift of God* in my essay "On the Evolutionary Impulse to Individuate: A Response to the Spiritual Path of Evolutionary Enlightenment," so I need not go into detail here; suffice to say that in my quest for resolution to the issue of the self, I came to the conclusion that we are all born with a spark of divine consciousness that evolves through life into an individual and autonomous self; and the self evolves naturally through the karmic process of being and becoming. To *be*, we have to *become*; and we *become* who we are according to how we live our life. That's the central mystery of the human condition that I explored in my book *The Pearl of Great Price*

Given my personal perspective, then; I see the matrix of consciousness that we call our reflective self not as a by-product (epiphenomenon) of our brain (our neurology), but as an autonomous self that exists independently of our body; but what other proof do we have?

In the movie *Still Alice*, Alice Howland loses her self-identity as her memory is erased by early-onset Alzheimer's; but was her self-identity a by-product of her neurological system which disappears into oblivion when that part of her brain is ravaged by her disease, or does it recede elsewhere where it cannot be seen?

In other words, is Alice *still* Alice despite the loss of her memory of who she is? Would Alice *still* be Alice if she lost a leg, an arm, a breast, or a vital organ that had to be replaced, like her heart?

Many heart transplant patients have reported the phenomenon of taking on personality traits of their donors, like Jane Seymour did in the movie *Heart of a Stranger* that was inspired by the true story of Claire Sylvia's heart transplant; but that's a separate musing that I hope to write one day. The point of today's spiritual musing is this: is our self-identity limited to our memory alone, or does it pervade throughout the cells of our entire body as pioneer researcher in cellular consciousness Dr. Graham Farrant and Dr. Paul Pearlsall (*The Heart's Code*) have discovered, and even beyond cellular memory in non-biological form after our body dies? And if so, what proof do we have besides my own conviction?

On November 10, 2008 Dr. Eben Alexander, a practicing neurosurgeon for twenty-five years who was convinced that self-identity was an epiphenomenon of the brain, had a unique if not providentially inspired medical experience that changed his entire scientific perspective on consciousness and made him a believer in the independent existence of our individual and autonomous self, and he wrote a book on the experience that initiated him into the divine mystery of the self.

His book is called *Proof of Heaven, A Neurosurgeon's Journey into the Afterlife*; and it was on the New York Times bestseller list for 97 weeks. He wrote: "I was struck by a rare illness and thrown into a coma for seven days. During that time, my entire neocortex—the outer surface of the brain, the part that makes us human—was shut down. Inoperative. In essence, absent."

Dr. Alexander believed that "the brain is a machine that produces consciousness," and when "the machine breaks down, consciousness stops." But the rare illness that he contracted (which proved to be a rare virus) shut his brain down and sent him into a seven-day coma that should have shut his consciousness down according to his scientific paradigm, but Dr. Alexander instead experienced himself outside his body in what Dr. Raymond Moody

(*Life After Life*) described as the most astounding near-death experiences that he had studied in more than four decades of researching the incredible phenomenon of near death experiences.

In the Prologue to *Proof of Heaven*, former non-believer Dr. Alexander contritely wrote: "My experience showed me that the death of the body and the brain are not the end of consciousness, that human experience continues beyond the grave. More important, it continues under the gaze of God who loves and cares about each one of us and about where the universe itself and all the beings within it are ultimately going," which means, quite simply, that Alice was *still* Alice despite her loss of memory!

Once again, another example in Dr. Eben Alexander's out-of-body experience *(the literature is replete with anecdotal experiences of one's soul self)*, of someone who hit their impenetrable wall of unknowing and had a divinely inspired experience that initiated him into the sacred mystery of the final stage of evolution to wholeness and completeness; that's why I find it a waste of time to prove to anyone that our soul self is not an epiphenomenon of our brain. But this begs the deeper question: what is it about our reflective self that denies its own existence? Must take pause...

6. The Paradox of Our Shadow Self

Carl Jung came up with the word shadow in his study of the human personality. In his essay "On the Psychology of the Unconscious" he speaks of the shadow as the other in us, the unconscious personality of the same sex, the reprehensible inferior, the other that embarrasses or shames us.

"By shadow I mean the 'negative' side of the personality, the sum of all those unpleasant qualities we like to hide, together with the insufficiently developed functions and the content of the personal unconscious," said Jung; which makes the shadow "both the awful thing that needs redemption, and the suffering redeemer who can provide it," as the editors of *Meeting the Shadow: The Hidden Power of the Dark Side of Human Nature*, Connie Zweig and Jeremiah Abrams, describe the hidden dark side of our personality.

In a word, <u>**our shadow self is who we are not that desperately wants to be who we are. It is our paradoxical self that we don't want to acknowledge. It is the hidden, repressed dark side of our conscious ego personality, and just because we refuse to acknowledge our dark shadow self does not mean it does not exist**</u>. We behave as though it doesn't, but it exists despite our refusal to acknowledge it. This is why Jung said that it takes great moral courage to see our own shadow, which points to the creative imperative of *One Rule to Live By: Be Good*—the redemptive power of goodness that Socrates called the most noble virtue.

But it's much too soon yet to get to the point of my imperative, both personal and literary. I need sufficient context to make the point relevant, let alone credible. So, let me quote a spiritual musing that I posted on my Spiritual Musings blog *Saturday January 20, 2018* that speaks to the reality of the self that is who we are not but desperately wants to be who we are:

One Rule to Live By

The Eyes Behind Her Eyes

"The poet is the seer; the poem is the act of appropriation."

SOUL *at the* WHITE HEAT
—*Joyce Carol Oates.*

    I knew I was being called to write a poem as I watched an interview with the writer Iris Murdoch on the program *Modern Philosophy* on YouTube, hosted by the eloquent professor of philosophy and author Bryan Magee, the topic being "Philosophy and Literature," but I wasn't called by what the Oxford professor and novelist Iris Murdoch had to say about philosophy and literature, but by the beguiling look of her eyes, a look that I often see in deeply shadow-afflicted people, but never as pronounced as it was in Iris Murdoch's wary blue eyes that inspired my poem *The Eyes Behind Her Eyes* that I've been summoned by my muse to expand upon in today's spiritual musing—

The Eyes Behind Her Eyes

She had four eyes, two eyes
to look, and two eyes to see,
and she could not tell which
eyes were which.

Oxford Professor, writer, wife,
and childless by choice, a fluid
woman like no other, and the
breach of her eyes grew wider.

Tutoring young Oxfordian
minds by day, she stalked the
corridors of culture by night
to appease her hunger.

Danger abounded as she looked

for what she could not see,
and the harder she looked, the
more the danger grew.

Novel after novel, essay after
philosophical essay, but the
breach grew wider and wider
as her mind grew darker, —

And she died of Alzheimer's.

    The magic of poetry is its power to see into the mystery of life, and I had no idea what my poem was trying to tell me; all I knew was that the first two lines came to me unbidden and that I had to work out the rest of the poem, which I did. I went online and researched Iris Murdoch's life, and then I did some thoughtful editing and rewriting; but this did not alter the essential insight of my poem, which had to do with giving visual clarity to the Jungian concept of the shadow that I saw in Iris Murdoch's eyes; it only enhanced the poetic imagery. This is how the cognitive mind works with the writer's creative unconscious.

    Actually, the first two lines of my poem were not what they turned out to be in the finished poem; the first two lines went like this: *"She had four eyes, /two up front, and two in the back."* This is how my muse captured Iris Murdoch's shadow, which was so obvious to me that I could see her shadow as another personality with its own mind and emotions and distinct identity, hence the four eyes; and when the first lines of a poem come to me, I *have* to unpack them to see what my muse is trying to tell me. Nonetheless, I had to change the first two lines, because they created the wrong impression of having a set of eyes at the back of her head instead of having eyes within her eyes, which was more accurate.

    As I came to see after years of writing, our creative unconscious is infinitely wiser than our cognitive mind, but the cognitive mind has to do the work, and when the first lines of a poem come unbidden (sometimes, though rarely, a whole poem comes to me unbidden and word perfect, like my poem *What the Hell Is Going on Out There?*), I have no choice but to explore the given lines with thoughtful reflection, because if I don't, I will jeopardize my gift for writing poetry; which only means, really, that I'd have to work much harder to pry out of my unconscious the glimmer of my poetic insights.

But not with *The Eyes Behind Her Eyes*. This poem was easy to write once I had the first two lines, because they told me everything that I needed to say about the shadow I saw in Iris Murdoch's eyes. Which isn't to say that I was specifically given a poetic imperative to explore Iris Murdoch's shadow, which I did anyway by researching her life online, but because the creative imperative of my poem was to introduce the idea that the shadow can be seen in a person's eyes, and I had never seen the shadow as distinctly as I did in Iris Murdoch's eyes. That's why I *had* to write my poem *The Eyes Behind Her Eyes*.

So, how did I know that she had such a distinct shadow personality? What made it stand out for me? What was its most distinguishing feature? What gave her shadow away?

This is almost impossible to answer, but I will try; and the best way to resolve this mystery would be to provide a context that allows for the shadow to be seen in a person's eyes, a context that took me years to work out and which I creatively explored in my literary memoir *The Lion that Swallowed Hemingway* and its sequel, *My Writing Life: Reflections on My High School Hero and Literary Mentor Ernest "Papa" Hemingway,* which brought my perspective on Hemingway's paradoxical personality to resolution.

In effect, then; like a mystery writer who knows the solution to his mystery before writing his novel (or discovers the solution in the process of writing his novel), I will resort to the old saying that you can always tell a tree by its fruit. Let me say up front then, with all the gnostic certainty of personal experience and all the reading and writing and years of stalking the elusive shadow *(my own primarily)* that **the shadow is the unconscious persona of one's most private, most selfish nature; and it follows that the more selfish and self-centered a person is, the more shadow-afflicted one will be.** This is what inspired *The Lion that Swallowed Hemingway* and its sequel three years later, and what also gave Iris Murdoch's shadow away in her conversation with her brilliant host Bryan Magee.

Selfishness is the essential nature of our shadow, and all of its consequent behavior, *(the most bitter fruits of the shadow self are self-deception, vanity, and blind insensitivity),* which I saw in Iris Murdoch's eyes that set free the first two lines of my poem; so, I wrote my poem while I was in the grips of my *daemon,* and then I went online to research her life so I could flesh in my poem with biographical details that would confirm and expand my intuition, like the telling detail that Iris Murdoch had numerous sexual affairs before and after her marriage to the novelist and literary critic John Bayley, casual and passionate affairs with both men and women which were later verified by her posthumously published private letters.

I learned that Iris Murdoch was "gender fluid," so I added the phrase "a fluid woman like no other" in my poem to reflect this detail of her private life, a critical detail that spoke to her voracious sexual appetite that compelled her to gratify her sexual desires over, and over, and over again.

"Memoirs by her husband, John Bayley, and Richard Eyre's film *Iris,* in particular, defined her life around the poles of her defiant insistence on following her sexual desires where they took her," wrote Sarah Churchwell in her review of Murdoch's novel *The Sea, the Sea.* Which isn't to judge her morally; all that mattered to the imperative of my poem was the selfish nature of her private self, because **the more rapacious one's shadow is, the more distinct its identity will be,** and I could see Iris Murdoch's private shadow self as distinctly as I could see her erudite, sophisticated ego personality.

In my online research, it did not surprise me to learn that the basic themes of all her novels were "good and evil, sexual relationships, morality, and the power of the unconscious," because the more shadow-afflicted a person is, the more morally-conflicted they will be, and Iris Murdoch was a very conflicted woman which was revealed to me by the "breach of her eyes," as I wrote in my poem, the distance between her two sets of eyes that was later confirmed by my research on her life, both private and public.

"Iris Murdoch is an odd and difficult subject. Both in artistic and personal terms, she is a one-off. She does not fit comfortably into any literary history and her life was a series of contradictions," wrote Bryan Appleyard in his review of *Iris Murdoch: A Life,* by Peter Conradi, which is a perfect description of a deeply shadow-afflicted person, which Iris Murdoch's eyes revealed to me.

One Rule to Live By

Ironically, I've never read any of her novels or essays; but I did see the movie *Iris* based upon John Bayley's first two memoirs of his wife, starring Kate Winslet as the young Iris and Dame Judi Dench as the older Iris who was ravaged and died of Alzheimer's, a poignant portrayal of a philosopher/writer's life who creatively explored truth through her novels, as novelists tend to do; and all I wanted to do with my poem was to give the reader a glimpse into the creative process of truth-seeking through poetry, which can be eerily revealing when inspired, because there is often much more to a poem than even the poet can see; and in *The Eyes Behind her Eyes* I caught a faint glimmer of an insight into the possibility that Alzheimer's may just be as much psychologically induced as it is biologically based, an insight that is far beyond the scope of today's medical science and far more telling about the shadow than even the bravest poet would dare imagine.

Suffice to say then that the insight of my poem came to me unbidden to catch the shadow out, because the shadow is next-to-impossible to see. Only the inspired sight of a poet or mystic can see that the shadow is who we are not, the repressed and unresolved karmic energy of our ego/shadow personality, and what creates the "breach" between who we are not and who we are was what my muse was trying to tell me with *The Eyes Behind Her Eyes,* which I was called to expand upon in today's spiritual musing.

There we are, then; a perspective on the shadow self from that state of enlightened awareness that poets and mystics are blessed with. But who in the hell wants to believe that our shadow is as real as our ego personality? And yet writers have always explored the shadow side of the personality, like Dostoevsky in his angst-ridden novel *The Double;* and as *Oscar Wilde* in his soul-baring novel *The Picture of Dorian Gray;* and Robert Louis Stevenson in the best-known novel in the world on the darkest aspect of the human personality in his shocking tale of *The Strange Case of Doctor Jekyll and Mr. Hyde;* three exceptionally gifted novelists who dared to explore the unconscious—not to mention Edgar Allan Poe whose horror stories delved into his dark side, like "William Wilson" and "The Cask of Amontillado," which are classified as "tales of the double (or evil) personality."

Those are the most obvious examples. But exploring the shadow side of life makes for the most compelling reading, and this theme can be found throughout literature; like in James Joyce's *Dubliners*, specifically his story "The Counterpart," or in Hemingway's much more nuanced story "The Snows of Kilimanjaro" that he said was his most autobiographical story, but which I seriously doubt because Hemingway was dangerously more revealing of his self-deceiving ego/shadow personality in *Across the River and Into the Trees* in which he projected his own pathetically besotted love for a 19-year-old Venetian girl called Adriana onto his fictional self Colonel Cantwell's pathetic infatuation with an 18-year-old Venetian girl called Renata, and I explored Hemingway's shadow-possessed personality in *The Lion that Swallowed Hemingway* that I sent to professor Peterson before he came into public prominence, followed three years later with my sequel *My Writing Life, Reflections on My High School Hero and Literary Mentor Earnest "Papa" Hemingway*, in which I brought to resolution my understanding of the tortured writer's paradoxical personality.

I've been studying the shadow ever since I became aware of my own shadow in high school *(around grade ten I began to have an eerie sense of my own mercurial falseness)*, and I've become very familiar with the psychology of the shadow self; but it's next to impossible to expose the shadow to the light of common day. I tried with my first novel *What Would I Say Today If I Were to Die Tomorrow?* and Penny and I paid dearly for my valiant but outrageously foolish literary effort.

My hometown of Nipigon and surrounding communities were so outraged by my novel—*like an angry dog that had been rudely awakened and turned on us with a vengeance!* —that

One Rule to Live By

Penny and I had to relocate to Georgian Bay for peace of mind; so, I know what it can cost a writer for exposing the dark shadow side of life. Thomas Wolfe paid dearly for his autobiographical novel *Look Homeward Angel,* and look at what happened to James Joyce who not only turned his home town of Dublin against him with his stories in *Dubliners,* but his whole country; and now they celebrate him as one of Ireland's greatest writers. *Resentment runs deep, but it runs dry eventually.*

This is why I admire professor Peterson for speaking truth to power to defend our right to free speech, and for putting himself out there with his *12 Rules for Life: An Antidote to Chaos* that scares the bejesus out of the nefarious spirit of postmodern nihilism, self-negating identity politics, and political correctness gone loony. The dogs are snapping at his heels.

But like everyone whose path can take them no further on their destined journey to wholeness and completeness, Jordan B. Peterson was called to a higher purpose; and being painfully true to himself, he heeded the call to be a hierophant for today's crazy world...

7. The Mystery of Personal Identity

> "These leaves, our bodily personalities, seem identical,
> but the globe of soul-fruit we make,
> each is elaborately unique."
> —*Jalaluddin Rumi*

Personal identity. That's a hot topic today. Do we evolve in our personal identity existentially, through millions of years of natural evolution from the lowest life form all the way up to higher primates and then into human beings with a reflective self-consciousness? And if so, at what point did our "I" come into being? That's the mystery of personal identity.

I began my quest for my true self because of a sexual experience I had in my early twenties that brutally shocked my conscience awake and I could not live with myself, but I knew that the person who did what he did that night was not me; it was me, but not me, and I vowed to find out who this other me was or die trying.

That was the existential beginning of my journey of self-discovery, which I resolved when I gave birth to my immortal self in my mother's kitchen one fine summer day when my inner and outer selves became one self, whole and complete. What I want to make clear now is that there is more to the "I" of our *existential* life than we can see, because the "I" of our *existential* life is ensouled with the "I" of our evolving *essential* self; but who would believe this? Who would believe that we have two selves?

There are any number of theories about the "I" of our personal identity. Carl Jung told me in a dream one night that the burning question of his life was the alpha and omega of the self—*where does the self come from, and where does it go?* That's why I dropped out of university in my third year of philosophy studies, because I felt myself drifting out into a sea of endless philosophical speculation, the why and where and when and how of man's *being* and *non-being*, an endless mentation that would have drowned me; and I left university to look elsewhere for the answer to the question that had compelled me to go to university in the first place, *who am I?*

Philosophy means love of wisdom, and I needed all the wisdom I could get to find my true self; so, where else would I go to find the answer to my haunting question but to the mother of all disciplines? But I did not leave university empty-handed. I "found" Gurdjieff's teaching at university, and with his system of "work on oneself" through *conscious effort* and *intentional suffering* I went out into the world of order and confusion and set my feet firmly into the *"terra firma"* of my own existential life; and I built my life upon the gnostic truth of my own *lived* experiences.

I *knew* in my soul that the me who did what he did that evil night was me but not me, but how could this be? I did not plan to do what I did that night after shutting down my pool hall business for the day, I became possessed by this other me that compelled me to do what I did; but it wasn't the me that I knew myself to be. It was another me, a false me; and I dropped everything and went on a quest to find out who this other me was. That's how my quest for my real self began.

I gave up the lease on my pool hall business and boarded an ocean liner in New York City and sailed to Naples, Italy, and from there I took a bus to Paris and then a train to the Alpine city of Annecy in the *Haute-Savoie* region of France where I lived for a year before returning home to face the music. An Italian friend in Canada, who worked in one of the bush camps where I had worked before taking over the pool hall business in my hometown, had a brother and sister living in Annecy who welcomed me; and that's when my quest for my real self began in earnest, despite the fact that I had been called to become a seeker in high school when Somerset Maugham's novel *The Razor's Edge* inflicted me with an immortal wound that set my soul on fire. And while living in Annecy, I accidentally opened up the chakra at the base of my spine and awakened the kundalini (the "serpent fire") while meditating on a maple leaf one evening, and the kundalini energy set my mind on fire; and though it nearly drove me out of my mind like it did in my past lifetime as Salaam the mendicant Sufi *(it took a good ten years of relentless effort to harness the wild energies of the kundalini which was responsible for many of my personal aberrations that I will never live down)*, it provided me with all the energy I could ever need to continue my quest for my real self, and I went wherever I was beckoned by the most meaningful signs and symbols that life offered me and my own gut feelings pointed me to, paying whatever it cost me; until one day I was called to pay the final price, which I wrote about in *The Pearl of Great Price* that I sent to professor Jordan Peterson.

So I *experienced* the alpha and omega of my personal identity, from my embryonic un-self-conscious soul self in the Body of God to the birth of my reflective self-consciousness in my first primordial human lifetime as a higher primate, which I confirmed in my fourth past-life regression, and all the way up through many more incarnations to the happy resolution of my *existential* and *essential* self in my current lifetime when I gave birth to my immortal self in my mother's kitchen one summer day while she was kneading bread dough on the kitchen table; and when I hear all of this talk today on the hot topic of personal identity and gender politics, which got professor Peterson into hot water, I find myself smiling at all the confusion that I would also have been lost in had I completed my academic studies and garnered a master's degree, or PhD in philosophy.

But I would never have ventured down the path I was called to had I not believed in God, the immortal soul, and the afterlife; this was implicit to my belief system, and in my quest for my real self, I became more and more conscious of what I believed in. This is what *inspired* the spiritual musing that I posted on my blog *Friday, February 2, 2018*:

One Rule to Live By

Why People Don't Believe in God, the Immortal Soul, or Afterlife

From the earliest age, I never doubted the existence of God, the immortal soul, or afterlife; on the contrary, it was because of my belief that I suffered the anguish I did as I grew up in my Roman Catholic faith. I felt trapped, and I had no idea why. All I knew was that I was born with a purpose, but I had no idea that this purpose was to find my lost soul. And then in grade twelve Somerset Maugham's novel *The Razor's Edge* inflicted me with what professor Harold Bloom called an immortal wound of wonder, and I became an inveterate truth seeker like Maugham's intrepid hero Larry Darrell.

But I've covered a lot of ground since I began my quest for my lost soul, which, ironically, I had presciently foreseen in my poem *Noman* that I wrote that same year for my grade twelve English teacher (who must have found it bewildering, to say the least; especially the closing lines when Noman shouts as he falls from heaven, *"Open you vile, voracious, loveable sweet whore! /God, why hast thou forsaken me?)* but which I finally resolved fifty years later in the memoir of my parallel life, *The Summoning of Noman* (which I sent to my English teacher who was still living but who must have been no less shocked again because he never got back to me; I also sent him a copy of *The Pearl of Great Price* and *In the Shade of the Maple Tree*, my first volume of dialogues with St. Padre Pio, which probably baffled him even more than my poem); but in my awareness that I was a lost soul whose compulsive imperative was to find my true self, I solved the riddle of the human condition which I worked out in *My Writing Life,* the sequel to my literary memoir *The Lion that Swallowed Hemingway.*

And herein lies the mystery of why some people believe in God, the immortal soul, and afterlife and others don't; and it all has to do with where one's "I" is centered. And by "I" I mean the reflective consciousness of one's individuating soul self, which is the central problem of the human condition that the great writer Leo Tolstoy tried to explore in his novel *The Death of Ivan Ilych,* a problem that stems from the paradoxical nature of our reflective self—our *existential* and *essential* self, as the German mystic teacher of the gnostic way

Karlfield Graf Durckeim described the dual consciousness of our soul self.

"We are citizens of two worlds, an 'existential' one which is a conditioned reality, limited by time and space, and an 'essential' one unconditioned and beyond time and space, accessible only to our inner consciousness and inaccessible to our powers," said K. G. Durckeim in Alphonse Goettmann's book, *The Path of Initiation*. And he goes on to say: "***Only this union of the existential self with the essential self, dealing with the whole of man, carries him to his full maturity and bears fruits, the first and most important of which is to be able to say "I am" in the full meaning of the word.*** From this becoming of the "I" in the full blossoming depends the relationship between man and the world, man and himself, man and Transcendence. At the beginning and at the end, at the origin and in the development of all life is found this transcendent "I am." At the heart of all that is, man secretly senses this great "I Am" from which comes and to which returns all life. ***Each being is called to realize in his own way to this divine "I am" which seeks to express itself in modalities as varied and diverse as are all creatures of the universe***" (*The Path of Initiation, An Introduction to the Life and Thought of Karlfield Graft Durckeim*, by Alphonse Goettmann, pp. 33, 36, 37, bold italics mine).

And now comes the tricky truth; which is to say, the unrealized truth of our soul self as I have come to experience it and which will no doubt be subject to the ridicule and resistance of arrogant incredulity before it will ever be accepted as an incontrovertible fact of the human condition.

As K. G. Durckeim realized (as have many mystics, poets, and God knows who else), it would appear that we have two selves; one self, or "I" that is born of our life in this world, which makes it our ephemeral *existential* self, and an a priori *essential* and immortal self that we are born with. But what Durckeim did not express in his apperception of the double self of man, was the dual consciousness of our *existential* ego/shadow personality that I spent most of my life exploring as I lived my own gnostic path of conscious self-individuation inspired by Gurdjieff's teaching and chronicled in *The*

One Rule to Live By

Pearl of Great Price, the unbelievable true story of the self-realization of the "I am" consciousness of my soul self.

Without going into detail, which I've done in my twin soul books *Death, the Final Frontier* and *The Merciful Law of Divine Synchronicity*, suffice to say here that we all come into the world as sparks of divine consciousness, embryonic souls pre-destined to grow and evolve through life into fully self-realized individual souls, which K. G. Durckeim defined as the blessed fruit of the "I am" consciousness of God; but to bear the fruit of our own individuation process, we have to make one "I" out of our *existential* ego/shadow self and our *essential* soul self, one "I" whole and complete unto itself, just as Jung realized in his own gnostic path and which his unconscious confirmed in a dream he had just before dying at the ripe old age of 85. In his dream he saw, high up on a high place, a boulder lit by the full sun, and carved into the illuminated boulder were the words: *"Take this as a sign of the wholeness you have achieved and the singleness you have become."* This was the blessed fruit of his life, his precious pearl of great price.

As incredible as it may seem (this would be the resistance stage that the world will have to my spiritual rebirth), I also experienced wholeness and singleness of self, which I spelled out first in *Gurdjieff Was Wrong, But His Teaching Works* and later in *The Pearl of Great Price*; that's how I solved the riddle of our paradoxical nature that bedevils everyone, especially philosophers and scientists, and it all has to do with what Jesus revealed in his cryptic teachings of the **secret way** about making our two selves into one.

In the *Gospel of Thomas,* the Master was asked by someone when the kingdom would come, and Jesus replied*:* **"When the two will be one, and the outer like the inner, and the male with the female neither male nor female."** And Thomas added, "Now the two are one when we speak truth to each other and there is one soul in two bodies with no hypocrisy" (*The Unknown Sayings of Jesus,* by Marvin Meyer, p. 95); which simply means, at the risk of inviting further ridicule and resistance, that we have to reconcile the ephemeral consciousness of our ego/shadow personality with our eternal soul self, which we can only do when we live by transformative values that are inherently self-transcending, as all great spiritual teachers of the world like Socrates, Jesus, and Rumi have told us; values like truthfulness, kindness, and goodness.

"These leaves, our bodily personalities, seem identical, /but the globe of soul fruit /we make, /each is elaborately /unique," said Rumi, which speaks to what pioneering depth psychologist C. G. Jung came to call the individuation process of the archetypal self of man, *"a bliss peculiar to each one by individual existence,"* said John Keats in his letter "The Vale of Soul Making," and herein lies the quandary that bedevils the world about God, the immortal soul, and the afterlife…

This is going to be a very hard if not impossible truth to swallow, but there is no other way of saying it: our *essential* self is our inner, true soul self, and our *existential* self is our outer, ephemeral self; and those of us who have an innate belief in God, the immortal soul, and afterlife have been born centered in our *essential* self, or shift our center of gravity, the "I" of our *existential* self, to our *essential* self in the course of living our life; and those of us who have doubts about God, the immortal soul, and afterlife have been born centered in our ephemeral *existential* self, or shift our center of gravity to our ephemeral self in the course of living our life, and by ephemeral self I mean the unresolved ego/shadow consciousness of our individuating *essential* soul self. In effect, we only have one "I", but it is bifurcated; and our destined purpose in life is to reconcile our false ego/shadow self with our inner, true soul self. *This is the human predicament.*

This of course presupposes the principles of karma and reincarnation (again, subject to the incredulity, if not violent resistance by some quarters like Christianity which disavows reincarnation that was once part of its belief system), because our *existential* ephemeral self is the unresolved consciousness of all the ego/shadow personalities that we have created over the course of our reincarnational history and which we bring with us unconsciously with each new life that we are born into; and it's to the ontological nature of our ephemeral self that determines why so many people have doubts about God, the immortal soul, and afterlife.

One Rule to Live By

Strictly speaking, belief and non-belief in God, the immortal soul, and afterlife all comes down to the degree of the blended consciousness of one's ephemeral *non-being* and the eternal reality of one's *being,* which determines the degree of one's belief or non-belief in God, the immortal soul, and after life—which, truth be told, will vary over the course of one's life as one shifts between their *being* and *non-being* selves.

But why? What is it about the consciousness of our ephemeral self that grows and evolves with the *existential* self of our ego/shadow personality of each new life that we are born into that leads one to doubt the existence of God, the immortal soul, and afterlife? *What?*

That was the quandary of my lost soul self that horrified me when my *daemon* spouted my poem *Noman* out of the profoundest depths of my *non-being* self like a volcanic eruption and which I finally resolved in my memoir *The Summoning of Noman* fifty years later after I found my lost soul self; but the short answer for today's spiritual musing can be distilled from my experience of finding my true self, which should be convincing in itself but I *know* will not be because, as Gurdjieff said, "There is only self-initiation into the mysteries of life." Nonetheless, the answer is simple enough, if totally incomprehensible to the cognitive mind; but how can one possibly believe in God, the immortal soul, and afterlife if their ephemeral self *is* the I-consciousness of one's *non-being*, the paradoxical self of one's *essential* self?

The ephemeral self that everyone experiences in moments of deep despair as that unbearable sense of one's own nothingness is *ipso facto* incapable of believing in God, the immortal soul, and afterlife, because this is the self of one's own *non-being*, and one cannot possibly believe in God, the immortal soul, and afterlife if they are centered in the consciousness of their *non-being*; the ontology of one's own *nothingness* simply precludes it. Which explains why one would be an atheist and non-believer.

Our ephemeral self is the self of who we are not, the self of who we are yet-to-be, the unresolved *non-being* of our *essential* nature, the consciousness of our *existential* self that is only conscious of its own mortality and consequent meaninglessness that Shakespeare described as "a tale told by an idiot full of sound and fury signifying nothing." This is the same self that Sartre gave voice to when he said, "I am what I am not, and I am not what I am." This is why he called man "a useless passion," because he could not resolve the *enantiodromiac* dynamic of soul's imperative to wholeness and completeness. Jean-Paul Sartre, like every unbeliever in the world, was centered in his *non-being* self and could not find his way out; hence his monumental work *Being and Nothingness* and his play *No Exit*.

In effect, this is what a lost soul is, a soul born centered in the unresolved ephemeral self of its *non-being*; and if not born this way, it becomes this way according to the values that it has been brought up with or chosen to live by, values that compromise one's destined journey to wholeness and completeness, values that serve the ego/shadow personality and not one's inner, true soul self.

And, at the risk of offending non-believers even further, not until one has grown enough through the natural individuation process of karma and reincarnation and is ready to take evolution into their own hands to complete what Nature cannot finish will one be free to reconcile their ephemeral self with their *essential* nature and become one self whole and complete; only then will this truth become self-evident. That's the mystery of the human predicament that the poet Emily Dickinson spoke to when she wrote: "Adventure most unto itself /The Soul condemned to be; /Attended by a Single Hound— /Its own Identity."

———

This is why I cannot get caught up in the gender politics and identity confusion of the LGBTQ community that called professor Jordan Peterson to refute Bill C-16, the amendment to the Human Rights Act that would have compelled him and all Canadians to use gender neutral pronouns to identify whatever the gender variations wished to call themselves, because he felt—*and rightly so, as most of us believe*—that it was a violation of our freedom of speech (and by extension, freedom of thought as well), and he refused to be compelled by government fiat to use gender neutral pronouns that weren't organic to the language. It was an obscene piece of badly reasoned legislation.

The established pronouns for the male and female genders (he/him/his, she/his/hers, they/them/theirs) were sufficient to define the existential gender binary reality of human nature, and he shouted NO! to the amendment Bill C-16 and was heard loud and clear by the common-sense folk who are sick and tired of all this identity politics and political correctness nonsense that has made a travesty of truthfulness and good-faith logic; and that's what catapulted Citizen Peterson onto the world stage when his protest videos went viral on YouTube. And then he published his shadow-shocking, character-building book *12 Rules for Life: An Antidote to Chaos* to push back the toxic tide of neo-Marxist postmodern nihilism and bad-faith logic that has fostered the mind-boggling chaos that is fueling the divisive ideology of identity politics and mindless political correctness.

Of course, I'm speaking from a perspective that presupposes the reincarnational history of one's personal identity, the many lifetimes of growth and individuation of one's *essential* self that is genetically imbedded in the cellular memory of each new incarnation; this is why I've come to believe that this whole LGBTQ gender confusion issue has less to do with nature and nurture and more to do with the history of one's own past lives. And in *Seth Speaks, The Eternal Validity of the Soul,* by Jane Roberts, the psychic who channeled the higher collective entity called Seth, Seth verifies this shocking, but irrefutable outside-the-box perspective:

"As I mentioned earlier, each person lives both male and female lives. As a rule, conscious memory of these are not retained. To prevent oversimplification of the individual with his present sex, within the male there resides an inner personification of femaleness. This personification of femaleness in the male is the true meaning of what Jung called the 'anima.'

The anima in the male is, therefore, the psychic memory and identification of all the previous female existences in which the inner self has been involved. It contains within it the knowledge of the present male's past female histories, and the intuitive understanding of all the female qualities with which the personality is innately endowed...Maleness and femaleness are obviously not opposites, but merging tendencies...The animus and anima are, of course, highly charged psychically, but the origin of this psychic charge and the inner fascination are the result of a quite legitimate inner identification with these personified other-sex characteristics. They not only have a reality in the psyche, however, but they are imbedded in genetically codified data by the inner self—a genetic memory of past psychic events—transposed into the genetic memory of the very cells that compose the body.

Each inner self, adopting a new body, imposes upon it and upon its entire genetic makeup, memory of the past physical forms in which it has been involved. Now, the present characteristics usually overshadow the past ones. They are dominant, but the other characteristics are latent and present, built into the pattern" (*Seth Speaks, The Eternal Validity of the Soul,* by Jane Roberts, pp. 219, 220, 221).

So, there's more to personal identity than meets the eye then; and I've come to believe that this whole LGBTQ gender confusion issue stems from our past lives, as this entity of higher collective energy called Seth confirmed. But I worked this out long before I found confirmation in my reading, and I came to the conclusion that a soul that lives three or four *consecutive* lifetimes as a female and is reborn a male will have overshadowing memories of being a woman, and these pressing memories of its female gender will push up into the mind of its male body; this is why a gay man will say, "I was born in the wrong body. I should have been a woman." And the same with a soul that lives three or four *consecutive* lifetimes as a man and reincarnates as woman; it will have such strong memories of being a man that it will say, "I was born in the wrong body. I should have been a man." This is what causes gender confusion; and as offensive as this may be to some people, I believe this is a deep soul-betrayal of one's sexual identity and morally torturous for the LGBTQ person who cannot resolve their trans feelings of being the wrong gender. This is why Dr. Peterson rightly calls trans people confused, and why he has been called transphobic by the LGBTQ community—*a total misperception of the behavioral psychologist's understanding of the binary nature of the human condition.*

But to come to a clear perspective, one has to take evolution into their own hands and resolve their inner and outer self and become one self, whole and complete; and that speaks to the imperative of *One Rule to Live By: Be Good,* which has a long way to go yet before I have enough context to do the noble virtue of goodness the justice it deserves...

8. The Unbearable Anguish of Being Called

While going to high school, I had four or five past-life recollection dreams. As much as I felt myself fully present in my dream-life experiences *(especially in my lifetime as a North American Indian when I had to endure a painful rite of passage which I had to undergo twice because the first time I did not have the courage to see it through and was banished from our village until I grew strong enough to be initiated into manhood)*, I did not know they were past-life recollection dreams until I began reading books on reincarnation and the "Sleeping Prophet," as America's greatest psychic Edgar Cayce was called; but I always felt that there was something different about me that I could never put my finger on; I did not belong in my family.

I was so different from my parents and siblings that I felt I had been born into the wrong family; but from all the reading that I did on reincarnation I came to learn that we choose the family we are born into. But why did I choose my family?

Then I read Jess Stern's book, *The Search for a Soul: Taylor Caldwell's Psychic Lives* (Taylor Caldwell was the hugely successful historical novelist who received the information for her novels from the Akashic Records), and I knew that one day I would write a book on my own past lives, which I did when Penny Lynn and I moved to Georgian Bay, South Central Ontario, and I had seven past-life regressions that became the inspiration for my novel *Cathedral of My Past Lives;* and though it's not published yet, I connected the dots while writing this novel and saw the big picture of life, and my own life in particular, because I finally understood why I had the strangest feeling growing up that I was going to be *"the last of my own line,"* whatever that meant.

At first, I thought this strange feeling meant that I would not have any children (I don't); but the more I studied what

Socrates called "a doctrine uttered in secret," the more I began to suspect that my current lifetime was going to be my last incarnation. Which led me to believe that the "gadfly" of Athens, who was tried and condemned for defending free speech (*see how far we've come, Jordan!*), was only telling half the story when he said that the unexamined life was not worth living; because in light of karma and reincarnation, I came to see that every life we live is necessary for our destined purpose of becoming what we are meant to be, a realization that inspired the following spiritual musing that I posted on my blog *Tuesday, January 20, 2018*:

The Sanctity of Individual Experience

One of the most difficult decisions of my life was dropping out of university in the second semester of my third year of philosophy studies, but I *had* to; I had been called to the gnostic path of my own life with Gurdjieff's teaching of "work on oneself," which *the merciful law of divine synchronicity* provided for me with the serendipitous gift of P. D. Ouspensky's book *In Search of the Miraculous* in my second year of studies. I didn't know this at the time, though; that's what made my decision to drop out of university so excruciating, because the humiliation of dropping out would be devastating.

I began to feel it around the middle of my second year, a terrifying feeling of being cast adrift in a sea of endless philosophical speculation, seductively brilliant but speculative all the same; and then I began to feel a growing sense of panic that I would be cast so far adrift I would lose my way and drown before I found what I had gone to university to look for, and by the second semester of my third year I heard the call of the *way* so loud and clear in Gurdjieff's teaching that I had to sever my relationship with academia because philosophy had done all it could for me, and that's not where I was meant to be.

"*What am I doing here?*" I asked myself, in the darkness of my bedroom of the house I shared with three male students in the winter of my second year; but I persisted in the hope that I would find the path to my true self in philosophy. And that's the subject of today's spiritual musing, the path that we are called to when we're ready to be called by life to our destined purpose.

I didn't want to write this spiritual musing, because it meant dredging up all those feelings of dropping out of university; but, as the Algerian-born French philosopher Albert Camus wrote in *The Myth of Sisyphus* (though I did not agree with him that one must imagine Sisyphus happy in his punishment of rolling a rock up a hill for all eternity for offending the gods), *"crushing truths perish from being acknowledged,"* and only by coming to terms with my humiliation of dropping out of university would I finally resolve those still-anguishing feelings; but let me explain first how I was called to write today's spiritual musing…

I went on YouTube one evening and came upon a video that caught my attention, titled *The C.G. Jung Foundation Presents*, which I watched with growing fascination when I learned that Dr. Stevens had serendipitously come upon his own life-path through his research on attachment behavior in infants for his doctoral thesis, which in turn brought him to the Jungian therapist who had analyzed him when he was a student, because he wanted to ask her if Jung's theoretical approach of the archetypes would help him in his doctoral research on infant attachment behavior, and he was so taken by what she told him that this led him to change his course and become a Jungian analyst himself; and he went on to write many books on the individuation process, starting with his best known book, *Archetype: A Natural History of the Self.*

Dr. Stevens set free the idea for today's spiritual musing (though the title that came to me was "One of the Most Difficult Decisions of My Life," which I instantly changed when I heard the phrase "the sanctity of individual experience" in a follow-up video, because this phrase honored the gnostic wisdom of personal experience); and when I finished watching the tribute to Dr. Stevens, I went on Amazon and put *Archetype: A Natural History of the Self* on my Amazon wish list; but because serendipity had provided Dr. Stevens with the discovery of his new life-path in C.G. Jung's psychology just as serendipity had provided me with mine in Gurdjieff's teaching, I felt compelled to watch a video link of a talk on synchronicity by Frank Joseph, which (*oh happy coincidence!*) gave me exactly what I needed to help make the point of today's spiritual musing: **the only truth we can count on in life is the gnostic truth of our own *lived* experience.**

    That's why I dropped out of university. I could no longer trust what the great thinkers of the world—Sartre, Camus, Nietzsche, Schopenhauer, Kierkegaard *et al*—had to say, because it finally dawned on me that that was *their* truth and not mine, and in the final analysis it was all very personal and speculative, however true or false it may have been; and to find my true self, I *knew* that I would have to build my life upon the only truth that I could count on, and that was the truth of my own *lived* experience; and I could only do so by going out into the world and living my own life with the guidance of Gurdjieff's teaching of "work on oneself," because the call of his teaching was strong enough to sever me from the path of philosophy that I had grown to distrust, and I tortured myself for days over my decision to leave.

    But why not pursue my degree in philosophy and still employ Gurdjieff's teaching to help me find my true self? Would not that have been the prudent thing to do?

    That would have been the logical thing to do, but I couldn't. I went to university because that's where my quest for my true self had taken me, and in my second year down the philosopher's lonely path serendipity introduced me to the gnostic way of life through Gurdjieff's teaching, because in its infinite wisdom *the omniscient guiding principle of life* knew that this was the path to my true self and not philosophy, and even though I did not know this consciously, I felt it so deeply in my soul that I *had* to leave; that's why it was so painful to drop out of university in the second semester of my third year.

    I *knew* that if I pursued philosophy, I would have gone down a path that was no longer right for me; and this brings me to Frank Joseph's talk on synchronicity, which was drawn from his book *Synchronicity and You: Understanding the Role of Meaningful Coincidence in Your Life.*

As original as Frank Joseph's paradigm-shifting synchronicity experience was, it did not come as a surprise to me, because I had long been aware of how *the omniscient guiding principle of life* works in the world; and the wilful young atheist Frank Joseph was summoned to his gnostic path of self-discovery by a mind-blowing meaningful coincidence late one afternoon while driving home from work in the spring of 1992 in Chicago where he lived and worked as a courier.

For no apparent reason, as he was driving home the name "Rushdie" popped into his mind and would not go away. "Rushdie, Rushdie, Rushdie," over and over again, and he couldn't figure out why the author of *The Satanic Verses*, a novel that had stirred the ire of the Muslim world enough to threaten Rushdie's life and force him to go into hiding for years, would pop into his mind and not go away until he willed it to go away; but just as he willed it out of his mind, a dark blue Buick drove up along the off-ramp on his right side and pulled out in front of him, and that's when he had the synchronicity that set him on the course to his new path in life, because, believe it or not, the licence plate of that Buick read: RUSHDIE.

The odds of those two events—the name popping into his mind for no apparent reason and then on the licence plate—were astronomical, if the event was even mathematically possible, which after much research on the synchronicity principle led Frank Joseph to believe that it was not a random event at all but providentially designed, and this compelled him to pursue his new path wherever it took him.

Without going into detail, which he does in his book *Synchronicity and You,* after he had that meaningful coincidence with the licence plate he kept a journal of his own and other people's coincidences, and after six years of recording all of those coincidences he wrote a book on the subject, and as he wrote about all of those coincidences he began to see a pattern emerge out of every person's coincidences, which blew his mind again, because the pattern of each person's coincidences spelled out the script of their life story, as if one's life was being choreographed by an invisible guiding principle; and that's when Frank Joseph shed his willful atheism and became a believer in a benevolent guiding principle, and

One Rule to Live By

I couldn't help but smile when I read this, because that was the same conclusion that I had come to and written about in my own book, *The Merciful Law of Divine Synchronicity*.

Robert H. Hopcke, the author of *There Are No Accidents: Synchronicity and the Stories of Our Lives*, wrote: "…our lives have a narrative structure, like that of novels, and at those moments we call synchronistic this structure is brought to our awareness in a way that has a significant impact on our lives." And in *The Power of Coincidence: How Life Shows Us What We Need to Know*, David Richo wrote: **"Synchronicity shows us that the world orchestrates some of our life events so they can harmonize with the requirements of our inner journey."** Which was the same conclusion that Frank Joseph came to while writing his book *Synchronicity and You* (to be followed with *The Power of Coincidence: The Mysterious Role of Synchronicity in Shaping Our Lives)*; but this begs the question: what does the narrative structure of our life lead to?

We all have our own individual story, and these authors came to the conclusion that the imperative of our own story compels us—in the words of Joseph Campbell, author of *The Hero with A Thousand Faces*—to be true to ourselves and follow our own bliss; but all this means is that one must be true to the path they have been called to, like Dr. Anthony Stevens and Frank Joseph were; but again, why?

This is the real mystery, and not until one gets to the end of their story will one resolve it, as Jung did by living his own path, which was confirmed by a dream he had several days before dying, a gnostic truth that he explored in *The Red Book*, the same gnostic truth of one's true self that became the premise of my own book *The Pearl of Great Price*; suffice to say that <u>**the more true one is to their life-path, the more they will grow in personal meaning and gnostic wisdom that satisfies the longing in their soul for wholeness and completeness**</u>.

This is why I *had* to drop out of university. Philosophy wasn't giving me what I needed to satisfy the longing in my soul for wholeness and completeness, and *the omniscient guiding principle of life* called me to live my own life and find my own truth with the guidance of Gurdjieff's teaching of "work on oneself," which is why I chose the title "The Sanctity of Individual Experience" for today's spiritual musing. As Jung said in *The Red Book*, **"The way is and always will be an individual path."**

POSTSCRIPT

This is pure conjecture, but as I reworked this spiritual musing to make it as reader-friendly as possible for my Spiritual Musings blog (not easy to do, given the subject matter), it dawned on me why the name Rushdie popped into Frank Joseph's mind the day he had his life-changing experience. Everything happens for a reason, and synchronicities do not just drop out of the air for nothing; they happen to startle our mind and wake us up to the deeper mystery of our life's purpose, and Frank Joseph's life needed re-alignment. In effect, his outer self had to be brought into alignment with the destined purpose of his inner self.

Salman Rushdie was a confirmed atheist and gifted writer who had the courage to be true to his own calling, and he was called to write *The Satanic Verses* that shocked the Muslim community out of its spiritual complacency; but that's what writers do, shine the light of creative insight into social consciousness to break up inflexible patterns of thought to help expand old paradigms of meaning that have long served their purpose.

That's why Rushdie's name popped into Frank Joseph's mind, his higher self gave him a symbolic, albeit ironic imperative in Salman Rushdie's name to explore a different path to his true self, because his willfully defiant path of atheism had blinded him to his destined purpose of wholeness and completeness as it had done to Salman Rushdie who got stuck in the closed paradigm of atheism, and Frank Joseph was ready to move on to a new path, which he discovered as he dug deeper and deeper into the mystery of the synchronicity principle that began to erode his belief in the closed belief system of atheism.

Every path in life serves its purpose; and when one's path can do no more to satisfy the longing in one's soul for wholeness and completeness, *the merciful law of divine synchronicity* kicks in to reconnect one with their destined purpose, which is how I found my new path in Gurdjieff's teaching through the serendipitous gift of

One Rule to Live By

Ouspensky's book *In Search of the Miraculous* when I got the uneasy feeling that philosophy could do no more for me, just as Frank Joseph's belief in atheism could do no more for him and *the merciful law of divine synchronicity* kicked in to save him from himself.

It's sweetly ironic then that the cynical atheist Salman Rushdie should pop into the defiant young atheist's mind that day; but that's the playful side of the synchronicity principle, which Frank Joseph was blissfully unaware of. Nonetheless, his is an amazing story of how he found his new path in life, just as all life-changing stories of synchronicity are, another favorite of mine being how the pattern of meaningful coincidences wrote the script of Sir Winston Churchill's life to become the Prime Minister of England who saved his country from the Nazi war machine; but that's a spiritual musing for another day.

So, I got severed from the academic life because I was called to forge my own path through life with Gurdjieff's teaching of "work on oneself," which was one of the most excruciating decisions of my entire life; but not the most anguishing.

My most anguishing experience was being severed from my life when I became possessed by a sexual desire that so brutally traumatized my conscience that I could not live with myself, and I dropped my comfortable life (I was going on twenty-three and doing very well in my pool hall and vending machine business) and fled to Annecy, France where I began my quest for an answer to the terrifying mystery of my dual nature—because the person who did what he did that godforsaken night was me, but not me; and I had to find out who this other me was.

As the Stoic poet Cleanthes put it, we can walk alongside our destiny or be dragged by it, and I was not mature and wise enough to walk alongside my destiny; I had to be severed from my life and be dragged by my destiny to the path that would best satisfy the longing in my soul for wholeness and completeness. That's why *the merciful law of divine synchronicity* provided me with Gurdjieff's teaching when I began to get the uneasy feeling that philosophy was not the path for me; and by the second semester of my third year, I panicked.

That's why I left university with nothing but Gurdjieff's teaching to guide me through life; and, believe me, this was not an easy decision to make. It cost me in more ways than I care to remember. As professor Peterson would say, I stepped out of a world of order into chaos, and I did not know what monsters were out there waiting for me. *God, did I not know!*

So, I know a call when I hear it; and when professor Peterson put his career on the line when he stood up for free speech by refusing to comply to Bill C-16 that would compel him, and all Canadians, to use gender neutral pronouns, a courageous stand for free speech that would threaten both his academic career and clinical practice, I *knew* he had been called to a higher path, and I *knew* just how terrifying it was going to be for him...

Sixteen months after his courageous decision, having survived the initial horrors of the malevolent forces of identity politics and radical political correctness that were out to destroy him, professor Peterson was asked by Dave Rubin on *The Rubin Report* (streamlined *January 31, 2018*): "As these last couple of years have happened, and as you both (Ben Shapiro, another staunch defender of free speech and enemy of identity politics and radical political correctness, was Rubin's other guest) have risen in profile, and you're out there saying what you think all the time, and defending your beliefs, what's been the most personal thing that you've struggled with along the way?"

And the good professor and seasoned clinical therapist, honest to the bone, took his time and thoughtfully replied, with poignant self-conscious awareness: *"Well, for me it's two things. One is—it's not so bad now. It's still pretty bad. I've lived in constant existential terror of saying something that will be* fatal...I've had to watch myself in a hyper-vigilant manner to provide those who regard me as their enemy with the tools to dispense with me...you know, I have my family resting on me as well as whatever else I happen to be doing; so, it's been extraordinarily intense. And the other thing is the persistent feeling of surreality of what's happening to me..."

Given his exponentially rising number of followers on YouTube and other venues *(they lined up by the hundreds to hear his book tour talks, giving more and more credence to a real life allegory of the Sufi poet's Conference of the Birds as all those wayward souls flocked to him for guidance)*, it was only natural that he would find the effect he was having surreal, especially the life-transforming effect on disaffected young men who had nowhere to turn; professor Peterson was called for a reason, and in my soul I *knew* that he was called to answer the angry question of my poem, which spoke for me and the collective unconscious of society. I *felt* his terror, and my heart went out again to this "deeply, deeply good man," as one of his closest friends described the good professor...

9. The View from Where I Am

A writer is not fledged until he finds his own voice. Until then, he's only doing what most writers do—learning the craft until he finds his writer's voice, if he's lucky; only then can he take flight and claim a point of view that is uniquely his own.

I heard the call to writing in grade school, and in high school I fell in love with the romantic ideal of becoming a writer like Earnest Hemingway, who became my high school hero and literary mentor; but my call to writing was supplanted by my call to become a seeker like Larry Darrell in Maugham's novel *The Razor's Edge,* and my life no longer became my own because I forfeited my call to writing to the guiding principle of my life that kept dragging me by the scruff of the neck to find the right path that would fulfill my soul's plan for this life and find a way out of the recurring cycle of karma and reincarnation through my own efforts—*an unbelievably foolish imperative that I demanded of myself;* and I chose the family that I was born into, because my family's shadow was deeply rooted in what I needed most to realize my true self—*the alchemical gold of irreducible conceit.*

But who would believe this but another soul with a point of view from that transcended state of resolved self-consciousness where one is both what he is and is not and something other, a fully realized soul self, that state of resolved self-consciousness that Jesus pointed to with his saying that the kingdom of God would only come when one has made his two selves into one, neither male nor female with no hypocrisy? *"A man without quotation marks,"* as Gurdjieff defined this rare type of individual. But can there even be such a person? And would we know one if we met them?

"Ye shall know them by their fruits," said Jesus, telling us how we would know them. **"Do men gather grapes of**

thorns, or figs of thistles? Even so every good tree bringeth forth good fruit; but a corrupt tree bringeth forth evil fruit. A good tree cannot bring forth evil fruit, neither can an evil tree bring forth good fruit. Every tree that bringeth not good fruit is hewn down and cast into the fire. Wherefore by their fruits ye shall know them..." (Matthew 16-20).

What then would be the rare fruit of this fully developed soul that has realized wholeness and completeness if not the consummate goodness of their individual virtue—*the* best music from the musician, *the* best poetry from the poet, *the* best healing from the physician, *the* best of one's chosen field? A fruit so sweet in its goodness that one would not help but see their difference, people of distinction like Abraham Lincoln, Winston Churchill, Mahatma Gandhi, Nelson Mandela, and Doctor Albert Sweitzer whose call to serve humanity gave birth to his philosophy of reverence for all life, highly evolved souls who chose to come back to this world to serve humanity with their precious gift of consummate goodness—Mozart, Beethoven, Shakespeare, Wordsworth, Rumi, and countless unsung heroes who affected and continue to affect the world with the rare fruit of their highly evolved individual virtue, be it whatever life path they were called to.

Would this be why Socrates deemed goodness to be the most noble virtue? Given the logic of the individuation process, which I've been studying since I began "working" on myself with Gurdjieff's teaching, Christ's sayings, and my own Wordsworthian ideal, I would think so, despite a person's unconsciousness of their own resolved inner nature *(which is why great souls simply know who they are and what they are destined for, be it art, politics, medicine or whatever)*; and the more I grew in my own virtue, the more I *saw* shades of goodness and evil in people; and then one day I became acutely aware of the connection between good and evil and the values that people lived by.

So, I had a very difficult choice to make; and I chose to live by values that made me *the* best person that I could possibly be. And I made it the ethic of my life to be a good, kind, honest and truthful person, idealized by Wordsworth's poem *Character of the Happy Warrior*.

That was my *conscious* intention, my gnostic path to personal virtue. And then one summer day, to my amazement, while standing in the doorway of my mother's kitchen while she was kneading bread dough on the kitchen table, talking about what I cannot remember, I had the most astonishing experience of my life. A quiet feeling washed over me that I was immortal and would never die. That's it. No angels singing, no heavenly choir, no golden trumpets; just a quiet feeling that I was immortal and would never die, and all fear of death vanished. As did the longing in my soul for wholeness and completeness. And I no longer longed to be me. I just *was*!

I *was* me, whole and completely myself, a feeling that has never gone away some forty years later. And as much as I wanted to share this with my mother, I could not. She would not have understood. I did not understand either. And it took more than twenty years to work out what happened to me that day in my mother's kitchen, but I finally solved the mystery; and as my muse would have it, I finally worked my "spiritual rebirth" into a poem—

I Am

> I felt ashamed of life when I saw her frail body
> fighting for its life in the Emergency Room,
> emaciated and heaving like a bellows for air;
> I saw no dignity in the physical struggle
> to stay alive, no grace, no hope, no honor,
> just a bodily organism in the throes of death.
> I walked home alone from the hospital,
> the lonely moon as big as the Eye of God
> and the stars sparkling like lost souls in heaven,
> and I thought of life and death and everything
> in between, and in my heart I smiled for all

of my efforts, struggles, and humiliations to find my true self, because as I spied death steal my lover's mother's life I knew, I simply knew, that I am, and life is merely something that I do.

By "working" on myself with pathological commitment to Gurdjieff's discipline of *conscious effort* and *intentional suffering* (including his no-less demanding techniques of *non-identifying* and *self-remembering*), plus my *Royal Dictum* (my edict of self-denial), and my Wordsworthian ideal of laboring good on good to fix, I created enough virtue to shift my center of gravity (my "I") from my *existential* outer self (my ego/shadow personality) to my *essential* inner self (I *coincided* with myself and become one self, whole and complete; that's when I experienced my own eternal life that Jesus referred to as being born again); and from that moment on to this very day, I lived my life from the perspective of my resolved dual self, which is the viewpoint of the third and final stage of evolution that is realized when the inner and outer selves become one self, and everything that I wrote from that day to this I have written from this unique perspective, my own writer's voice, like the light-hearted spiritual musing that I posted on my blog *Wednesday, December 20, 2017*:

A Room of My Own

I've been meaning to write a spiritual musing on my writing room for years, but the idea never possessed me until I read Lindall Gordon's biography, *Virginia Woolf, A Writer's Life,* while I was in the middle of painting my writing room this summer; and, of course, the idea was set free by Virginia Woolf's Victorian convention-breaking comment that sparked a fire in the soul of women everywhere and set the stage for the modern feminist movement, and which became the theme of her iconoclastic little book *A Room of One's Own:* "A woman must have money and a room of her own if she is to write fiction."

But that comment could apply to any writer. And if they have the money to be free to write, all the more power to them. But life doesn't work like that. Ask Alice Munro, who had to squeeze in her writing time whenever she could between household chores (she was married with two small children); but she persevered and wrote, and wrote, and wrote, and at the respectable age of 82 was awarded the Nobel Prize for Literature in 2013 for her "mastery of the contemporary short story."

Which suggests much more than having a room of one's own to write in, and the money to be free to write; it suggests that a writer will write no matter what, because if they do not write they will feel like they have betrayed themselves, something that my high school hero and literary mentor Ernest Hemingway explored in his most autobiographical story, "The Snows of Kilimanjaro," and which haunted me most of my life also because my call to creative writing was superseded by my call to find my true self, and only when I had satisfied the longing in my soul for wholeness and completeness was I free to devote more time to creative writing; which brings me to my writing room in the two-story house that Penny and I built in Blue Water, Tiny Beaches in beautiful Georgian Bay, Ontario…

I've always wanted a room of my own to write in, and I went out of my way three times to build a room of my own; the first time when I built an addition onto my parents home in Nipigon, in Northwestern Ontario when I opted to stay at home for my mother's sake (my father's closet drinking was too much for her) after I left university to start my own contract painting business, and for the next fourteen years I stayed at home in my attached but separate apartment unit and worked my trade and read and wrote until my father died; and the second time I built a room of my own was in the triplex that I built in Nipigon by converting the loft of the top apartment unit of our triplex into my writing room where I wrote every morning for eleven years until Penny and I built our new home in Tiny Beaches, Georgian Bay (on STOCCO CIRCLE, a street with my name; a divine coincidence that blew my mind that would require a whole novel to do it justice and which I plan to write one day with the title, *We May be Tiny, but We're Not Small*) in which I converted the empty space above our double garage called the "bonus room" into my writing room but which I never got to finish painting until this summer, fourteen years after our house was built.

So, a room of my own to write in was precious to me, despite the fact that my writing room was also my sanctuary and haven of safety while searching for my true self which began in high school when Somerset Maugham's novel *The Razor's Edge* struck me with the immortal wound that called me to become a spiritual seeker like his protagonist hero Larry Darrell; and I did most of my seeking through reading in the privacy of my writing room until I found my lost soul that I had come into this world to look for and which I wrote about in *The Pearl of Great Price*. And after I found my lost soul and wrote all the books that my *daemon* beckoned me to write (the last being my twin soul books, *Death, the Final Frontier* and *The Merciful Law of Divine Synchronicity*), I was finally free to do justice to creative writing that I was called to in high school by the writer who became my high school hero and literary mentor, Ernest "Papa" Hemingway whom, ironically, I've just finished writing about again in *My Writing Life,* which was inspired by the gift of an *Indigo Hemingway Notebook* that I got from Penny's sister last Christmas and which morphed into a sequel to my literary memoir *The Lion that Swallowed Hemingway* that I wrote three years ago.

Not that I didn't write creatively all these many years (my novel *Tea with Grace* is still my favorite of all my fiction writing), I simply could not devote all of my precious time and energy to creative writing (which, as any writer knows, demands total attention); I had to work my trade to make a living first and foremost, and I also had to heed the call to tell the story of my quest for my true self, which to date numbers two dozen books and counting; so I had very little time for creative writing.

But now that I've finally told the story of how I found my true self, I am free to write all the poetry and short stories and novels that I am called to write (not to mention my spiritual musings, which always come unbeckoned, like today's spiritual musing on a room of one's own); and, in all honesty, I could not wait to finish painting the faded and boring primed white walls of my writing room, because after fourteen years it deserved to be dignified with a color best suited to the creative writer in me, a colour that my life partner Penny Lynn chose at Home Depot last weekend—*HOPEFUL BLUE*.

And why did Penny choose this colour, other than the fact that we both loved it? As she said to me, without a trace of irony: "I just hope it gets on the walls, that's all."

Not only do I have a room of my own to write in (I love the metaphor of "bonus room," which in our house plans referred to the empty space above our double garage that I had our builder convert into my writing room), I also have the "bonus" of a fully-fledged voice of my own in the point of view that I realized in my quest for my true self; a unique perspective from that state of resolved self-consciousness that can only be realized in the third and final stage of evolution, and it goes without saying that writing from this extreme outside-the-box perspective can be quite threatening to conventional wisdom, which could be why behavioral psychologist and clinical therapist professor Jordan Peterson never responded to the books I sent him, before and after he stepped onto the world stage with his *12 Rules of Life: An Antidote to Chaos*; but again, I'm only guessing.

But why? What can be so threatening about a perspective that reflects life from a state of resolved self-consciousness that takes God, the immortal soul, and the afterlife for granted? Why would the world be threatened by this point of view? And I know it is, because this has been my experience, starting with my first novel *What Would I Say Today If I Were to Die Tomorrow?*

The short simple answer, which presupposes initiation and gnostic awareness of the **secret way**, is **MORAL RESPONSIBILITY**, because the only way to resolve the dual nature of our *essential* and *existential* self is by taking moral responsibility for our own individuation process, and this is not an easy responsibility to bear. But despite how hard we try, we cannot deny the divine imperative of our inner self to wholeness and completeness—a*nd that's our bloody dilemma!*

So, there we are, driven by the teleological imperative of our inner self to grow and evolve and become what we are meant to be, *"a bliss peculiar to each one by individual existence,"* as Keats described the identity of our soul self, trapped in our physical body that is biologically driven by the selfish imperative of our ego/shadow personality; it's no wonder that man is torn in two, because we cannot realize our real self without sacrificing our false self. And that's the dilemma that drove brilliant little Friedrich Nietzsche, infamous author of the God-is-dead philosophy, crazy.

"Two souls, alas, are housed within my breast, /And each will wrestle for the mastery there," wrote the German philosopher/poet Goethe; and I spent the most creative years of my life resolving this monstrous conflict in my breast, and I know just how threatening my point of view can be to those who are not yet ready to bear the moral responsibility of taking evolution into their own hands to complete what Nature cannot finish. **"Many are called, but few are chosen,"** said Jesus.

That's why my heart goes out to professor Peterson. His maps of meaning have taken him as far as they possibly can in his profound study of the human condition, which he articulates with scholarly erudition and uncanny gnostic wisdom; and as always happens when one's path can take them no further on their journey to wholeness and completeness (which he rendered into 12 *Rules for Life* that is quickly becoming a global bestseller*)*, life calls them to a higher purpose; and the good professor was called to the hero's journey in his defence of free speech, a moral imperative to be a shining light for our crazy modern world, which will go a long way to initiating him deeper into the mysteries of the **secret way** and his own divine nature, because that's how good karma works.

And what a journey! I just love watching him slaying all those pesky postmodern neo-Marxist dragons, like the resentful writer Pankaj Mishra, who not only skewered Peterson's *12 Rules for Life: An Antidote to Chaos* but took a pathetic cheap shot at his character in *The New York Review of Books,* and all those pesky little politically correct demons out to take him down, like nasty little Cathy Newman on Britain's Channel 4 News and the malevolent Nellie Bowles in the *New York Times,* who identified Peterson as an "icon of toxic masculinity" and "custodian of the patriarchy," because I have never seen the hero's journey play itself out with such ferocious integrity, like a modern day Knight Templar defending to the death the sanctity of the Holy Grail!

It's no wonder that Jordan Peterson lives in constant existential terror. But he's a "deeply, deeply good man" driven by the Logos, and it gives me great joy to see how many souls he's setting on fire with the moral imperative of his *12 Rules for Life: An Antidote to Chaos,* leading them through the darkest impasses of their mind with his hierophantic message of hope—just like the hoopoe bird in the Sufi poet's *Conference of the Birds...*

10. The Jordan Peterson Phenomenon

> "Know then thyself; presume not God to scan,
> The proper study of mankind is Man."
> —*Alexander Pope*

I've been reflecting on my poem *What the Hell Is Going on Out There?* since I began writing this book on one rule to live by (while reading Peterson's *12 Rules for Life: An Antidote to Chaos* and watching his YouTube lectures and interviews), and it didn't occur to me how woefully ignorant I was of the political reality of the world today until I was drawn into the Jordan Peterson phenomenon, because the more I listened to him defending our right to free speech and expound upon his hierophantic message of self-reconciliation, the more I became aware of what the hell was going on out there? But why was I so woefully ignorant?

It's not that I didn't follow the news. I watched TV and listened to CBC radio regularly (Michael Enright defaulted to becoming my favorite host when Charlie Rose fell from grace for his arrogant sexual indiscretions), and I read the *Globe & Mail*, *National Post*, and *Toronto Star* every weekend (not to mention the occasional *Walrus*, *Maclean's*, *Zoomer*, *Atlantic*, *Harper's*, and *New Yorker* magazines), and I saw what was going on in the world; but I was truly puzzled by the logic of man's behavior, especially the political circus playing out in the United States with Donald Trump at the helm, which is why my muse brought my bewilderment to my attention with the spontaneous eruption of my poem *What the Hell Is Going on Out There?*

My poem came to me unbeckoned and word perfect; and upon reflection, I realized that my poem not only voiced my own bewilderment, but the collective bewilderment of society, because that's what inspired poetry does. It speaks for the zeitgeist of one's time and place, and this explained the sudden and unexpected meteoric rise of professor Jordan Peterson's popularity.

When David Fuller, host of the *Rebel Wisdom* podcast, asked biologist and evolutionary theorist Bret Weinstein why he thought Jordan Peterson had become so popular and what could possibly account for the Jordan Peterson phenomenon, he replied:

> "There is a drought of authenticity and courage, and Peterson has found that hunger and he's tapped into it. And I admire his ability to detect it and to speak to it plainly and in a way that it resonates with. When you live in a world that is so full of crap as the world we live in, where people are advertising bullshit from the moment you get up to the moment you go to sleep and then somebody finally tells you some truth that you need to hear, it's a relief just to know there's some other channel that's not compromised, and I don't think he's the only one speaking truthfully, but I think he is speaking from the heart, and people know it" *(Bret Weinstein, Commentaries on JB Peterson: Rebel Wisdom).*

When Jordan Peterson spoke truth to power with his recalcitrant defense of free speech (which not only threated legal action for not complying with Bill C-16, but his position at U of T and twenty-year clinical practice as well), he woke people up to the toxic spirit of neo-Marxist postmodern nihilism and the in-your-face idiocy of political correctness gone loony and identity politics that have permeated our western culture; and this catapulted him onto the world stage.

And then he published his pull-no-punches shadow-shocking, character-building book *12 Rules for Life: An Antidote to Chaos,* which became an overnight Amazon bestseller that landed him an unbelievably propitious interview with Cathy Newman on Britain's Channel 4 News that instantly endeared him to the world for skillful slaying Cathy Newman's ideologically possessed left-wing personality that ferociously tried to take him down with all the devious craftiness of her profession—*"So, you're saying..."* (she used this line 28 times to twist his words). The interview went viral, and tens of millions more viewers gravitated to the good professor's irrefutable dragon-slaying logic.

The Jordan Peterson phenomenon was explaining to me and everyone listening just how our crazy modern world worked from his profoundly studied point of view *(starting with his lobster thesis that illustrated the instinctual imperative for hierarchy in human nature)*, and I began watching his *Maps of Meaning* lectures on YouTube, which were drawn from his book *Maps of Meaning: The Architecture of Belief* that took him fifteen years to write working three hours a day (how many hours of reading he must have done for that book, one can only guess); and that's when the penny dropped, and I *saw* why I was called to write *One Rule to Live By: Be Good*.

In *Maps of Meaning: The Architecture of Belief*, professor Peterson works out a comprehensive theory for how people construct meaning in a way that is compatible with modern scientific understanding of how the brain functions. He examines the "structure of systems of belief and the role these systems play in the regulation of emotion, using multiple academic fields to show that connecting myths and beliefs with science is essential to fully understand how people make meaning," which gave the good professor the well-researched and studied understanding of his complex subject (*"The proper study of mankind is Man,"* said the poet Alexander Pope) that instantly appealed to what the author of *The Sun Also Rises*, my high school hero and literary mentor Ernest "Papa" Hemingway, were he alive today, would probably call "the new lost generation."

This is Jordan Peterson's sudden pop star appeal, especially to all the disaffected young men lost in the wilderness of our crazy world. They are the angry voice shouting, *"What the hell is going on out there?"* They are the new lost generation that has given up on religion, science, and politics that cannot provide the guidance and direction they need to negotiate their way through this life; and their hunger to satisfy the desperate longing in their soul has pulled them into the good professor's orbit with such gravitational force that he's still reeling from the tsunami effect of his polyphonic answer to my poem's angry question. And after watching his online lectures and podcasts and interviews, I *finally* made sense of why the world was listening to what he has to say:

There's an old saying attributed to the ancient Greek philosopher Aristotle that Nature abhors a vacuum, and for years now the hole in the soul of the world has grown larger and larger, and no one seems to know how to fill it (religion, science, and politics have failed miserably); but along comes a fledgling hierophant from the northern prairie town of Fairview, Alberta with cowboy boots and an outlier attitude, a professor of evolutionary psychology and a twenty-year veteran clinical therapist with a finely honed holistic philosophy wrought out of a lifelong obsession with man's capacity for evil who dared to risk his academic career and clinical practice and stood up to the wickedly myopic spirit of Canada's Bill C-16, and his Solzhenitsynian pushback caught the attention of the world because decent people everywhere are sick and tired of political correctness gone loony, socially disruptive identity politics, faithless soul-sucking nihilism, and postmodern neo-Marxist ideology responsible for the death of millions of people, and the more professor Peterson pushed back at these evil forces with his studied maps of meaning, the more he explained what the hell was going on out there, and the more the world listened to what he had to say. There's a ravenous spiritual hunger in the world today, and in the words of Bret Weinstein, an articulate member of the Intellectual Dark Web, "Peterson has found that hunger, and he has tapped into it." That's why he's been called "an unignorable cultural figure of our time," a psychologist, philosopher, and spiritual guide all rolled up into one!

Which isn't to say that he doesn't get his share of criticism for his heroic effort (*the good that we do never goes unpunished,* goes the old saying), of which there seems to be no end of criticism for people whose views threaten the malevolent spirit of postmodern nihilism, like Tabatha Southey's cheeky article in *Maclean's* magazine (*November 17, 2017: "Is Jordan Peterson the stupid man's smart person?"*) that disparages the good professor with typical Southey mock irony— "It's easy to assume Peterson is deserving of respect. A lot of what he says sounds, on the surface, like serious thought. It's easy to laugh at him; after all, most of what he says is, after fifteen seconds' consideration, completely inane. But in between his long rambling pseudo-academic takes on rambling self-help advice and his weird fixation on Disney movies, is a dreadfully serious message..."

Really, Tabatha? *"Sounds like serious thought?" "Pseudo-academic?" "Rambling self-help advice?" "Weird fixation on Disney movies?"* And all of this coming from a man with a PhD in clinical psychology who lectured at Harvard for six years and at the University of Toronto for twenty more and is a twenty-year veteran psychotherapist who treated people in their most desperate time of need and who traced the narrative of mankind in his pioneering work *Maps of Meaning: The Architecture of Belief* that revolutionized the psychology of religion? And what are your qualifications, Tabatha Southey? What authority do you have to criticize professor Dr. Jordan Peterson?

There are none so blind as those who refuse to see, and it puzzles me how people can be so resentful and willfully pernicious; but then, that's precisely what professor Peterson was explaining to the world with his profound understanding of political extremism, toxic feminism, and soul-crushing neo-Marxist postmodern nihilism—all the pesky dragons of our crazy modern world.

I read a few more of these bad-faith reviews *(even more resentful than Tabatha Southey's),* which were more revealing of their author than they were of Jordan Peterson; but the good professor is taking all of this malice and resentful hostility in stride and marches on triumphantly, always rendering the complex narrative of his maps of meaning into the simple message of taking responsibility for one's own life that the world is hearing loud and clear in his book tour talks, interviews, and podcasts that have attracted millions of followers and counting, a message of hope for today's desperate world that, as coincidence would have it, perfectly reflects the inspired message of a spiritual musing that I posted on my blog *Tuesday, October 10, 2017*:

The Two Ends of the Stick, Shania Twain and P. D. Ouspensky

I woke up at 2:30 yesterday morning with Gary Lachman's book *In Search of P. D. Ouspensky* on my mind and with a very strong compulsion to read it, so I got up and read the book until 4 A. M., and then I put coffee on and continued reading until Penny got up at seven and joined me for coffee in my writing room, coughing and wheezing.

I had read *In Search of P. D. Ouspensky* once already, finding it an engaging rehash of material I was familiar with from my extensive library on Gurdjieff, but for some reason, I took a greater interest this time around in the author who introduced me to Gurdjieff's teaching with his book *In Search of the Miraculous*, as though I had missed something about Ouspensky's life the first time, little realizing that my oracle had called me to read *In Search of P. D. Ouspensky* for today's spiritual musing which had not yet conceptualized as an idea in my mind and would not do so until later in the day after I had read the *National Post* (*Wednesday, October 11. 2017*) that I picked up in Midland when I drove in to get some cough syrup and lozenges for Penny who had come back from her niece's wedding in Ottawa with a bad cold, and the article in the *Post* that set the idea free for today's musing was on the singer Shania Twain, headlined in bold caps, IT'S HER TURN NOW, which brought forth

One Rule to Live By

the third connecting factor that set my idea for today's spiritual musing free, something that the mystical Jeshua said in Glenda Green's book *Love without End, Jesus Speaks*: ***"There is no other time or place to find yourself. Now is your only context,"*** because these words spoke directly to Shania Twain's and P. D. Ouspensky's life-journey; but I would not be free to write my spiritual musing until I had finished reading *In Search of P. D. Ouspensky*, which I did throughout the day

But before I get pulled into today's spiritual musing, I feel compelled to say something about how my spiritual musings come to be, which speaks to the mystical nature of the creative process (and, as coincidence would have it, to the very theme of today's spiritual musing which centers upon our journey through life to wholeness and completeness, in this case the disillusioned teacher of Gurdjieff's System, P. D. Ouspensky, and the iconic singer Shania Twain), because this is the first time that I've actually caught a glimpse of my creative unconscious at work as it coalesces the requisite variables into an idea for a spiritual musing, and, believe me, I *know* that the idea for today's spiritual musing is going to demand the most of me because it impels me to give gnostic clarity to the meaning and purpose of our existence and which definitely falls into the category of a very dangerous spiritual musing. Why very dangerous, though? What is it about this spiritual musing that makes me so uneasy? Let me pause for thought, if I may…

Misoneism. That's the word that my oracle popped into my mind. According to my sidebar Merriam-Webster dictionary, misoneism means: "a hatred, fear, or intolerance of innovation or change," and I first became acquainted with this word in C. G. Jung's book *Modern Man in Search of a Soul*; that's why today's spiritual musing can be very dangerous, because I have to step far outside the paradigm of conventional thought to give gnostic clarity to the meaning and purpose of our existence. This is why Padre Pio, the Roman Catholic Saint who made his presence in my novel *Healing with Padre Pio* through a gifted psychic medium who channeled him, said that my writing will **"open the door to a new way of perceiving, a new way of thinking and understanding,"** just as all creative thinkers do who blaze a new trail for man to follow, as C. G. Jung did with his psychology of individuation that addresses man's longing for wholeness and completeness, and which just happens to be the subject of today's spiritual musing.

This, then, is what I caught a glimpse of with the idea for today's spiritual musing: **the creative unconscious is not bound by time.** I *know* this, because of how the three factors that my creative unconscious brought together throughout the day to coalesce into an idea for today's spiritual musing: 1., waking up at 2:30 A. M. yesterday with a very strong compulsion to read Gary Lachman's book *In Search of P. D. Ouspensky*, the man who introduced me to Gurdjieff's teaching that awakened me to the **secret way of life**; 2., reading the article on Shania Twain's successful comeback in the *National Post* later in the day; and 3., a quotation from Glenda Green's book *Love without End, Jesus Speaks* that popped into my mind later in the day that connected the other two dots to manifest into the idea for today's spiritual musing on the gnostic way of life, which can be expressed in the simple realization: **NOW is the only time and place to satisfy the longing in our soul for wholeness and completeness.**

But what was the relationship between the long-deceased writer P. D. Ouspensky and Shania Twain's comeback after a fifteen-year hiatus that my creative unconscious wanted me to explore in today's spiritual musing? I knew that an idea for a new spiritual musing was forming in my mind, but I couldn't connect the dots until I finished reading Gary Lachman's biography on Ouspensky, which I did after I read the article on Shania Twain's comeback with her new album, *Now*.

As I was reading the last chapter of Lachman's book titled "The End of the System," in which Ouspensky, whose book *In Search of the Miraculous* is considered to be the best book on Gurdjieff's System, abandon's Gurdjieff's System after a lifetime of teaching it because it failed to satisfy the longing in his soul for wholeness and completeness, Shania Twain's new album *Now* popped into my mind, which automatically called forth Jesus's words in Glenda Green's book *Love Without End, Jesus Speaks*, **"There is no other time or place to find yourself. Now is your only context,"** thereby connecting the dots for today's spiritual musing on the gnostic way of life, and by gnostic way of life I mean the natural way of life through personal experience to wholeness and completeness.

Ouspensky went to his grave a broken, disillusioned man. He spent his life teaching Gurdjieff's System that failed to satisfy his longing for wholeness and completeness, but I knew from personal experience that Gurdjieff's System worked because I had realized my true self with his teaching, which is why I wrote *Gurdjieff Was Wrong, But His Teaching Works;* and I knew, from my own self-initiation into the **secret way of life**, that Shania Twain was living the gnostic way in her own journey of self-discovery which she courageously shared with the world in her music, as she did in her new comeback album *Now* that speaks to her "heartbreak, loss, and survival," the continued narrative of her journey to wholeness and completeness, and I found it sweetly ironic that she should title her comeback album *Now* given that Jesus said, *"There is no other time or place to find yourself. Now is your only context."*

Aside from her incredible singing voice, what makes Shania Twain so popular is her honesty about her own life's journey through struggle and heartache which touches the heart of the world in her songs, and her courage to not give into the soul-crushing nihilistic forces of life, as she poignantly illustrates with the first song of her new album *Now*: *"I wasn't just broken, I was shattered,"* which leads to the triumphant chorus, *"Life's about joy, life's about pain /It's all about forgiveness and the will to walk away /I'm ready to be loved, and love the way I should /Life's about, life's about to get good."*

Since her last album, 2002's *Up*, Shania Twain (whose parents died in a car accident when she was young, taking odd jobs to support her siblings and all the while writing songs to nurture her dream of becoming a singer), has been through a heart-wrenching divorce (her husband cheated on her with her best friend), battled Lyme disease, and overcame dysphonia (which she says forced her how to sing again); and she chronicles this harrowing phase of her journey through life in her album *Now*, and so personal and courageous and indomitable is she that her songs speak to the spiritual alchemy of the human condition, the natural *enantiodromiac* process of becoming whole and complete. That's why she's so popular; her songs are about *her* life, *her* story through her ups and downs, which is the impenetrable secret of the gnostic way of life that satisfies the longing in one's soul for wholeness and completeness.

Gary Lachman's book *In Search of P. D. Ouspensky* brought me to tears, because if such a great thinker and dedicated truth seeker as the philosopher/mathematician and foremost exponent of Gurdjieff's System could become so disillusioned by life, what hope was there for the rest of the world? Which is why my muse wanted me to connect Ouspensky's disillusioned life with the young (she's 52) Shania Twain whose spirit could not be broken, because I was called to explore in today's spiritual musing what Gurdjieff referred to as "the two ends of the stick." Specifically: *Shania Twain's* **hope** *and Ouspensky's* **despair**.

As gloomy and pessimistic as Gurdjieff's teaching can be, because it's founded upon his misperception that we are not born with an immortal soul, with *"conscious effort"* and *"intentional suffering"* we can "create" our own immortal soul (a teaching that broke the spirit of many followers, i.e., P. D. Ouspensky), Shania Twain's incorruptible innocence offers hope for all the those souls caught in the wretched currents of life's struggles; and it doesn't matter if one believes in eternal recurrence (as Ouspensky did and explored in his novel *Strange Life of Ivan Osokin*), or in one lifetime only as Christianity would have us believe, or in reincarnation and our autonomous and immortal self as I do, NOW is the only context to satisfy the longing in our soul for wholeness and completeness, as long as we are true to the divine imperative of our life to be all that we are meant to be; and that's the message of Shania Twain's new album *Now*, a truth that Ouspensky failed to discern because he could not break the gnostic code of the **secret way of life** with Gurdjieff's System as Shania Twain did with her gnostic path of music.

"Life's about joy, life's about pain /It's about forgiveness and the will to walk away," sings Shania Twain from her sacred place in the gnostic way of life. *"I'm ready to be loved, and love the way I should /Life's about, life's about to get good,"* she adds, glorifying the gnostic process of self-individuation that Gurdjieff's System failed to do; that's why Gurdjieff broke the spirit of so many seeker/followers, as he did his most famous student P. D.

One Rule to Live By

Ouspensky's. But not mine. I took his teaching to heart and broke the code of the gnostic way of life and love him dearly, as I love Shania Twain's indomitable spirit.

  Shania Twain is living proof of professor Peterson's message that life is full of pain and heartache as well as love and joy *(order and chaos, the two ends of the stick)* and what we do with our life is entirely up to us; that's why my heart went out to him when life called upon him to share the gnostic wisdom of his own remarkable journey to wholeness and completeness and explain to our crazy modern world what the hell was going on out there.
  And like his champion Aleksandr Solzhenitsyn (Jordan Peterson was asked by an editor of Vintage Classics at Penguin Books to write the Forward to the 50th Anniversary Edition of the single volume abridged version of *The Gulag Archipelago*— *"perhaps the single greatest honor that has ever befallen me, given the historical importance of Solzhenitsyn's book, as well as its great personal impact on me,"* said Peterson), he had to heed the call to his hierophantic purpose, because it wasn't in his character to turn a blind eye to the malevolent spirit of neo-Marxist postmodern nihilism, identity politics, and radical political correctness gone loony that have infected our crazy modern world like a soul-sucking super virus that has become immune to common sense and good-faith logic; and unlike the dystopian poet who asks *"what hope is there?"* the good professor shines a light into the darkest corners of our soul with his maps of meaning lectures and shadow-shocking, life affirming antidote to chaos, offering a lifeline to every forsaken soul out there—*"You saved my life,"* said one young man to the good professor at the signing of his book, reflecting the sentiment of thousands of followers. *"Thank you, Dr. Peterson!"* said another, and another, and another…

Jordan Peterson may not have a golden voice like Shania Twain *(actually, it's rather raspy; more like Kermit the Frog)*, but they're both singing the same encouraging, soul-healing song of hope for these desperate, life-weary times; that's why the world loves Shania Twain and is listening with impassioned curiosity to the good professor's hierophantic message...

11. On the Effect of Jordan Peterson's Message

"God," said I, "be my help and stay secure;
I'll think of the Leech Gatherer on the lonely moor!"

RESOLUTION AND INDEPENDENCE
—*William Wordsworth*

I'm not one given to despair, though I've had more occasions than I care to remember to do so; but whenever the spirit of this soul-sucking demon tries to possess me, I turn to one of my favorite poems to chase this demon back to hell where it came from—William Wordsworth's devastatingly personal poem, RESOLUTION AND INDEPENDENCE.

Wordsworth was given to mood swings— "But, as it sometimes chanceth, from the might /Of joy in minds that can no further go, /As high as we have mounted in delight /In our dejection do we sink as low..." And it so happened that one morning when he went for a walk in the moors, as was his habit, he began full of cheer; but then despair began to set in, a despair so deep that it cast a devastating pall over his creative spirit— "We Poets in our youth begin in gladness, /But thereof come in the end despondency and madness."

And here the poem takes a turn that speaks to the mystery of *the merciful law of divine synchronicity* (why the world refuses to see the miraculous choreography of *the omniscient guiding principle of life* continues to beggar my mind), the poet comes upon a stranger, "The oldest man he seemed that ever wore gray hairs" whose indomitable spirit would chase Wordsworth's cursed demon back to hell where it came from, a lonely Leech Gatherer who seemed to the poet "Like one whom I had met with in a dream; /Or like a man from some far region sent, /To give me human strength, by apt admonishment..."

One has to read the entire poem to appreciate the healing grace that Wordsworth experienced from his synchronous experience with that decrepit old man "with so firm a mind" conning for leeches in the lonely moor just as his black demon possessed him but which could not withstand the might and dignity of that decrepit old man's noble spirit and had to flee back to hell where it had come from, an experience that affected William Wordsworth so deeply that he made a point to remind himself of the Leech Gatherer on the lonely moor whenever his black demon tried to possess him again—"God," said I, "be my help and stay secure; /I'll think of the Leech Gatherer on the lonely moor!"

I intended to start this chapter with a thought that came to me on my drive to my hairstylist's home yesterday morning, a thought which strangely enough was coincidentally confirmed by something she said to me while cutting my hair; but the creative impulse has a mind of its own, and I was compelled to introduce Wordsworth's experience with the Leech Gatherer instead, and as preposterous as it may seem, I think I know why now.

On my drive to my hairstylist's home (I can't call her my barber, or hairdresser; so I opted for hairstylist), the thought came to me that the reason professor Peterson's message—and there's no doubt about it now, he does have a core message that he's rendered from all of his maps of meaning and psychology lectures and years of clinical practice, a message of hope to stave off and transform the disruptive forces of chaos—has affected so many young people that have followed his lectures on YouTube and read his *12 Rules for Life: An Antidote to Chaos* and listened to his book tour talks, podcasts and interviews, was not unlike the message that Wordsworth revealed in his poem RESOLUTION AND INDEPENDENCE, a message of how to deal with the influence of the dark shadow energies of one's personality and the dark shadow energies of these crazy times.

That's why I suspect that the choreographer of life arranged for Donald Trump to become president of the United States *(the odds were so against him that no one believed he would win without divine intervention),* so the people of America could get a good hard look at the dark shadow side of the archetypal American personality that Donald Trump ensouled *ad nauseum*—the beam in their own eye, as it were; because only then can one integrate one's shadow energy into one's ego personality and become a whole person, because we have to see the shadow energies of our own life before we can deal with them, which is not easy to do because it takes great moral courage to look into the dark corners of one's own soul; and if I were to distill professor Peterson's message for this crazy world, and in particular to our wayward younger generation, it would be this: **your shadow is real, and here's how to integrate your shadow self with your ego personality;** ergo, *12 Rules for Life: An Antidote to Chao.* This is why I was compelled to introduce this chapter on the effect of Jordan Peterson's message with William Wordsworth's poem, because they both spoke to the same message to always try and be resolute and independent, whatever our walk of life may be. *Bravo, Jordan!*

But because the shadow is such an illusive creature, it behoves me to shine more light onto this dark side of our personality with a spiritual musing that I wrote for my fourth volume of spiritual musings, whose ironic title Penny provided for me, *The Armchair Guru*:

The Shadow Personality

The best piece of advice that I ever got in my life came from a source I would never have imagined, because that just wasn't my reality at the time; and although it pierced my heart with the deadly accuracy of a skilled swordsman, I had to laugh at the blissful sweetness of the humble monk's advice that was revealed to me through a gifted psychic medium who channeled St. Padre Pio for my novel *Healing with Padre Pio*: "He told me to tell you to **resist the urge to be right**," said the psychic medium.

In one blinding flash of insight, I saw through my tragic character flaw that was responsible for so much aggravation in my life; and every time I got the urge to correct someone, the Good Saint's words popped into my mind and I had to bite my tongue.

I went to this gifted medium for a spiritual healing, and out of this experience came my novel *Healing with Padre Pio;* and had I not personally experienced what I did with the departed Capuchin monk who suffered the stigmata most of his adult life (fifty years of daily anguish), I would have questioned the reality of the whole experience. This is why I have taken Gurdjieff's words literally that there is only self-initiation into the mysteries of life. But why did I have the urge to be right all the time? What was this compulsive need to correct people whenever I felt they were wrong?

I did it without thought, and it always got me into trouble because it set me apart as arrogant and insensitive; but I couldn't help myself and did it anyway, because I was the victim of my own shadow. And that's the subject of today's spiritual musing, the shadow side of our personality...

The shadow is a Jungian concept. It is the dark, repressed side of our personality, and it is not who we think we are. The shadow is our false self, and it is both our damnation and salvation; but because our shadow resides in the unconscious part of our psyche, we are blind to it, and we even resist the slightest hint of being made aware of our false shadow self because it threatens our perfect self-image.

"The shadow by nature is difficult to apprehend. It is dangerous, disorderly, and forever in hiding, as if the light of consciousness would steal its very life," wrote the co-editors Connie Zweig and Jeremiah Abrams in *Meeting the Shadow, The Hidden Power of the Dark Side of Human Nature*; but not until we become aware of our shadow and integrate it into our conscious personality will we ever be a whole person, and happy. But where does the shadow come from, and why does it have so much power over us?

In all honesty, I had no awareness of my compulsion to be right all the time; but after the humble saint *(no one can suffer the holy wounds of Jesus Christ for fifty years and not be humbled)* brought it to my attention, I began to notice that I was not alone in my compulsive need to be right, and I soon began to see that this was a defining trait of the shadow personality.

Why, for example, would that Muslim woman that made the national news risk sabotaging her Canadian citizenship just to wear her niqab during the oath-swearing part of the ceremony if she did not believe that she was right in her religious conviction? What compelled her to take such a dangerous risk of not getting her citizenship if she was not under the influence of her shadow personality? Would her faith have collapsed had she shown her face while swearing allegiance to her new country during the oath-taking ceremony? Why would she do what she did if she wasn't convinced that she was right in her conviction?

"The shadow personality develops naturally in every young child," said Connie Zweig and Jeremiah Abrams; and they explain that children identify with ideal personality traits in their respective cultures to create a socially acceptable persona, and they repress all those qualities that their culture rejects into the shadow part of their personality because they don't fit into their evolving self-image. So, **"the ego and the shadow develop in tandem, creating each other out of the same life experience."**

But not only do we create our own ego and shadow personality out of our own life experiences, we also inherit our family shadow—the archetypal matrix of unresolved family karma, the consciousness of all those experiences that one's family has repressed to the unconscious family psyche; and this can make our life very difficult depending upon our family's karmic history, which is why it is written that the sins of the parents are visited upon the children. But, still, the mystery remains; why the urge to be right?

The Sufis have a saying: "There are as many ways to God as there are souls." Which simply means that every soul is its own way to God. Would this be the source of my compulsive need to be right? Would this be why that Muslim woman risked her Canadian citizenship, because she believed her way was more right than the simple decorum of showing her face for the oath-swearing ceremony?

I suspect so, but I cannot solve this mystery on my own; and so, I'm going to call upon my muse to help me work out the answer...

Can a person live a lie and still be authentic? Let's, for argument's sake, say that we do not live one lifetime only, but many lifetimes; and let's further say that there is no eternal damnation, that this is just a prop used by Christianity to keep people on the straight and narrow. And let's now say that one believed in sin and eternal damnation in everlasting hellfire, like I did in my Roman Catholic youth; wouldn't that be my personal reality, then? But given my argument that we live more than one lifetime and that there is no eternal damnation, my personal reality would not have been real; it would've been false. And by living a false reality, was I authentic?

That's the issue of the shadow personality: I would be authentic in my Roman Catholic belief, but my personal reality would be false *(as I literally proved for myself with my quest for my true self);* it would be my life-lie, which characterizes the shadow personality that is real in its falseness.

This is the mystery of human nature, which is paradoxical in its ontology because we are a complex mixture of the consciousness of the real and false, the *being* and *non-being* aspect of our ego/shadow personality; but some of us are more real than false, and some of us are more false than real, and if we are more false than real then our shadow has unconscious power over our conscious ego and can make our life difficult, like the Muslim woman whose religious convictions compelled her to risk her Canadian citizenship for her religious belief. No doubt, she was genuine in her conviction that she had the right to wear her niqab while swearing the oath of allegiance to her new country, but was her personal reality real or false?

As someone wrote into the *National Post*, it seems that "her religious/cultural practices are more important than the cultural norms of her newly adopted country," and although she was granted the right by the Canadian Charter of Rights and Freedoms to not show her face during the public oath-taking ceremony for her citizenship, her behavior flew in the face of our Canadian Prime Minister, and many Canadians; myself included. But why, if not because she was a victim of her own recalcitrant shadow personality?

"If we don't acknowledge all of who we are, we are guaranteed to be blind-sided by the shadow effect," said Debbie Ford in her introduction to *The Shadow Effect*, co-written with Deepak Chopra and Marianne Williamson. "Our shadow incites us to act out in ways we never imagined we could and to waste our vital energy on bad habits and repetitive behavior," she adds, which can throw one's life into disarray as it did mine and the Muslim woman with our blind and foolish need to be right; but not since I became aware of that aspect of my shadow personality and began to integrate it into my conscious ego.

But, again, why does the shadow have this need to assert itself, which in my case was compulsive? Why did Padre Pio tell me to resist the urge to be right?

"How can you find a lion that has swallowed you?" asked the psychologist Carl Jung, with playful humor; which is why he also said that it takes great moral courage to see our shadow. By lion, Jung meant our unconscious shadow that can take control of our ego personality, which I explored in my memoir *The Lion that Swallowed Hemingway;* and the conclusion that I came to was that **the shadow has to assert itself to prove to the world that it is authentic and real,** as Ernest Hemingway did *ad nauseum* to the despair of everyone who knew him, especially his third wife Martha Gellhorn who described the great writer as an apocryphiar and pathological liar and cruelest man she knew. And **the more power the shadow has over our ego, the more real we think we are**. And that's the bitter irony of our reality.

This is why Debbie Ford wrote, "The conflict between who we are and who we want to be is at the core of the human struggle," which was why my compulsive need to be right made my life miserable, and why St. Padre Pio told me to resist the urge to be right.

"The shadow," said Connie Zweig and Jeremiah Abrams, "is both the awful thing that needs redemption, and the suffering redeemer who can provide it," and not until we smelt the alchemical gold out of the dross of our shadow personality will we be whole, and happy.

I'm not quite finished reading his book yet, but without reading the rest of *12 Rules for Life: An Antidote for Chaos* I can sum up Jordan Peterson's core message in the same two words that reveal the message of Wordsworth's inspiring poem, a moral imperative to take charge of our life and do our very best to be **resolute** and **independent**; that's how we can stave off the inevitable forces of chaos. Hence the first rule of *Twelve Rules for Life:* '**Stand Up Straight with Your Shoulder's Back**," a vernacular poetic iteration of Shakespeare's aphoristic *"Assume a virtue, if you have it not."*

I have no idea if Jordan Peterson writes poetry (like most creative people, I'm sure he's dabbled in the genre), but given how he expresses himself in his book tour lectures and interviews, forever looking upward into the heavens whenever he's stuck for a word or thought, it suggests to me that he has the probing mind of a poet that he stretches to the limits of cognition and into the limitless horizons of his imagination; that's why I see him as a hierophant.

In his brilliant essay, "A Defense of Poetry," which he concludes with a line that has been rendered into a golden precept, Percy Bysshe Shelley wrote: "Poets are the hierophants of an unapprehended inspiration; the mirrors of the gigantic shadows which futurity casts upon the present; the words which express what they understand not; the trumpets which sing to battle and feel not what they inspire; the influence which is moved not, but moves. **Poets are the unacknowledged legislators of the world**."

Why did professor Jordan Peterson speak up against Bill C-16, the amendment that now legislates Canadians to use gender neutral pronouns upon the request of the LGBTQ community, if not because he had the strength of character to refute that morally bankrupt amendment that was driven by identity politics and radical political correctness gone loony?

One Rule to Live By

Professor Peterson may not be a poet by natural imperative, but he's certainly a magnanimous poet in spirit; and it's a blessing for the world that he spoke against legislation that curtails free speech. Shelley must be smiling in his grave...

12. The Mystique of Jordan B. Peterson

Our life gives birth to its own wisdom through personal experience. By wisdom, I mean the sacred knowledge of life that nourishes our soul with meaning and purpose, and which for all intents and purposes can simply be called the Logos; a wisdom, incidentally, that professor Peterson declares is best realized by assuming responsibility, both moral and practical, for one's own life, which is the imperative of his *12 Rules for Life: An Antidote to Chaos* and all of his talks and lectures.

My sidebar Merriam-Webster Dictionary defines Logos as the divine wisdom manifest in the creation, government, and redemption of the world. Logos is also defined as the Word of God, or principle of divine reason and creative order, identified in the Gospel of John with the second person of the Trinity incarnate in Jesus Christ, which is why Jesus said, **"I am the way, the truth, and the life. No one comes to the Father except through me."**

By Father, Jesus meant Logos. This is why he said, **"I and my Father are one."** Which did not make Jesus the sole savior of the world as Christianity contends; it made him one with the *way*, the redemptive spirit of the Logos. In the most esoteric language possible, Jesus became his own *way* when he became one with the Logos; just as anyone can become their own *way* when they become one with the Logos. This was Christ's message to the world, a message that Carl Jung conveyed with stinging irony to Jungian analyst Barbara Hannah (*Jung, His Life and Work: A Biographical Memoir,* by Barbara Hannah) when he said, "Thank God I am Jung, and not a Jungian."

In my efforts to become one with the Logos, I "worked" on myself with such pathological commitment to my personal ethic (made up of Gurdjieff's teaching, the sayings of Jesus, my edict of self-denial that I called my *Royal Dictum*, and my personal ideal of being good, kind, honest and truthful—*God, was this ideal difficult to live by being in business for myself, which often called for Herculean moral integrity, and my conscience still stings with regret at the times I compromised my ideal for the sake of my business!*) that I developed a sixth sense for the Logos whenever it spoke to me through life experience, regardless of what I was doing—working, reading, writing, watching TV, or whatever; and I grew to understand what Jesus meant when he said that his sayings were for those who had ears to hear and eyes to see, which became the inspiration for my novel *Jesus Wears Dockers* in which my narrator self and my archetypal Jesus decode the meaning of Christ's sayings.

    I never knew when the Logos (I didn't call it Logos then; I recognized the sacred knowledge of life simply as the *way*—the **secret way** and *omniscient guiding principle of life* that inspired my memoir *The Merciful Law of Divine Synchronicity*) would speak to me, but the more I nourished my soul with the sacred Logos, the more I grew in spiritual consciousness and put myself in danger of becoming infected with the redemptive spirit of the Logos that I came to call the "messiah virus."

    Many people become infected with this treacherous virus, and there has never been a shortage of cult leaders that seduce people with their teachings, like the duplicitous leader of an offshoot Christian solar cult teaching that I practiced for three years which did irreparable damage to my eyesight before I saw it for what it was when I flew to Reno, Nevada for a weekend seminar where I met the cult leader for the first time after the seminar and shook his hand and *saw* him for the deceitful manipulator that he was. But that's a story I've reserved for my fiction (my working title is *The Sunworshipper*), if I can ever summon the courage to write it, as well as another spiritual teaching that I lived for over thirty years when Gurdjieff's teaching had done all it could for me.

    This was a New Age spiritual teaching of The Light and Sound of God that I finally walked away from when it had nothing more to teach me about the seductive power of Spiritual Masters (that's when I was "nudged" to go for a spiritual healing with the gifted psychic medium who channelled St. Padre Pio for my novel *Healing with Padre Pio*, which gave me the spiritual strength I needed to break away from the seductive hold of this New Age teaching), and I'm still waiting for my muse to call me to write about my experience with this purloined teaching and Shadow Master who professed to be the "Mahanta," the Outer and Inner Master of all his chelas (this Master's influence upon a friend of mine who died of cancer is central to my story *The Pearl of Great Price*); and the point of these humiliating personal disclosures is that gnostic wisdom comes with a great price, as the spiritual musing inspired by the movie *The Light Between Oceans* that I wrote last summer sadly illustrates with the lighthouse keeper Tom Sherbourne's moral cowardice:

Chemistry of the Soul

Friday, April 21, 2017, not yet summer but nearing the end of what the poet T. S. Eliot called the cruelest month of the year, a dull grey dismal day too cold to sit on the front deck to have a tipple, or finish reading my book *Paris Without End, The True Story of Hemingway's First Wife*, so I asked Penny if she wanted to watch a movie in the cozy comfort of my writing room.

She said yes, and I "chanced" upon a movie on Netflix called *The Light Between Oceans,* starring Michael Fassbender as the lighthouse keeper, whose portrayal of C. G. Jung in *A Dangerous Method* completely won me over, Alicia Vikander as the lighthouse keeper's wife, whom I didn't know, and Rachel Weisz who played the birth mother of the infant child in this poignant drama, and whom I fell in love with the first time I saw her starring with Ralph Fiennes in *The Constant Gardner*, and we cozied up in our sofa chairs and watched the movie that so moved me to tears it stirred up the root of an idea that I've had gestating in my unconscious for several years, and that's the subject of today's spiritual musing….

One Rule to Live By

I had unfinished business with Hemingway since I wrote *The Lion that Swallowed Hemingway* three years ago, or I would not have been called back to Hemingway by my relentless muse to write the sequel *My Writing Life, Reflections On My High School Hero and Literary Mentor Ernest "Papa" Hemingway*; and all of my new reading on the iconic writer whose simple prose introduced the modern world to a new style of writing was giving me a deeper insight into the *enantiodromiac* process of Hemingway's conflicted ego/shadow personality, which was brought to light with spontaneous delight when the lighthouse keeper Tom Sherbourne in *The Light Between Oceans* had to wrestle with a moral dilemma that he knew in the pit of his stomach would one day come back to haunt him if he did not choose wisely, just as Hemingway did when he was torn between his deep love for his wife Hadley and the other woman he had fallen in love with, Pauline Pfeiffer who ended up becoming his second wife.

"That's it!" I exclaimed, when the lighthouse keeper Tom Sherbourne chose against his gut feeling to comfort his grieving wife who had just suffered her second miscarriage, jarring Penny from her comfort. *"That's the human condition in action! That's the grinding of the soul that makes for great literature! That's the chemistry of the soul!"*

Penny was puzzled by my outburst, but I was excited, as I always am when an idea for a spiritual musing springs free from my unconscious, and I shot out of my chair and jotted down the title of today's spiritual musing in my *Indigo Hemingway Notebook* that Penny's sister had given me for Christmas— *"Chemistry of the Soul."*

But what was the lighthouse keeper Tom Sherbourne's moral dilemma that set this idea free, a moral dilemma that by miraculous happenstance was no less soul-wrenching and life-changing than Ernest Hemingway's marital dilemma that I was just reading about again in *Paris Without End, The True Story of Hemingway's First Wife?*

First, let me spell out what I mean by this exciting, gnosis-laden idea "chemistry of the soul," and then I will explain how it was set free by the lighthouse keeper's moral dilemma that instantly brought to mind Hemingway's marital dilemma that I was all-too familiar with and just "happened" to be reading about again in Gioia Diliberto's biography *Paris Without End, The True Story of Hemingway's First Wife*.

The phrase "chemistry of the soul" just came to me out of the blue when I made the connection between the lighthouse keeper's moral dilemma and Ernest Hemingway's marital dilemma, but this is the phrase that my creative unconscious gave me to capture my spontaneous insight of what a moral dilemma can do to one's soul, because I *knew* from all the reading I had done on Ernest Hemingway what his marital dilemma had done to him when he chose to betray his wife Hadley for his lover Pauline, which gave me the insight to foresee what the lighthouse keeper's moral dilemma would do to him if he made a decision that went against his gut feeling; that's why I burst out: *"That's the human condition in action! That's the grinding of the soul that makes for great literature! That's the chemistry of the soul!"* Because I *knew*, I simply *knew* that the lighthouse keeper was going to put his soul through the grinding mill of life if he chose against his conscience, and he was going to suffer just as Hemingway suffered for choosing to go against his better nature when he chose to betray his loving wife Hadley for his seductive, inveigling lover.

"Thus conscience does make cowards of us all," said Shakespeare; but why? Why would conscience, man's moral center and guiding star, make cowards of us all if not for the onerous responsibility that goes with making a decision that conscience demands of us?

Hemingway's conscience demanded of him the moral imperative to be true to his wife Hadley, which meant that he would have to fight off his sexual/romantic attraction for Pauline Pfeiffer; but he could not. He wanted to have his cake and eat it too, and he was too weak to fight off his attraction for his lover.

That's what made the budding young writer, who would one day win the Nobel Prize for Literature, a moral coward. Ironically, his moral cowardice caused the fatal wound in his soul that gave him the *daemonic* fuel for some of his best short stories and novels; that's what I meant by "chemistry of the soul," because Hemingway's fatal wound ground his soul from lover to lover until he could bear himself no longer and he killed himself, and I knew that the lighthouse keeper

One Rule to Live By

Tom Sherbourne would put his soul through the same grinding mill if he capitulated to his grieving wife's desire to keep the infant child that they found in the boat with her dead father that had washed up on the shore of Janus Island in Western Australia where he was the lighthouse keeper; he knew in his gut that they should seek out the infant child's birth mother, but they didn't, and that decision came back to haunt them. A story that made for a great novel by M. L. Stedman, which became a great movie by the same title, *The Light Between Oceans*.

Ernest Hemingway left his wife for his lover, and that decision haunted him for the rest of his life, which he sadly owned up to in his bitter/sweet memoir *A Moveable Feast* that he was still working on just before taking his own life with his favorite bird shotgun at his home in Ketchum, Idaho. *"When I saw my wife again standing by the tracks as the train came in by the piled logs at the station, I wish I had died before I ever loved anyone but her,"* he wrote, regretting his decision to leave Hadley for Pauline so much that he would rather have died had he known what his moral cowardice would do to him.

I watched *The Light Between Oceans* with anxious anticipation, because I *knew* that once Tom Sherburne and his wife Isabel decided to keep the infant child and raise it as their own instead of notifying the authorities that one day life would call them to account for their moral transgression; and that's what I meant by "chemistry of the soul," which is a poetic way of saying that life has a way of grinding down the moral grist of one's soul, and I was no less angry at the lighthouse keeper for not being true to his conscience than I was at my high school hero and literary mentor Ernest Hemingway for betraying his faithful and loving wife Hadley for his calculating, seductive lover Pauline Pfeiffer. But then, where would we get our great literature from if not for the moral grinding of our soul?

When Carl Jung wrote in *The Red Book*, *"This life is the way, the long sought-after way to the unfathomable, which we call divine. There is no other way, all other ways are false paths,"* I understood exactly what he meant, because I exhausted many paths (both light and dark, though I did not know some were dark paths at the time; that's what made me wise to Shadow Masters) before I realized that life itself *is* the way to one's true self; but how? And why?

These are the questions that underlie the message that professor Jordan Peterson points to in *12 Rules for Life: An Antidote to Chaos*; and because he does not yet know the how and the why of the imperative of the *way* to one's true self, his message bears the existential anxiety of unknowing. But the imperative of the *way* is and has always been to reconcile one's outer life with one's inner life and resolve the paradox of one's *enantiodromiac* nature.

"Get your life in order!" exclaims the good professor to the young people (mostly young men 25 to 35) who attend his book tour lectures, and they resonate with his redemptive message of the *way* but cannot quite apprehend the imperative of the *way*; and that's the mystique of Jordan Peterson that imbues him with a charisma that mystifies everyone, including himself...

13. There Are No Right or Wrong Paths in Life

If life itself is the *way*, it follows logically that there are no right or wrong paths in life; but this only makes sense from the perspective of the third and final stage of evolution which transcends the unresolved paradox of one's nature; this is what can make Jordan Peterson's book *12 Rules for Life* so damn infuriating—*because it's right without knowing why!*

And that's the irony of the human condition. Conscience tells us what is right and what is wrong; but if there are no right or wrong paths in life, what does it really matter? The nihilists tell us that morality is relative, so one way is as good as another—which is only true from the perspective of one's unresolved nature *("I am what I am not, and I am not what I am,"* said Jean-Paul Sartre, which led him to the nihilistic conclusion that "man is a useless passion"); so, what does it mean then that there are no right or wrong paths in life? And if this is the case, why are so many young men resonating with Jordan Peterson's message? And why are his numbers exploding?

On his book tour for *12 Rules for Life* professor Peterson gave a talk in Los Angeles, and the following day he was out walking in the city with his wife when a car pulled over and a young Latino jumped out. He recognized Jordan Peterson and told him he had been to his talk the night before and had been following his lectures on YouTube, and he had to thank him for what he had done for him and his father, and excitedly the young Latino got his father who was in the car with him and full of emotion father and son hugged and thanked the good professor for reconciling their broken relationship; and there are many stories of a similar nature.

In a conversation with John Anderson, the former Deputy Prime Minister of Australia, he shared a story of a young man who had come up to him at the book signing after his talk but who was so overwhelmed with gratitude that he had to thank him for getting him back together with his father whom he hadn't seen in ten years. Jordan Peterson was so moved when he shared this with the former Deputy Prime Minister John Anderson that he choked up and broke into tears.

So, it's no wonder that he's been described as a prophet for his message of hope. But not everyone would agree. Cynical critics have called him a "a prophet for profit," because he's making tons of money from his book tour talks and sales of his book, which have hit the million mark and soon to be translated into forty languages, plus his Patreon platform that generates a monthly revenue of thousands of dollars; but he smiles at his resentful detractors and continues to march to the beat of his own reverberating drum. *Bravo, Jordan!*

In the epilogue to his remarkably erudite book *How to Read and Why*, professor Harold Bloom, who calls himself a Gnostic Jew, brings his brilliant and staggeringly comprehensive life-long study of literature to the simple, but unresolved conclusion with the words of Rabbi Tarphon: *"It is not necessary for you to complete the work, but neither are you free to desist from it."*

The work? What **work**? Life? To live life with purpose and meaning? Is that **the work**? And if so, how? But more to the point, why?

All of his life, professor Bloom sought an answer to life's purpose and meaning in the great literature of the world (he was born with preternatural reading skills, reading up to one thousand pages an hour in his early years but only five hundred or so pages an hour in his eighties, and he was also gifted with a "scandalous memory" and can recite poetry and passages of prose at will), and of all the thousands of writers that he read, studied, and taught at Yale University for more than half a century, he declared William Shakespeare to be his god; but for all of his genius, even Shakespeare could not satisfy the longing in his soul for wholeness and completeness, which is why he concluded his book *How to Read and Why* with Rabbi Tarphon's saying: *"It's not necessary for you to complete the work, but neither are you free to desist from it,"* which leaves us hanging.

But the wise Rabbi also said: *"The day is short and the work is great, and the laborers sluggish, and the wages are abundant, and the master of the house is demanding,"* which, when decoded, gives us a clue to the gnostic wisdom of his cryptic saying of not desisting from doing **the work**.

Work is life itself, which bears its own meaning and purpose; **the day is short** means that we have to get the most meaning out of life in the short period of time we have to live it; **work is great** means that life is hard; **the laborers are sluggish** means that life can get weary and fatiguing; the **wages are abundant** means that life is rich and rewarding in meaning and purpose; and **the master of the house is demanding** means that the divine imperative of our guiding inner self demands that we do our best in life, whatever our task may be.

But again, this leaves us hanging. It certainly left professor Bloom hanging, because it did not resolve his life-long need to know the meaning and purpose of life that literature could not satisfy; and he brings his book *How to Read and Why* to closure by turning to his god of literature.

"Why, if the work cannot be completed, are we not free to desist from it?" professor Bloom asks, puzzled by what seemed like a contradiction; and he goes on: "To answer that is not a simple matter, particularly since the greatest of all writers, Shakespeare, did desist from his marvelous labor of reinventing the English language and human personality (Bloom credits Shakespeare for much of Freud's psychology). It fascinates me and saddens me that Shakespeare gave up writing, after his collaboration with John Fletcher on *The Two Noble Kinsmen* in 1613. Shakespeare was just forty-nine, and he lived another three years. Perhaps illness dimmed Shakespeare's final years, but the Shakespearean parts of *The Two Noble Kinsmen* show a new style and a new consciousness, which should have been developed. In the remainder of this epilogue, I want to contrast Shakespeare's abandonment of the work with Tarphon's insistence that we are not free to abandon it," and then professor Bloom sums up Shakespeare's "new consciousness" with the moral injunction to live out one's life with equanimity, because that's the best that we can do.

"Does it matter whether one is required to complete the work or whether one is free to desist from the work if you must meet a final appointment (death) that certainly you did not make?" asks professor Bloom. "Is bearing yourself with equanimity sufficient?"

"At sixty-nine, I do not know whether Tarphon or Shakespeare is right. And yet, though the moral decision cannot be made merely by reading well, the question of how to read and why are more than ever essential to help us decide whose work to perform," Bloom writes, bringing to closure *How to Read and Why* but never really penetrating the secret of **the work.**

He was sixty-nine when he wrote *How to Read and Why*, and he continued to read and write and teach well into his eighties (*The Daemon Knows*, written in his mid-eighties, is my personal favorite, but I cannot wait to read his work-in-progress, *Possessed by Memory*, which may be his final work, to be released April, 2019); but literature still could not satisfy the longing in his soul, and good old Bloom had to satisfy his longing by adopting a Falstaffian attitude to life.

Shakespeare's Falstaff had an enormous appetite for life, whom professor Bloom explores in *Falstaff: Give Me Life* that was published on *April, 4, 2017*; but it saddens me that such an unbelievably gifted reader and scholar and teacher who has been called "the world's greatest literary critic" *(I honestly believe he was born a savant with a rare gift for literature)* could not satisfy the longing in his soul with all the wisdom to be found in the great literature of the world and had to resign himself to "take what time remains pretty much as it comes," but dignified with equanimity.

And this is why the gifted New Zealand short story writer Katherine Mansfield sought Gurdjieff out at his Institute for the Harmonious Development of Man in Fontainebleau, France to satisfy that longing in her soul that literature could not satisfy either.

"*Literature is not enough,*" she said to her editor of the *New Age* journal in London, Alfred R. Orage, who also became a follower of the enigmatic mystic/philosopher, because Gurdjieff's teaching, which strangely enough he called **the Work,** promised to fill the hole in Katherine's soul; but I've written about this in *Gurdjieff Was Wrong, But His Teaching Works* and need not bother here. I simply want to emphasize that life is not enough to satisfy the longing in our soul for wholeness and completeness; but life can make one ready, which brings me back to professor Peterson's book *12 Rules for Life* and a spiritual musing I wrote that makes this very point:

What Does Life Expects of Us?

I picked up an old *Psychology Today* magazine (*June 2012*) from the stack of magazines on my book shelf by the door of my writing room on my way to the john this morning, because I cannot go to the john and not read something. I get some of my best ideas in the john, and as I read an old article, which I had highlighted with a blue marker, titled "The Atheist at the Breakfast Table" by Bruce Grierson, one of my highlights jumped out at me and an old idea for a spiritual musing grabbed me with *daemonic* intensity because this idea has tried to grab me before but not quite enough to compel me to explore it; but like all of my ideas for poetry, stories, and spiritual musings, when its time has come to be given expression I have no choice but to see it through. So, what was the highlight that set the idea for today's musing free?

This is the paragraph that grabbed me: "Tepley was raised by observant parents who celebrated the holidays and kept a kosher home. He and his brother were bar mitzvahed. But cognitive dissonance soon ensued. 'In religious school, God was frequently presented as just and merciful. *But how could a just and merciful God allow the Holocaust?* I know I wasn't unique in asking that.'"

"Why cognitive dissonance?" I asked myself, and my idea for today's spiritual musing was set free. I have put the sentence that liberated the idea into bold italics, the idea that people are puzzled by a just and merciful God allowing such horrendous suffering in the world like the Holocaust, which seemed like a contradiction in terms *(hence the cognitive dissonance),* and when I finished my business in the john, I jotted the idea down in my notebook to expound upon in today's spiritual musing...

I sense that this is going to be another one of those dangerous spiritual musings, because it's going to step so far outside the box of conventional thought that it will make most readers uneasy; but this is what writers do, explore new pathways for the mind to pursue. Isn't this what Shelley meant in his essay "A Defense of Poetry" when he wrote: "Poets are the hierophants of an unapprehended inspiration"?

This is what makes writers dangerous, because every now and then they are blessed with "an unapprehended inspiration" that threatens conventional thinking, as I was blessed with the idea for today's spiritual musing that opened a window onto human suffering that defies man's disbelief that a just and merciful God would allow such devastating suffering like the Holocaust, a cognitive dissonance that paralyzes the soul and keeps one a prisoner to himself.

But as serendipity would have it, once I committed myself to writing today's spiritual musing I was blessed with the surprising coincidence of two movies on Netflix which addressed my "unapprehended inspiration" of today's spiritual musing: *God's Not Dead*, Part 1, and *God's Not Dead,* Part 2, both movies speaking to the issue of God's existence *(just and merciful, notwithstanding),* which the truculent atheist Professor Radisson does not believe in but which his Christian student Josh does, because his faith won't allow him to deny the existence of God and sign a statement for Professor Radisson's philosophy class stating that God is dead. All the other students in the class have signed the statement denying God's existence, and Professor Radisson challenges Josh to defend his position to the class; and the ensuing drama of their conflicting points of view makes for surprisingly engaging movies.

So, just what was my "unapprehended inspiration" for today's spiritual musing? What did I see about man's relationship with God and suffering that is so far outside the box of conventional thought that it will be sure to take readers so far beyond their comfort zone they may might just think I'm crazy?

This insight did not come to me without a history, because no idea is born *ex nihilo;* it has a history, and its history was born of my quest for my true self, which I happily realized and wrote about in my memoir *The Pearl of Great Price,* a history that delves into the mystery of the evolutionary process of man's paradoxical nature—our real and false self, or *being* and *non-being* as the case may be; because in the resolution of my outer self (my ego/shadow personality) with my inner self, I came to the astonishing realization that **human suffering is Nature's way of resolving the *enantiodromiac* dynamic of man's paradoxical nature and making our two selves into one,** which absolves God of all responsibility for tragedies like the Holocaust, and personal suffering as well, like professor Radisson's mother's death by cancer which drove him to abandon his Christian faith and embrace the doctrine of atheism. This also happened to a Canadian writer and social activist whose obdurate pride gave me the insight I needed to know why someone would abandon God and become an atheist, and I wrote a poem on my insight—

The Making of an Atheist

She stared out her living room window
lost to the world she knew and loved; three
hours later she returned from the farthest
regions of her mind where the great void had
swallowed her whole, and she gave the rest
of her life to helping others, founding a home
for unwed mothers and an AIDS hospice for
gays among many other charitable causes,
and all because a drunken driver had run
over her golden boy. She went to church and

knelt for hours begging God to tell her why her twenty-year old son had to die, but God did not respond, and she walked away with her unyielding pride leaving her simple faith that she had inherited from her caring mother and philandering father who had abandoned her when she was twelve behind her. "Saint Joan," they called her, for all her good works, and they named a street after her when she died of inoperable cancer.

Vanity dies hard. That's what makes this spiritual musing dangerous, the unbearable realization that human suffering serves Nature's purpose for man's evolution, which is to resolve the dual consciousness of our paradoxical nature and make us whole.

As each plant grows from a seed and becomes in the end an oak tree, so man must become what he is meant to be. He ought to get there, but most get stuck," said Carl Jung; but this can only make sense in light of karma and reincarnation, because man cannot possibly realize his true self in one lifetime alone. It may be impossible to comprehend, but suffering is our friend.

My "unapprehended inspiration" for today's spiritual musing then came to me again while reading "The Atheist at the Breakfast Table" the other morning, which was consolidated with the coincidence of the two *God's Not Dead* movies that delved into the lives of believers and non-believers alike; but as informative as the *Psychology Today* article and the movies were, I drew upon my own life to flesh in today's spiritual musing, because like the student Josh and professor Radisson in the movies, the only truth that really matters in the end is the truth of one's own experiences, and mine initiated me into the divine mystery of human suffering that speaks more to a just and merciful God than it does to the non-existence of God. And what a relief it is to know that even atrocities like the Holocaust serve Nature's purpose of bringing man's evolving self-consciousness to spiritual resolution; but only within the context of karma and reincarnation.

That's the answer that Victor Frankl, the author of *Man's Search for Meaning,* was seeking for all the brutal suffering that he and his fellow inmates in the Nazi concentration camps had to endure, the merciful answer to the question that haunts every person, **what does life expect of us?** Because suffering that appears on the surface to be senseless and gratuitous resolves our paradoxical nature and makes us whole. And that's probably where the gnostic saying that suffering is good for the soul came from.

I may be stretching it, but I don't believe it was a coincidence that Gurdjieff called his teaching **the Work**, which he defined as "work on oneself" (a transformative teaching of making our two selves into one), and Rabbi Tarphon saying that *"It's not necessary for you to complete **the work**, but neither are you free to desist from it,"* because my instincts tell me that Gurdjieff's meaning of **the Work** and Rabbi Tarphon's **the work** are the same; and, in the simplest terms possible, <u>the meaning of</u> <u>**work** for both of these mystic philosophers is the fulfillment of the</u> <u>imperative of our inner self, which is to realize wholeness and</u> <u>completeness.</u> This is why Gurdjieff said that man must complete what Nature cannot finish and Rabbi Tarphon said that man must not desist from doing **the work.**

I lived Gurdjieff's teaching and "worked" on myself with pathological commitment, and it awakened me to the **secret way of life**, and I realized my true self; so I know what it means to realize wholeness and completeness, and I can say with gnostic certainty what Gurdjieff meant by **the Work** and what Rabbi Tarphon implied with his saying that one must not desist from doing **the work**; but neither Gurdjieff nor Rabbi Tarphon spelled out the vital fact that one simply cannot complete **the work** in one lifetime alone *(this is what makes this spiritual musing so dangerous)*, because Nature can only take one so far on their destined purpose to wholeness and completeness.

One has to take evolution into their own hands to complete what Nature cannot finish; this is what Gurdjieff's "work on oneself" is all about and why Rabbi Tarpon said that it was not necessary to complete **the work** but neither was one free to desist from doing it. And this is the context from which I drew the inspiration for my spiritual musing "What Does Life Expect of Us?"

But I would be remiss if I did not also credit Dr. Victor Frankl's book *Man's Search for Meaning* for the question of my spiritual Musing "What Does Life Expect of Us?, because while in the concentration camp the young doctor came to the paradigm-shifting realization that to survive the horrific conditions in the camp they had to change their attitude about life.

The suffering was so unbearable that many inmates gave up on life completely and wanted to die. "I have nothing to expect from life anymore," said one inmate after another; and Dr. Frankl, who was a psychiatrist when imprisoned and working on his new method of healing which he called Logotherapy, had to do something to lift the spirit of his fellow inmates; and he tells us in *Man's Search for Meaning* how he stepped out of the paradigm that kept them trapped in a perspective that simply could not make sense of all their suffering:

"What was really needed was a fundamental change in our attitude toward life. We had to learn ourselves and, furthermore, we had to teach the despairing men, that *it did not really matter what we expected from life, but rather what life expected from us.* We needed to stop asking about the meaning of life, and instead to think of ourselves as those who were being questioned by life—daily and hourly. Our answer must consist, not in talk and meditation, but in right action and in right conduct. **Life ultimately means taking the responsibility to find the right answer to its problems and to fulfill the tasks which it constantly sets for each individual**" (*Man's Search for Meaning*, Victor E. Frankl, p. 98; bold italics mine).

One Rule to Live By

I highlighted that sentence in bold italics, because it's the core message of Dr. Jordan Peterson's *12 Rules for Life: An Antidote to Chaos*. The good professor came to see that we are all trapped in the existential paradigm of life that is (*please, pardon the comparison*) not unlike a concentration camp, and the inevitable suffering of life can get to the best of us; and we despair.

Professor Peterson had the wisdom—which he drew from Dr. Frankl's *Man's Search for Meaning*, and especially from his hero Aleksandr Solzhenitsyn who also suffered in the Soviet Gulag and chronicled in *The Gulag Archipelago*—to articulate this unbearable truth and confront it with the courage of the archetypal hero that he was called upon to become when he could no longer suffer the coercing forces of political correctness and *had* to speak to Bill C-16 that threatened free speech and thought. This was the good professor's tipping point, the defining moment of his life when the gravitas of his character was tested, and the world finally got the hierophant that the collective voice of my poem *What the Hell Is Going on Out There?* was calling for…

14. The Existential Conundrum

Professor Harold Bloom brought me to tears, again. For all of his literary genius, he could not transcend the existential paradigm that burdened him with the unbearable anxiety of unknowing; and by the logic of his own wisdom, drawn primarily from his unbelievably expansive knowledge of literature, he resigned himself to the Shakespearean injunction to bear his life with equanimity, because he could not complete **the work** that Rabbi Tarphon's injunction said he should not desist from doing; that's why I was brought to tears again when I listened to the *Harold Bloom Interview on RTE* on YouTube the other day, his voice so full of longing that my heart went out to him, as it did to professor Jordan Peterson who was also up against his own wall of unknowing. From the interview, this is the essential Harold Bloom in all of his gnostic wisdom and heart-wrenching vulnerability that reflects the same unbearable anxiety of professor Jordan Peterson's unknowing:

"William Hazlitt got it right, it is we who are Hamlet; women and men alike, we are all of us Hamlet. We are all of us, our mind struggling with the prospect, with the imminence or delayed, of annihilation. The rest is indeed silence for him, because he knows that whether you take the rest as remainder or as solace and sleep, that's all there is, silence. But then, I differ from most people who write about Shakespeare these days. **I think that ultimately the elliptical burden of what he gives us is a breathtaking kind of nihilism more uncanny than anything that Nietzsche apprehended**. I think in the end he, among so much else, (is) telling us that there are no values, or value except those that we create or imbue events, people, or things with. Emerson beautifully said, no world; there is no next world. Here and now is the whole fact. And I think Hamlet understands that very well indeed that here and now is the whole fact; or (in) that beautiful phrase, is it a Victor Hugo that the sublime Walter Pater repeats? '**We have an interval and then our place knows us no more.**' But that I think is what the highest literature is finally about. I tell my students that appreciation, to use Pater's wonderful word, is what I think our stance towards the highest imaginative literature should be, and that what we have to appreciate are the only values that matter in the highest literature, which are cognitive and aesthetic values quite cut off from societal and even historical considerations. Immanuel Kant, I think it was in the first *Critique*, says that time and space are indeed appearances and therefore in a sense illusory. But nevertheless, he says there is something numinal, there is something permanent in these appearances, and I think you don't need Kant if you have Shakespeare. Of course, Hamlet, among so much else, is telling you that. Our yearning is at least transcendental..."

What a conundrum! Good old professor Bloom, doomed by his own logic to be but an interval in time and space and then to be no more, whose yearning for the transcendental cannot be sated by literature, resigning himself to take the rest of his life as it comes and bearing it with equanimity; but what's the difference from professor Bloom's resignation and Albert Camus' "one must imagine Sisyphus happy"? Both have imprisoned themselves in the same existential paradigm of meaninglessness and absurdity, and it doesn't matter if one bears their life with equanimity or imagines Sisyphus happy, Sterling Professor of the Humanities or Nobel laureate of literature, one will never satisfy the longing in their soul for wholeness and completeness until they find a way out of the conundrum that man is born into. This is the existential dilemma that inspired a spiritual musing that I posted on my blog *Saturday, January 27, 2018*:

A Way Out of the Darkness

I've been steered in this direction for quite some time now, and I went online the other day to research David Foster Wallace, who wrote the novel *Infinite Jest* that stirred up the literary world with the promise of a new literary light; but DFW committed suicide on *September 12, 2008* at the age of 46, just when he was coming onto his own as a writer, and I wrote a poem to air my frustration with literature—

The Way of Literature

> Deeper and deeper into the mix,
> he's the zeitgeist behind the chaos
> of a tortured mind, exposing himself
> like a trench-coated compulsive proudly
> showing himself to strangers, an aberrant
> tick, never telling us why he is this way
> (wearing a bandana because he can't stop
> sweating), only doing what he must do to
> satisfy his self-obsession. DFW, what a
> genius, what prophetic wizardry, what a
> tortured soul you are; no wonder you chose
> to exit to the other side, this world was too
> much for your rapacious mind to process,
> resolve, and understand, a joke, an infinite
> jest; but your light will continue to shine
> until another light shines brighter, and
> there will always be another light from
> the eternal fire of man's struggle, a
> new zeitgeist for a new time, for
> such is the way of literature.

In David Foster Wallace, I saw the existential dilemma of life writ large, the same dilemma that Camus (about whom I had recently heard on CBC's *Ideas*, asserting to how much influence his philosophy still has in the world today) explored in *The Myth of Sisyphus,* the dilemma of man's inner and outer self; and despite his literary genius, which was acknowledged by most critics who reviewed *Infinite Jest* (he also received a "genius grant" from the MacArthur Foundation in 1997), DFW, who saw life as a joke not unlike the fate of Sisyphus, was unable to resolve the dilemma that finally drove him to suicide, a fate that Camus considered to be the only truly serious philosophical problem; an act of courage, or desperation?

Of course, they blamed it on his life-long depression for which he took medication; but despite all the medication and therapy that he received for clinical depression and drug and alcohol addiction (which were central to his novel *Infinite Jest*), he still got swallowed up by his shadow and hung himself to put an end to his unbearable suffering, which leads to today's spiritual musing—that aspect of human consciousness that is responsible for inducing the insufferable

One Rule to Live By

conviction that life is meaningless and absurd, that dreaded state of depression that we all experience at one time or another as our own nothingness, and which was given the most exquisite expression in literature by Macbeth's much-too-blithely quoted, *"Life is a tale told by an idiot full of sound and fury signifying nothing."*

This is not an easy state of consciousness to apprehend, let alone explain; but it's felt by anyone who suffers from life-long depression, like David Foster Wallace. And even those who do not suffer from deep depression experience it, because this state of consciousness defines the dark shadow side of our personality. But herein lies the quandary, because who wants to believe that our shadow self is real? It's much easier to repress our dark shadow self than to acknowledge its existence, until it's too late.

Three years ago I wrote *The Lion that Swallowed Hemingway* in which I explored the shadow side of Ernest Hemingway's personality, because I wanted to flesh in this concept of the elusive shadow with the real life story of my high school hero and literary mentor, but even after all the fleshing in that I did with Hemingway's shadow-afflicted personality, I still feel some apprehension as I write today's spiritual musing; but I must be true to my calling, because this unresolved state of consciousness is responsible for the existential dilemma that can pull one so deep into the despair of their own nothingness that it can drive one to desolation and suicide, like it did Ernest Hemingway and David Foster Wallace.

So, what is this consciousness of our own nothingness? How does it come about? This is the mystery of the repressed dark side of our personality. The novelist John Irving made a comment so arrogantly offensive that I had to respond to it by writing a spiritual musing, "Chicken Little Syndrome and the World According to John Irving," that I posted on my blog; he said, **"You don't choose your demons, they choose you."** This is why I was never attracted to read any more of his novels after reading *The World According to Garp* that launched his career, because the central ethic of his life was delusory, which I confirmed by quoting something in my John Irving spiritual musing that America's greatest seer Edgar Cayce revealed:

> "While we are all at different stages of development and may be working on different lessons, we do not make much progress until we can recognize our

problems as opportunities. *We begin to grow when we face up to the fact that we are responsible for our trials and misery. We are only meeting self. Our present circumstances are the result of previous actions whether long removed or in the recent past. So, if we are beset with problems, blame not God, for they are of our own making.* Our miseries are the result of destructive or negative thoughts, emotions, and actions. We can avoid trouble and misery if we live lives of noble thought and action" (*Edgar Cayce's Story of Karma*, by M. Woodward, pp. 219-220; bold italics mine).

In *Meeting the Shadow: The Hidden Power of the Dark Side of Human Nature*, editors Connie Zweig and Jeremiah Abrams tell us why we have a problem, especially writers who are always trying to come to terms with the human condition and the existential dilemma of life, the seemingly irreconcilable problem of our paradoxical nature: "Our shadow self remains the great burden of self-knowledge, the disruptive element that does not want to be known." And why does our shadow not want to be known? The editors of *Meeting the Shadow* tell us: ***"The shadow is by nature difficult to apprehend. It is dangerous, disorderly, and forever in hiding, as if the light of higher consciousness would steal its very life"*** (*Meeting the Shadow*, Introduction, pp. XVII and XXI, bold italics mine).

But didn't Edgar Cayce say, "We can avoid trouble and misery if we live lives of noble thought and action"? Doesn't this suggest that there is a way out of the darkness of our own nothingness?

It certainly does for me, which is why I made this moral imperative the guiding principle of my life and my writing; but then, as they say, the proof of the pudding is in the eating, and unless one lives a life of noble thought and action one will never know why they are the author of their own misery, because **living a life of noble thought and action makes one a good person, and the law of karma has to bring goodness into one's life, not misery!** This is the logic of life that every person must see to make sense of suffering.

A tad far-fetched? Perhaps. But where does a writer go when they have come to the limits of their paradigm of meaning? Depression and suicide, like Hemingway and Wallace, both gifted but self-obsessed writers who wanted to have their cake and eat it too?

"Literature is not enough," said Katherine Mansfield, who tragically died of tuberculosis at the age of 34 at the Gurdjieff

One Rule to Live By

Institute for the Harmonious Development of Man in Fontainebleau, France where she sought out a teaching to expand her paradigm of meaning, as did I with the same teaching; but to expand the paradigm of literature by including the principles of karma and reincarnation as Cayce deemed would seriously tax the credulity of the literary world, which is why the light of literature will never be bright enough to resolve the consciousness of our nothingness, and one must imagine Sisyphus happy in his struggle as the celebrated philosopher of the absurd was forced by his own egocentric logic to do.

But we keep hoping against hope; because, as the dystopian writer Margaret Atwood said in one of her dystopian poems, "All we have is hope, but what hope is there?" And another brilliant writer will always come along, like the Norwegian Karl Ove Knausgaard with his six-volume angst-ridden autobiographical novel that he, ironically, called, *"My Struggle."*

Perhaps one can now understand the gravitational attraction that Jordan Peterson's book *12 Rules for Life: An Antidote to Chaos* has for today's crazy world; his message has awakened the world to the existential crisis of meaning that religion, science, and politics can no longer address with conviction; and with the passion and certainty of an ancient prophet, the good professor has dared to stare the archetypal shadow of life in the eye and make it blink, and even shudder.

In the Overture to his *12 Rules for Life: An antidote to Chaos,* he tells us that while he was working on his book *Maps of Meaning: The Architecture of Belief* he had what his hero C. G. Jung called a "big dream" that gave him the insight he needed to break through his wall of unknowing. "Dreams shed light on the dim places where reason itself has yet to voyage," he explains, with Jungian conviction *(if anything, Jordan Peterson owns his knowledge, and he speaks with a gnostic certainty that gives him the authority of the hierophants of old),* and he writes:

"My dream placed me at the centre of Being itself, and there was no escape. It took me months to understand what this meant. During this time, I came to a more complete, personal realization of what the great stories of the past continually insist upon: ***the centre is occupied by the individual. The center is marked by the cross, as X marks the spot. Existence at that cross is suffering and transformation***—and that fact, above all, needs to be voluntarily accepted. It is possible to transcend slavish adherence to the group and its doctrines and, simultaneously, to avoid the pitfalls of its opposite extreme, nihilism. It is possible, instead, to find sufficient meaning in individual consciousness and experience.

"*How could the world be freed from the terrible dilemma of conflict, on the one hand, and psychological and social dissolution, on the other? The answer was this: through the elevation and development of the individual, and through the willingness of everyone to shoulder the burden of Being and take the heroic path*" (Overture to *12 Rules for Life: An Antidote to Chaos,* by Jordan B. Peterson, p. xxxiii; bold italics mine).

This is pure Jungian logic, and it's the same realization that the Logos grants to every person that life has made ready for the **secret way of life** (I also had several "big dreams," as well as a symbolic squaring-of-the-circle mandala experience in my second year at university that confirmed my path to wholeness and completeness in Gurdjieff's teaching, which I wrote about in *The Pearl of Great Price* that I sent to professor Peterson three years before he became a public figure to help him break through his wall of unknowing); and the good professor, being true to his oracle no less than his hero C. G. Jung, accepted the challenge of his prophetic dream to make the individual self the sacred center of life when he was called to stand up for free speech, and he offered his shadow-dismantling, character-building book *12 Rules for Life*: *An Antidote to Chaos* to help the world complete **the work** which the world cannot desist from doing, **the work** that satisfies the longing in one's soul for wholeness and completeness; that's why life came knocking on the good professor's home in Toronto "the Good" (*how ironic*) to be a hierophant for today's crazy world...

15. The Sacred Individual

In his first book, *Maps of Meaning: The Architecture of Belief*, professor Peterson wrote: "Every culture maintains certain key beliefs that are centrally important to that culture, upon which all secondary beliefs are predicated. These key beliefs cannot be easily given up, because if they are, everything falls, and the unknown once again rules. **Western morality and behavior, for example, are predicated on the assumption that every individual is sacred.**"

This is why young men everywhere are reading his *12 Rules for Life: An Antidote to Chaos* and flocking to his talks like lost souls to the hoopoe bird and viewing his podcasts and lectures, because his message confirms the sacredness of their individual being which they are desperate to hear, and why some young men shout *"We love you, Jordan!"* during his book tour talks.

Of course, Jordan Peterson blushes from all the adulation; he's much too modest to vaunt the effect he's having on them, which, in his own words, is simply speaking his truth. Here's what he said in an interview that I saw online the other day. The YouTube interview was labelled *Jordan B. Peterson Spring 2017 full-length interview* (IDEOLOGY, LOGOS & BELIEF, Two-part interview with Dr. Jordan B. Peterson, *April 2017*, in Vancouver, Canada):

"What I'm trying to do is say what I think as clearly as I possibly can and to listen to the feedback and modify my message when that seems to be necessary; and apart from that I'm willing to let the chips fall where they may, because that's also part of the decision. The decision is, if you believe, if you choose to believe, if you choose to act as if the truth brings Being into existence in the best possible manner, then you speak your truth, you examine your conscience, you listen to feedback, and you allow the events to unfold as they will."

Jordan Peterson is a firm believer in the Logos, which I've identified as one's muse, oracle, and *omniscient guiding principle of life* (as well as *the merciful law of divine synchronicity* and *the great choreographer of life*), and through courageous commitment to his own obsessive individuation process, he brought himself to the point where he trusts that speaking the truth brings the eternal reality of the Logos into Being; this is why he made speaking the truth *Rule 8* in his book of soul-making guiding principles, the premise of his favorite rule being to consolidate one's life and stave off the chaotic forces of nihilism and darkness: *"Tell the truth—or, at least, don't lie."*

The individual self is sacred to Jordan Peterson, as it was to his hero C. G. Jung, and as it is to every person who has the courage to look at life squarely (which his hero Aleksandr Solzhenitsyn finally did, as he tells us in *The Gulag Archipelago*); but because our vision has become obfuscated by moral relativism and the self-compromising inflation of our ego/shadow personality, which our modern world gratuitously panders to by granting our every desire, *the great choreographer of life* had to intervene—as it always does when the sacred individual self gets stuck and is desperate to get back to its destined purpose of wholeness and completeness; that's why professor Peterson was called by life to give his hierophantic message of self-reconciliation to the world.

"I'm really trying to help a person find his or her own way," said Peterson in the interview; and this is the imperative of his hierophantic message, which was my own inspiration when I wrote the spiritual musing that I posted on my blog *April 8, 2017*, but only I went much deeper into the metaphysics of the individuation process than the good professor Jordan Peterson:

The Mathematics of Life

One Rule to Live By

Over coffee in my writing room this morning, Penny and I shared our dreams and tried to decode their message (like C. G. Jung, we both believe that "dreams are the guiding words of the soul"); and in the course of our discussion, my transcendent function (what Jung called "superior insight") kicked in, and I was given a magnificent metaphor to help explain my literary hero Harold Bloom's existential dilemma.

I had just finished reading professor Bloom's big book *The Western Cannon* again and was well into my second reading of his ponderous book *The Daemon Knows,* and his existential dilemma was fresh on my mind, and it just happened to relate to Penny's dream and mine because they both spoke the omniscient guiding words of our transcendent self and superior insight.

Penny's dream was about someone stealing her Singer sewing machine. A man had put it into his yellow truck and was driving away, and Penny shouted, "Hey, that's my sewing machine!" And in my dream, I had just written five or six pages of a new story that I was showing to an old acquaintance, and the first sentence of my story read: "He was different."

My story was autobiographical, and I knew what my fictional self meant by that first sentence "He was different"—true to my literary mentor Ernest Hemingway's credo to begin every story with "one true sentence," as Penny vouchsafed with her comment, *"You're different, alright!"*

In my dream, I let an old acquaintance from my hometown read the first few pages of my story because I wanted to introduce him to the mystery that eluded the great literary scholar professor Bloom his entire life—the mystery of the **secret way of life** implicit to the archetypal imperative of literature, the secret of our *becoming* which resolves the existential dilemma of our dual nature.

And I saw Penny's dream as a good sign, the yellow truck symbolizing the mobility of Divine Spirit (yellow is always associated with the spiritual dimension of life), and I saw her sewing machine as a symbol for "stitching things up," which Penny has been doing all of her life (a metaphor for "making do"), so I said to her: "That's a good dream. Your dream self is telling you that the theft of your sewing machine means you will have more mobility and won't have to stitch things up anymore. Your dream augurs good fortune, because you will no longer have to make do."

Penny looked at me quizzically, but I did not explain further because symbolic dreams take time to sink in (it took me a few more weeks to see that Spirit, symbolized by the yellow truck, "stole" Penny's fear of having to make do); and my dream augured well for me also, because I've been called back to creative writing and am working on a new book of short stories with the conscious guiding principle of the resolution to man's existential predicament that literature cannot supply, and by letting a retired grocer read the first few pages of my new story, my dream was telling me that my stories will find public consumption (food for the soul, if you will; hence, the dream symbol of the retired grocer reading my story in my dream); that's why professor Harold Bloom popped into my mind.

As professor Bloom came to see with terrifying clarity, literature is all about individuation, the realization of self-identity—his best example at the center of his cannon being Shakespeare's conflicted Prince Hamlet of Denmark, which he expounds upon in his book *Shakespeare: The Invention of the Human*, and with deeper conviction in *Hamlet: Poem Unlimited;* but in the American bard Walt Whitman, professor Bloom found his most poignant expression of individuation, especially in Whitman's signature poem "Song of Myself" which professor Bloom described as "a psychic cartography of three components in each of us—soul, self, and real me or me myself."

The great tragedy of literature, and personally for the great professor Bloom, who suffers from what he calls a Shakespearean kind of breathtaking nihilism, is that literature cannot resolve the three aspects of man's nature—soul, self, and real me or me myself; and that's what Penny and I discussed over coffee this morning, because the central theme of all my books has to do with reconciling the separate aspects of our nature, thereby resolving professor Bloom's existential dilemma.

"The unconscious is neutral. It's neither good nor bad, neither right nor wrong; it just is what it is, a magnificent process of self-becoming," I said to Penny this morning. "Let me give you a metaphor to explain what I mean. This is what professor Bloom figured out about literature, but he got stuck in the labyrinth of his own brilliant mind and couldn't find his way out. Let's consign a number to every variable of life. Let's say one experience is consigned a number, and another experience, thing, thought, idea, or emotion are all consigned a number. Let's say that all of life is mathematical in nature, which is what the ancient Greek philosopher Pythagoras believed; so, when the variables of our life are put together in a certain way, there will be a mathematical truth to them. One plus three plus seven has to equal eleven. That's a mathematical certainty. That's life in a nutshell. It just *is*. But we have free will. We are primarily responsible in how we arrange the variables of our life, and when added up these variables make up who we are, the mathematical certainty of our life if you will. But what if we get stuck in our life and can't move on? What happens then?"

"Life can get pretty boring," Penny said, and laughed.

"Yes, or tragic," I added. "And this is where I part company with professor Bloom, because I happen to believe in an omniscient guiding principle of life that comes to help us get unstuck from the existential dilemma of life. That's what my book *The Merciful Law of Divine Synchronicity* is all about. And I believe this was the message of our dreams last night; yours to get you unstuck from your fear of always having to stich things up to make do, and mine confirming my call back to creative writing with stories that will expand not only my own literary horizons, but hopefully the horizons of literature as well."

"I've been telling you that for years," Penny said, with a generous smile.

"I know, sweetheart; but you know me, I have to do what I have to do to do what I'm called to do. That's why I'm different."

"You're different, alright!" Penny said, with a mirthful chuckle.

―――――

Perhaps we can better understand now what Rabbi Tarphon meant by **the work,** which we must not desist from doing, in light of professor Bloom's perception of the individuation process that he discovered to be the imperative of all literature, which is to reconcile "the three components in each of us—soul, self, and real me or me myself."

But herein lies the tragedy, because the most that literature can do is reflect the human condition (in poetry, stories, novels, and plays) that traps the self in the existential paradigm of our becoming which cannot reconcile the three components in each of us.

But let me spell out what professor Bloom meant by "soul, self, and real me or me myself" that he intuited with literary genius but could find no resolution for in literature, and which was responsible for his life-long melancholic longing for wholeness and completeness.

Soul is the spark of divine consciousness that we are all born with, which is teleologically driven to realize wholeness and completeness; **self** is the "I" of our ego/shadow personality that we create with each new incarnation from the *I Am*-consciousness of the *enantiodromiac* dynamic of our daily life experience (the inevitable conflict of our inner and outer self); and **real me or me myself** is our self-actualizing **soul self**, which is created through the natural process of individuating the paradoxical nature of our inner and outer self that we experience in our daily life, like the lighthouse keeper Tom Sherbourne's moral predicament in my spiritual musing "Chemistry of the Soul" which taught him the lesson of his life that self-betrayal always comes with a price. *In short, Tom Sherbourne grew in his soul self through the pain and suffering of his own making.*

But because the natural individuation process of our daily life cannot resolve the paradoxical dilemma of our inner and outer self (our real and false self), the sacred individual self needs help to become whole and complete. This is what Rabbi Tarphon pointed to, as does professor Jordan Peterson with his *12 Rules for Life: An Antidote to Chaos*, despite not being cognizant of doing this.

One Rule to Live By

Rabbi Tarphon's messages speaks to the imperative of **the work** that we must not desist from doing, which is to become whole and complete, but he doesn't tell us how; and professor Peterson's message in *12 Rules for Life* tells us how to do **the work** to become whole and complete but doesn't tell us why. Which is why I was called to write *One Rule to Live By: Be Good*, because from my perspective of having resolved the paradoxical nature of my inner and outer self, I can see both the how and the why of **the work** that one must do to honor the divine imperative of our sacred individual self to become whole and complete, and then one will realize that state of resolved self-consciousness that I have articulated in the following words in *The Pearl of Great Price*: **I am what I am not, and I am not what I am; I am both, but neither: I am Soul**. And this transcendent state of resolved self-consciousness was confirmed by a dream I had one night a few years ago; but before I relate my dream, let me explain what I mean by my resolved state of consciousness.

This may appear to be a digression, but it bears direct relevance to my resolved state of consciousness that I realized when I gave "birth" to my eternal self in my mother's kitchen one summer day many years ago, which was why I finally walked away from that New Age spiritual teaching of the Light and Sound of God after living it for more than thirty years, because I could no longer suffer the hypocrisy of putting the carriage in front of the horse, which this teaching did by proclaiming that we are all Soul and all we had to do was accept and realize it, which I *knew* from my own journey of self-discovery was misleading, because one has to *become* Soul, whole and complete, before one can state with gnostic certainty that one *is* Soul. In short, we have to *become* our true self before we can say that we *are* our true self, and this is the mystery of the individuation process that Carl Gustav Jung expounded upon with his inherently gnostic psychology of individuation.

This was my beef with Christianity as well, because it also short-circuited the process of self-individuation by proclaiming Jesus to be our savior, because Christ's real message was all about *becoming* our true self by "doing" his sayings. ***"Therefore, whosoever heareth these sayings of mine, and doeth them, I will liken him unto a wise man, which built his house upon a rock,"*** said Jesus, (Matthew. 7: 24). In other words, there are no shortcuts to our true self; and by true self (***"house upon a rock,"*** in Christ's words), I mean Soul whole and complete, the resolved consciousness of our inner and outer self, the self that is both real and false but neither, the self that Jesus called "eternal life" and "pearl of great price" in his sayings and parables.

Now, my dream that confirmed my resolved state of consciousness: Like Carl Jung, who realized wholeness of self through his own remarkable individuation process, a dream he had several days before dying confirmed that he had completed **the work**, as did I. In his dream, Jung saw, "high up in a high place," a boulder lit by the full sun. Carved into the illuminated boulder were the words: "Take this as a sign of the wholeness you have achieved and the singleness you have become." It was *carved in stone,* which symbolically confirmed that he had achieved wholeness and completeness—*the blessed fruit of his individuation process;* and in my dream, I was granted permission to look my name up in The Dictionary of Life; and this is how Life defined me: **Orest Stocco: Soul** (with a capital S)—*also the blessed fruit of my own individuation process, my true self whole and complete.*

Nothing more, just my name and the word Soul to define who and what I was; and it felt good to have inner confirmation that I had also completed **the work** and *become* Soul, my true self whole and complete, as had my hero C. G. Jung; and as cryptic as Rabbi Tarphon was in his saying about not desisting from doing **the work**, I suspect he knew much more than he implied.

One Rule to Live By

Which is why I have such deep respect and admiration for professor Jordan Peterson, whose message to the world not only honors and preserves the integrity of the sacred individual self, but offers a gnostic way to *become* one's true self by practicing, or "doing" his 12 Rules for Life, thus honoring Rabbi Tarphon's dictum to not desist from doing **the work**...

16. Live Your Own Path and be Cool

Cool people are charismatic. Jordan Peterson is charismatic; ergo, Jordan Peterson is cool. This is an irrefutable syllogism. So, how did Jordan Peterson become cool? And, better still, can his gnostic little book *12 Rules for Life: An Antidote to Chaos* make one cool?

Is this why his message is so attractive to the younger generation, especially wayward young men (to date, about 80% of his youth audience is male), because they find him cool and want to know his secret? And when he tells them the secret is to simply shoulder the responsibility for their own life— *"You can start by cleaning your damn room!"* —why do they not flee in horror but instead want more? That's the mystique of Jordan B. Peterson.

The concept of cool fascinated me no less than it did David Brooks, the *New York Times* columnist who called Dr. Peterson "the most influential public intellectual in the Western world right now" and whose column I follow in *The New York International Weekly* that's inserted into my *Toronto Sunday Star*, along with *The New York Times Book Review*; in fact, so fascinated was I by the concept of cool that I wrote a spiritual musing inspired by David Brooks, which I posted on my Spiritual Musings blog *Saturday, October 7, 2017:*

The Essence of Cool

I really didn't want to, but I jotted the idea down in my notebook just in case I ran into a dry spell (which happens rarely) and needed an idea to explore just to keep the creative juices flowing, and I forgot about it until this morning when I noticed the highlighted passage in David Brooks' op-ed piece in the folded newspaper page that I had on my desk which I intended to explore but never got around to until it caught my eye this morning as I was going through the notebooks and papers on my desk.

Brooks' piece is titled "What Has Replaced Cool in America" (*The New York Times International Weekly, Wednesday, July 30, 2017*), and I highlighted in blue marker the passage that inspired the idea for a short spiritual musing on the essence of cool: ***"The cool person is stoical, emotionally controlled, never eager or needy, but instead mysterious, detached and self-possessed. The cool person is gracefully competent at something but doesn't need the world's applause to know his worth. That's because the cool person has found his or her own unique and authentic way of living with nonchalant intensity."***

How cool is that? Given that description of what a cool person is, I can't imagine anyone not wanting to be cool; but that's why the idea for a spiritual musing on cool seized me, because not everyone can be cool. That's what makes one cool, if one can appreciate the irony. But just in case, let me explore the irony of being cool in today's spiritual musing…

For some reason known only to my muse, I was nudged to browse through one of the bookcases in my writing room yesterday morning, and as I went through the top shelf I came upon *The Seasons of the Soul*, a collection of poems by Hermann Hesse previously unpublished in English, translated and with a commentary by Ludwig Max Fischer and a forward by spiritual activist Andrew Harvey, and even though I had read it already, I felt strongly nudged to read it again, which I did throughout the day in the comfort of our front deck; and this morning I was called to read *My Belief,* essays on life and art, also by Hermann Hesse, which I had read two or three times already, and only upon reading the introduction again did I make the connection with Hermann Hesse and the idea for my spiritual musing on the essence of cool, and I had to smile at the remarkable coincidence, *because I never cease to be amazed at how the merciful law of divine synchronicity works in my life to make things happen for me, especially when I'm writing.*

I had highlighted one more passage in David Brooks' article, a single sentence that summed up what I felt to be the essential quality of a cool person, which popped into my mind while reading the introduction to *My Belief*, and I knew instantly why I was called to re-acquaint myself with the writer I had read many years ago while on my own spiritual quest like Hermann Hesse. The sentence that I highlighted said it all: **"The cool person is guided by his or her own autonomous values, often on the outskirts of society."**

That was Hermann Hesse to a tee, a man guided by his own autonomous values and on the outskirts of society, a definition which, at the risk of sounding immodest, applied to me no less than Hermann Hesse, because my whole life I've always lived by my own guiding inner light which set me apart from everyone; so, there it was then, my reason for being called to write a short spiritual musing on cool—to demystify the *je ne sais quoi* of this elusive quality of being cool.

In truth, I already have a gnostic awareness of what constitutes the essence of cool; but it would be presumptuous to state this up front without providing the context that gave birth to my realization of this elusive but alluring character trait, because it's in the context of my own quest for my true self that pulled Hermann Hesse into my life with his book *Journey to the East* first and then his magnificent novel *Magister Ludi*, also known as *The Glass Bead Game*.

I had already highlighted the passage, in yellow highlighter this time, but it jumped out at me again as I read the introduction to *My Belief* this morning: **"Hesse maintains that the idea of the underlying unity of all being is a synthesis that can be achieved only through a reconciliation of conflicting opposites. This dialectical process shows up over and over again in Hesse's novels."**

This dialectical process of reconciling conflicting opposites speaks to what C. G. Jung called the individuation process, the founding premise of his psychology (*it can't be a coincidence that Hesse underwent Jungian analysis during the most trying period of his life, which led him to meet Jung personally, after which he wrote his novel Demian that is replete with Jungian archetypes and symbols and explores the Jungian dialectic of individuation*); but not until one learns how to reconcile the conflicting opposites of their personality can one achieve what Jung's dream self called "wholeness and singleness of self." That's why Hesse became a cult figure for the mind-expanding, paradigm shifting counterculture movement of the mid-1960s, because his novels spoke to the longing in one's soul for wholeness and completeness.

Hesse's best-known works include *Demian, Steppenwolf, Siddhartha,* and *The Glass Bead Game,* each of which explores an individual's search for authenticity, self-knowledge and spirituality, and he was awarded the Nobel Prize for Literature in 1946; and it was their search for a way to reconcile the conflicting opposite aspects of one's ego/shadow personality with one's inner self that preoccupied both Jung and Hesse their whole life, with Jung succeeding and Hesse dying unresolved.

This is the context that awakened me to the **secret way of life** that both Jung and Hesse had become aware of, which Miguel Serrano alludes to in his short memoir *C. G. Jung and Hermann Hesse, A Record of Two Friendships;* and like Jung and Hesse, I came to the same realization that **self-reconciliation is the only way to one's true self,** and I embarked upon this perilous journey to authenticity that essentially makes a person cool. In short, *the more true one is to oneself, the more cool they will be;* but it wouldn't be cool to vaunt this, because the cool person just *is*, and that's the irony of being cool.

―――

A cool person, says David Brooks, "is guided by his or her own autonomous values, often on the outskirts of society," which describes outlier professor Jordan Peterson, who stands just outside the mainstream with his personal worldview that he expressed in his runaway bestseller *12 Rules for Life* that David Brooks, in his *July 18, 2018* review in *The New York Times,* says are "joyless and graceless calls to self-sacrifice." Undoubtedly, because they speak to the same dialectical process of self-reconciliation that Carl Jung and Hermann Hesse both explored in their separate ways.

But despite how harsh professor Peterson's *12 Rules for Life* may be in their imperative, they speak to the young people, especially to alienated young men who are so desperate to find a way out of the existential vacuum of this crazy modern world that they will do anything to fill the hole in their soul, and they take professor Peterson's joyless, self-sacrificing rules seriously—*because he made it painfully clear that the alternative would be more of the same soul-sucking nihilism that gorged the archetypal shadow of the world that gave rise to the brutal dictators Stalin, Hitler, and Chairman Mao who murdered millions of innocent people for the sake of delusory utopian dreams!*

"Stop doing what you know to be wrong," says professor Peterson. **"Say only those things that make you strong. Do only those things that you could speak of with honor. Pursue what is meaningful (not what is expedient.)"** Stern advice from an outlier, whose noble imperative to help young people find their way out of the social pressure cooker responsible for their stress and anguish has caught the ear of the world; but not to give the wrong impression, David Brooks' review of the good professor's *12 Rules for Life* was as negative (in a good way) as it was positive (in a better way), because from everything that I have read by David Brooks, he always comes across objective and fair in his opinions, as he does here.

"Parents, universities and the elders of society have utterly failed to give many young men realistic and demanding practical wisdom on how to live," he wrote in his *July 18, 2018 New York Time's* review, which he brings to honest and fair resolution. "Peterson has filled the gap. The Peterson way is a harsh way, but it is an idealistic way—and for millions of young men, it turns out to be the perfect antidote to the cocktail of coddling and accusation in which they are raised."

Curiously enough, David Brooks wrote his own little gnostic book on self-improvement that he called *The Road to Character,* and he was interviewed on CBC's *Tapestry*, which by another strange coincidence I just happened to listen to one Sunday afternoon.

"I wrote it to save my own soul," he told Mary Hynes, the smiley-voiced host of the show whose eager-seeker persona annoyed me in an opposite way that Stephen Fry annoyed me, especially her ready laughter; and I added *The Road to Character* to my Amazon wish list along with Peterson's *Maps of Meaning*, just to see how they would compare in their separate journeys to self-fulfillment, because no matter what path one takes in life, they all end up to that same terrifying place that Jesus called "the eye of the needle," which takes special wisdom to pass through.

Maybe this is why rumor has it that Jewish born and bred David Brooks may be converting to Christianity? Life, really, is strange; and when it calls it calls...

17. Outside the Box, or Cloud-cuckoo-land?

As I said, I never fit in with my family, and I found out why when I had my first past-life regression to my lifetime in London, England *(everyone in my family except my father were members of the British aristocracy, which finally explained my abhorrence for what I described in my past lifetime as that "foul blend of honour and deceit" in the upper circles of the aristocracy, a feeling that I brought with me into my current life and which I continued to see in my family shadow, the alchemical gold of irreducible conceit, my damnation and salvation)*; but truth be told, not only did I feel out of context with my family, but with my very own life and society as well, a strange feeling that I had my whole life and did not resolve until just a few years ago when I went for ten spiritual healing sessions with a gifted psychic medium who channelled St. Padre Pio for my novel *Healing with Padre Pio*.

Like C. G. Jung, who broke away from his mentor Sigmund Freud to establish his own discipline that he called Analytical Psychology, so too did Dr. Victor Frankl break away from the prevailing schools of psychotherapy to create his own discipline that he called Logotherapy; and as he tells us in *Man's Search for Meaning*, his therapy has to do with accepting personal responsibility for one's life *(Dr. Jordan Peterson owes much more to Victor Frankl than he dares to admit)*; and in one section of his book that he calls "THE ESSENCE OF EXISTENCE," Frankl writes:

> "The emphasis on responsibilities is reflected in the categorical imperative of logotherapy, which is: *'Live as if you were living already for the second time and as if you had acted the first time as wrongly as you are about to act now!'* It seems to me that there is nothing which would stimulate a man's sense of responsibleness more than this maxim, which invites him to imagine first that the present is past and, second, **that the**

past may yet be changed and amended. Such a precept confronts him with life's *finiteness* as well as the *finality* of what he makes out of both his life and himself" (*Man's Search for Meaning,* Victor E. Frankl, pp. 131-2; bold italics mine).

This may be hard to believe (*honestly, I never cease to marvel at the genius of the creative unconscious!*), but I was called by my muse last year to write a spiritual musing that creatively expounds upon Logotherapy's categorical imperative, offering a viable explanation drawn from the arts (literature and the movies, in this case) for why one should live one's life responsibly, and I posted my spiritual musing on my Spiritual Musings blog *Saturday, December 30, 2017:*

What's Life For?

Quantum physics theorizes that parallel worlds exist, and if they do exist so too would parallel lives, something that the German philosopher Friedrich Nietzsche (1844-1900) posited as a central concept in his most popular book *Thus Spoke Zarathustra* and which the writer and student of Gurdjieff's teaching P. D. Ouspensky explored in his novel *Strange Life of Ivan Osokin,* as well as the contemporary novelist Kate Atkinson with her novel *Life After Life*; but what if this theory were true?
This is the conceit of the movie *Before I Fall*, a fascinating story of eternal recurrence and self-redemption that is worth exploring in today's spiritual musing...

It was Boxing Day, and Penny and I watched the Netflix movie *Before I Fall*, based upon the best-selling eponymous novel by the prescient 26 year-old Lauren Oliver, a movie based upon the principle of eternal recurrence not unlike the movie *Groundhog Day* when Bill Murray keeps waking up to the same day, only in Oliver's story her protagonist Samantha (Sam) Kingston not only wakes up to the same day for seven straight days, but she explores her life of moral impunity and then finally comes to the realization that to give her life *meaning* she has to improve and make her life better, a captivating story of self-redemption that called for a spiritual musing on parallel lives and the Sisyphean struggle; but where did the mind-boggling idea of living our same life over again originate?

This idea goes back to pre-Socratic times, but the idea of living our same life over again came to the German philosopher Friedrich Nietzsche in a moment of desperate thought in August 1881 while out on a walk alongside Lake Silvaplana in Switzerland where he had gone to heal himself and write, and which he introduced as aphorism 341, entitled "The greatest weight," in Book IV of his book *The Gay Science*:

> "What, if some day or night a demon were to steal after you into your loneliest loneliness and say to you: "This life as you now live it and have lived it, you will have to live once more and innumerable times more; and there will be nothing new in it, but every pain and every joy and every thought and sigh and everything unutterably small or great in your life will have to return to you, all in the same succession and sequence—even this spider and this moonlight between the trees, and even this moment and I myself. The eternal hourglass of existence is turned upside down again and again, and you with it, speck of dust!
>
> "Would you not throw yourself down and gnash your teeth and curse the demon who spoke thus? Or have you once experienced a tremendous moment when you would have answered him: "You are a god and never have I heard anything more divine." If this thought gained possession of you, it would change you as you are or perhaps crush you. The question in each and every thing, "Do you desire this once more and innumerable times more?" would lie upon your actions as the greatest weight. Or how well disposed would you have to become to yourself and to life to crave nothing more fervently than this ultimate eternal confirmation and seal?"

For Nietzsche, this inspired idea became a thought experiment that he made central to his prophet-like figure Zarathustra's teaching, a philosophy of *amor fati* (love of one's fate), a life-affirming yae-saying to life as opposed to Christianity's life-denying nay-saying ethos because Christianity sees this world as inferior to another and this life as mere preparation for a life in paradise *(or so thought Nietzsche who completely misperceived Christ's teaching of "dying" to one's life to "save" one's life);* but in the mind of imaginative writers like Ouspensky, Atkinson, and Lauren Oliver one can change the recurring pattern of one's life and move on to a more perfect life, which opens up this spiritual musing to the terrifying issue of moral relativism that haunted me for years, because for the life of me I could not see where society was going, given that modern man was now free to posit his own personal sense of right and wrong, a ticking time-bomb that keeps exploding in the violent terrorist attacks on social order and human decency; but I finally brought this issue to resolution in my spiritual musing "The Stupidity of Moral Relativism," which I've included in my fourth volume of spiritual musings *The Armchair Guru* and need not explore here.

Suffice to say that moral relativism resists the teleological imperative of our destined purpose, which is to realize our wholeness and completeness; this is why the guiding spirit of our creative unconscious has introduced the principle of redemption through the concept of eternal recurrence in the medium of literature and the movies, with the anti-Nietzschean twist that we can change the soul-crushing recurring pattern of our same life if only we are willing to heed the redemptive principle of our destined purpose.

Our destined purpose is to become who we are meant to be, and I don't believe it was a coincidence that the motto **BECOME WHO YOU ARE** was shown on a poster in the high school student Kent's bedroom in the movie *Before I Fall,* which caught Sam's attention on one of her recurring days (and which quite possibly sparked her desire to improve her life and become who she was meant to be), and neither do I believe it was a coincidence that the high school teacher in the classroom that Sam keeps returning to on the morning of the recurring same day writes on the blackboard the word **HISTORY** in caps (implying that history repeats itself) and the word <u>Sisyphus</u> underscored, and then says to his students: "Sisyphus. Not an STD (sexually transmitted disease). What's he like? What does it mean when something is described as being Sisyphean? Does it mean pointless? Brave? *Late?* (Kent just walked into the classroom when his teacher said *"Late?"* and the class breaks into laughter.) What's his character like? Does he learn from pushing that boulder—" and just then three girls walk into the classroom delivering roses for Cupid's Day, the day before Valentine's, and the story now has its theme of eternal recurrence that Albert Camus made famous by allegorizing Sisyphus's fate with the drudgery of man's daily struggle in his famous essay "The Myth of Sisyphus," the theme of Samantha Kingston's recurring daily struggle.

Was there a point to Sisyphus rolling that rock up a hill only to have it roll back down of its own weight where he was fated to rolling it back up again, for eternity? Albert Camus couldn't see the point. The gods that condemned Sisyphus "thought that there was no more dreadful punishment than futile and hopeless labor," wrote Camus, comparing Sisyphus's fate with man's daily struggle, and he brings his iconic essay to ironic resolution by arrogantly thumbing his nose at the gods that had condemned Sisyphus: ***"There is no sun without shadow, and it is essential to know the night…The struggle itself toward the heights is enough to fill a man's heart. One must imagine Sisyphus happy,"*** which I could never do, because life for me was neither pointless nor absurd; it was *the* way to who we are meant to be, which Samantha finally figured out as she returned to live the same day over again and finally broke the pattern of her recurring life and was on her way to becoming who she was meant to be, her true self whole and complete, thereby resolving the conundrum of the Sisyphean struggle that she faced every morning of her recurring life.

But the question arises: why did Samantha want to redeem herself? What inspired her to change her recurring day into one that improved her life? Why not continue to live the same day over again doing whatever she wanted with moral impunity? Why improve her life, which she finally ended up doing, and by improving her life she meant becoming a better person?

Lauren Oliver answers this question in a letter that she wrote for the special enhanced edition of her novel *Before I Fall*; but before I reveal her answer, let me say something first about the creative spirit of a writer's life, the all-knowing *daemon* of one's creative unconscious that is infinitely wiser than our cognitive mind which Lauren Oliver makes clear in her inspiration for her novel *Before I Fall,* an inspiration that came from a childhood and adolescent ritual of putting herself to sleep when she had trouble sleeping by going over and over in her mind what made for a perfect day, a ritual which engaged the redemptive principle of life that seeks to reconcile one's existential outer life with one's destined inner purpose of realizing the wholeness and completeness of one's sacred self, a playful nighttime ritual that evolved into the idea of living one's life over and over again to improve and better one's life, which became the dynamic theme of her refreshingly iconoclastic, anti-Nietzschean and genuinely life-affirming novel *Before I Fall*.

Upon reflection on her novel years after she wrote it, Lauren Oliver came to realize that Samantha Kingston (her fictional self) was looking for personal *meaning*, what really mattered to her and what she wanted to be remembered for when she died, and she found this *meaning* by improving her life and becoming a better person; that was the driving aesthetic of her imagined but essentially autobiographical novel *Before I Fall*; but why *meaning*? Why not happiness and well-being? Material comfort, good health, pleasure, fame? Why *meaning*?

"Vanity of vanities, sayeth the Preacher, vanity of vanities; all is vanity. What profit hath a man of all his labor which he taketh under the sun?" asked the Preacher in *Ecclesiastes*, essentially the same question that Samantha asked as she relived her same day over again, and the answer that she came up with was that she had to improve and perfect her life because this would give her life the *meaning* for which she wanted to be remembered; but why? That's what the Preacher was trying to figure out, and every other person who asks the question, "What the hell's the point of it all, anyway?"

Albert Camus couldn't figure it out (he came dangerously close in his novel *The Fall*), and he relegates life to an absurd fate not unlike the futile and hopeless labor that Sisyphus was condemned to. But Lauren Oliver came to a different conclusion, and she did so by allowing the wisdom of her creative spirit to work it out for her in her novel *Before I Fall*, an imagined, but intuitive expression of the redemptive principle of life in Samantha's desire to become a better person, to make her recurring day as perfect as possible, which she did by acknowledging the worth and goodness in others; that's how she gave her life the *meaning* she needed. But this is a very difficult concept to convey, which I've explored in other musings; suffice to say here that *Before I Fall* is a story that addresses what we all ask, *what's life for?* To become who we are meant to be, our best and truest self intuited Lauren Oliver; that's what life is for.

Orest Stocco

POSTSCRIPT

It occurred to me as I edited and reworked this spiritual musing that Lauren Oliver's novel *Before I Fall* is an ironic, albeit unconscious literary response to Albert Camus's novel *The Fall*, the story of a French lawyer racked with guilt at the vanity, selfishness and duplicity of his former life as a lawyer. Camus's protagonist Jean-Baptiste-Clamence **falls** from grace and spends the rest of his remorseful life in Amsterdam wallowing in despair. Clamence recounts his story of woe and guilt to a stranger in a friendly bar called *Mexico City* in the red-light district that Camus metaphorically compares to "the last circle of hell," hence the title of his novel *The Fall*. In Lauren Oliver's novel *Before I Fall,* her protagonist Samantha Kingston safeguards her fall from grace by improving and bettering her selfish life. I'm only surmising, of course; but in my experience of how the creative spirit of a writer's personal *daemon* works, it has an omniscient quality that can draw upon the collective unconscious of the human psyche to make the point of the writer's story with an unconscious but all-knowing creative imperative, as it did with both Albert Camus and Lauren Oliver, only with Camus the point of his story was the ***absurdity of life,*** and with Oliver the point of her story was the ***meaning of life***, two distinctly opposite perspectives, but one no less valid than the other, as I spelled out in my spiritual musing "The Two Ends of the Stick: Shania Twain and P. D. Ouspensky." Both novels express the dual consciousness of human nature, one positive and one negative; and the choice is ours to make, as the young Samantha comes to realize in her recurring life of seven days. On a curious note, I wanted to know how Lauren Oliver came up with the title for her book; and in the special enhanced edition of *Before I Fall* she informs us that after she and her editor and agent went through a long list of titles, her editor Rosemary Brosnan *"dreamed"* (Oliver's italics) the title *Before I Fall*, which just happened to be the opposite end of the stick to Albert Camus's novel *The Fall*, confirming for me once again the guiding wisdom of the creative unconscious. *I never cease to marvel at how the merciful law of divine synchronicity works!*

One Rule to Live By

So, why did I feel out of context with my family, my own life, and society? Why did I feel like I was living a life apart? What could possibly explain this pervasive feeling?

I got an explanation late in life, but the seed was planted in a narrative poem that I was *inspired* to write in grade twelve—no, that's not the right word; I wasn't *inspired* to write my poem *Noman*, I was *possessed* to write it with a *daemonic* intensity that I have never experienced since; and it took me almost fifty years before I understood what my strange poem was telling me. Unfortunately, I no longer have a copy of my poem; but I remember the narrative like it was yesterday.

Noman was set free from the depths of my unconscious by the medieval morality play *The Summoning of Everyman* that I had read a week or so before I was summoned from sleep with the strongest desire to write a poem, and out poured *Noman* in a flood of images and words (all very biblical sounding, words like *thee* and *thou*) and I did not stop writing until I fell from heaven shouting as I fell, *"Open, you vile, voracious, lovable sweet whore! /God, why hast thou forsaken me?"* I was seventeen years old, and still a virgin; where did those words come from?

Like Everyman in the morality play, who symbolizes every person, Noman, who is the archetypal shadow side of Everyman, was summoned to God for a reckoning also. I was Noman, and as I stood before God, God said to me: "Noman, hast thou my fish's scale?"

I did not have God's fish's scale, and God gave me three days to find it in the "abyss with four corners," which I knew to be the world—North, South, East, and West; but it would take me one day to search each corner of the abyss, which meant that if I did not find it in three days there would still be one corner of the abyss left to search for God's fish's scale, and at the end of each day's futile search I heard God's booming voice, "NOMAN, HAST THOU MY FISH'S SCALE?"

It took me many years to realize what God meant by fish's scale, which turned out to be my own lost soul; and God wanted me to find my lost soul because it belonged to God. So, I searched and searched and searched and failed to find my lost soul, and I was summoned back to God for my reckoning; and God, in his mercy, condemned me to the fourth corner of the abyss for eternity to find my lost soul, and not until I found it and returned it to God would I be allowed back into heaven.

That was the gist of my poem *Noman*, which puzzled me for many years. But I finally worked it out after I had ten spiritual healing sessions with a gifted psychic medium who channeled St. Padre Pio for my novel *Healing with Padre Pio*, and I told the story of what my poem meant in my memoir *The Summoning of Noman*, which was inspired by something that Padre Pio told me in one of my spiritual healing sessions. To my astonishment, he told me that I had lived my same life over again three separate times in my reincarnational history, and my current lifetime was one of those times.

It blew my mind. *I, Orest Stocco, returned to live my same life over again as Orest Stocco!* How could that be? That's what I had to find out, and for months I went online researching the theory of parallel lives, and finally I had to turn to the only source of information that I could trust: my own dreams. My inspiration was Carl Jung, who always relied on his dreams for guidance, and the result was *The Summoning of Noman* that tells the story of my parallel life as Orest Stocco.

So, Victor Frankl; your categorical imperative was well-founded, because **I actually came back to live my same life over again to achieve a different outcome,** just as Padre Pio told me in my spiritual healing session, which I later explored in *The Summoning of Noman*; and the different outcome that I achieved was to pass through the eye of the needle that I could not find a way of doing in my first lifetime as Orest Stocco. In a word, I found my lost soul. *Unbelievable, but true!*

This means that professor Peterson's got it right with his book *12 Rules for Life*, because like Dr. Victor Frankl, he too worked out a therapeutic way of living one's life responsibly, which makes one a better person ready for the **secret way** that leads to wholeness and completeness; and this makes Dr. Peterson a logotherapist, whether he wants to call himself that or not...

18. The Crossroad of Jordan Peterson's Life

I should have been startled by Jordan Peterson's life-altering experience that he relates in *Rule 8: Tell the Truth—or, at least, don't lie,* but I wasn't; I laughed with joy, because I *knew* that he would have to have had a similar experience to mine in his journey of self-discovery, because that's just the way life works. But what was his life-altering experience, and just how was it so eerily similar to mine that it made me laugh with joy?

It always tickles me whenever another person's journey takes them to the crossroad of their life and they don't know which path to take to continue on their journey to wholeness and completeness, which Robert Frost epitomized in his poem *The Road Not Taken* that he summed up with poetic genius in the following lines: "Two roads diverged in a wood, and I— /I took the one less travelled by, /And that has made all the difference."

So, which road did truth-seeking young Jordan Peterson take that made all the difference in his life? He tells us in *Rule 8: Tell the Truth—or, at least, don't lie*:

"I had a strange set of experiences a few years before embarking upon my clinical training. I found myself subject to some rather violent compulsions (none acted upon), and developed the conviction, in consequence, that I really knew rather little about who I was and what I was up to. So, I began paying much closer attention to what I was doing—and saying. The experience was disconcerting, to say the least. I soon divided myself into two parts; one that spoke, and one, more detached, that paid attention and judged. ***I soon came to realize that almost everything I said was untrue***. I had motives for saying these things: I wanted to win arguments and gain status and impress people and get what I wanted. I was using language to bend and twist the world into delivering what I thought was necessary. ***But I was a fake.*** Realizing this, I started to practice only saying things that the internal voice would not object to. ***I started to practice telling the truth—or, at least, not lying.*** I soon learned that such a skill came in very handy when I didn't know what to do. What should you do when you don't know what to do? Tell the truth. So, that's what I did my first day at the Douglas Hospital." (*12 Rules for Life: An Antidote to Chaos*, p. 205, bold italics mine).

When I stopped laughing in joyful recognition of Jordan Peterson's dilemma, both his hero and mine, C. G. Jung, came to mind, because he too came to see the dual nature of his own self-consciousness, which he called Personality No. 1, and Personality No. 2, as everyone must see their dual self when their path can take them no further on their destined purpose to wholeness and completeness (David Brooks also came to see his two selves, calling them Adam 1 and Adam 2 in his book *The Road to Character*); and I reflected on the coincidental similarities of our paths.

Carl Jung had to live out his Personality No. 1 in his chosen path of psychiatry to grow in self-consciousness enough to take him to the crossroad of his life (which was in the fortieth year of his life, as he tells us in *The Red Book*), just as Dr. Jordan Peterson had to grow in his own path of psychology (teaching and clinical practice) and I had to grow in my chosen path (contract painting by vocation and writing by avocation), which brought us to the crossroad of our life that would make us ready for the **secret way** as it did our respective hero C. G. Jung; and this brings to mind the spiritual musing that I posted on my blog *Saturday, July 20, 2017* that speaks to the inability of the natural process of individuation to take us all the way to our destined purpose:

An Old Chinese Proverb

There's an old Chinese proverb, which is attributed to the Taoist Master Lao Tzu (author of the *Tao Te Ching*), that goes like this: *"Those who know, do not speak; those who speak, do not know."* Tao means the *way*, and the *way* is what C. G. Jung called the **secret way** in his commentary to Richard Wilhelm's translation of the ancient Taoist text *The Secret of the Golden Flower*, and reflecting upon this proverb, which took me years to resolve, one can see that Lao Tzu was referring to a secret knowledge of the Tao, or *way*.

Given this, this proverb can be broken down into the less enigmatic saying: those who know the *way* do not speak about the *way*, and those who do not know the *way* speak about it as if they know the *way*. Still, the unyielding mystery of this saying is the *way;* and this is the subject of today's spiritual musing…

Ideas for my spiritual musings can come to me from anywhere, and today's idea came from something that I read in my weekend paper, *Saturday, July 15, 2017 Toronto Star* Book Section, in James Grainger's review of Fiona Barton's new novel, *The Child*.

The first paragraph arrested my attention, and one sentence kept buzzing around in my head and would not go away; and this morning I felt compelled to abandon to my creative unconscious and explore this thought in a spiritual musing. I will quote the paragraph and highlight the sentence:

"In a culture where peace, political stability and relative prosperity have been the norm for over 50 years, the aspiring suspense or horror author may well ask: what is there left for readers to fear? **Not only are people living longer, healthier lives, they've stopped believing in an all-seeing God who punishes their transgressions.** The resounding answer, if the bestseller lists (and the plot lines of binge-worthy TV series) are anything to go by, is the fear of losing a loved one, especially a child."

This is where we are today, then; locked into an existential matrix where human life is characterized by the mortal limits of our biology and not by an expansive spiritual paradigm that includes the concept of an immortal soul that animates our body and continues to exist after our body has expired, as ancient wisdom teachings would have us believe, like the *Tao Te Ching* for example. It's no wonder then that the fear of death has such power over us!

It was because of this fear that I was called to write *Death, the Final Frontier,* which was immediately followed by my twin soul book *The Merciful Law of Divine Synchronicity,* to relieve the insufferable pressure upon social consciousness exerted by the existential dread of our mortality; but—*and this is the but that gave me the impetus to take the challenge of today's spiritual musing*—it has become painfully clear to me now that **society does not really want to know if there is more to life than our five senses (it does and it doesn't), because the answer is much more frightening than the fear of death itself,** as difficult as this may be to believe, an observation that has been confirmed many times talking with people.

Happily, there is much more to life than what we experience with our five senses, which the more intuitive among us can discern, as Psychologist Dr. Teresa DeCicco points to in her timely book *Living Beyond the Five Senses: The Emergence of a Spiritual Being* (which, as coincidence would have it, was the inspiring factor that called me to write *Death, the Final Frontier*), and the creative imperative of today's spiritual musing beckons me to spell out why man fears to expand the parameters of our existential paradigm of personal meaning that society, for whatever ungodly reason, cannot seem to transcend.

It happened innocently enough, as these kind of insights usually do. I was having a chat with my retired neighbor who was out walking his little Jack Russel and saw me reading on my front deck and stopped by to say hello, and he was telling me about his wife's early retirement and all the time she would have on her hands, and by happy coincidence I had just read a review in *The Walrus* magazine of a book called *The Power of Meaning: Crafting a Life that Matters*, by Emily Esfahani Smith, and I tore the page out of the magazine for his wife to look into, if she so wished; but, as irony would have it, my neighbor with his feisty little terrier and forlorn look in his eyes, revealed (whether it was a defensive response to the book I suggested his wife look into, or from a feeling of unfulfillment that he hoped would be satisfied by the good life that he and his second wife were embarking upon in her early retirement, I don't know) that he didn't think there was an answer to life's big question.

"This is all we got," he said, reigning tight his aggressive little terrier.

"Not so!" I reacted, with the instincts of a mongoose. "There is an answer, Lenny. I know there is, because I found it. But no one wants to know what it is, because with the answer comes the responsibility of living it; and that scares the shit out of people—"

I startled myself with my instinctive response, and Lenny was taken aback also; but this has happened to me many times before, as though I have an instinctive need to react to the pernicious shadow of the soul-crushing spirit of man's nothingness, which was best expressed by Macbeth's much-too famous, albeit exquisitely lugubrious soliloquy—

Tomorrow, and tomorrow, and tomorrow,
Creeps in this petty pace from day to day
To the last syllable of recorded time,
And all our yesterdays have lighted fools
The way to dusty death. Out, out, brief candle!
Life's but a walking shadow, a poor player
That struts and frets his hour upon the stage
And then is heard no more: it is a tale
Told by an idiot, full of sound and fury,
Signifying nothing.

But if Shakespeare, whose worldview the eminent literary scholar professor Harold Bloom called "a breathtaking kind of nihilism more uncanny than anything that Nietzsche apprehended," could not expand the existential paradigm of life beyond the values "that we create or imbue events, people, things with," then what hope was there for the rest of us to see the light at the end of the tunnel? It's no wonder that people are crushed by the weight of existential dread. But I could never imagine Sisyphus happy, as the iconic philosopher of the absurd Albert Camus did, because there *is* meaning and purpose to our existence.

That's the irony. But when one finds the *way,* one refuses to speak about it. For two reasons: 1, for fear of scaring people with the responsibility that goes with living the *way*; and 2, out of the knowledge that one will find the *way* eventually when life has made them ready, because that's just the way life works.

That's what Lao Tzu meant by his cryptic saying, and why I said to my friendly neighbor with his feisty little terrier that people don't want to know the answer to life's big question, because the responsibility of living the *way* would be too great to bear until life has made them ready to live the *way*.

I could have told him that one would find the answer eventually, but I didn't want to introduce the concept of reincarnation which would only have opened up a whole new conversation and scared him further; and yet, the mystic poet Rumi, who knew the *way* as intimately as Lao Tzu, shouted with clarion certainty: *"Tell it unveiled, the naked truth! The declaration's better than the secret."* Which put me in a tricky situation with my friendly neighbor, because I didn't know whether to speak or keep silent.

But Lenny plucked up his courage, as his feisty littler terrier circled around his legs anxious to walk some more, and asked me the dreaded question: "What's the answer?"

"Consciousness," I instinctively responded, like a deadly cobra. "The purpose of life is to grow in the consciousness of what we are, and what we are is more than our mortal body; but to grow in the consciousness of our essential nature asks much more than we're willing to pay. That's the premise of my book *The Pearl of Great Price* that was inspired by one of Christ's most cryptic parables. But we're getting into some very deep waters here, Lenny. Let me just assure you that there is an answer to life's big question, and one day, believe it or not, it will all make sense to you."

Again, he looked at me quizzically. "Well, I can't see it."

"Few people can. But it's there, I assure you," I responded.

"Would you stake your life on it?" he said, with a sly little grin.

"I already have. That's the price one has to pay to find it," I replied, and broke into an ironic chuckle that puzzled my neighbor even further as he held tight the leash to his little terrier.

In his book *In Search of the Miraculous,* Ouspensky quotes Gurdjieff, whose teaching I had taken up when I dropped out of university: **"To speak the truth is the most difficult thing in the world; and one must study a great deal and for a long time in order to be able to speak the truth. The wish alone is not enough. To speak the truth, one must know what the truth is and what a lie is, and first of all in oneself. And this nobody wants to know."**

There I was then, several years of living Gurdjieff's teaching with a commitment that I could hardly bear when I came to a crossroad in my life and could go no further until I found a way that would take me to wholeness and completeness—but I had no idea whatsoever what way to go, because when I dropped out of university I banked my whole life on Gurdjieff's teaching. But I hit a brick wall with his teaching, and I came to a stop so disconcerting that it shook me to the core of my being. *Where do I go? What do I do?*

The sad truth is that I did not even know that Gurdjieff's teaching could take me no further; and that's when my oracle, the inner guiding principle of my life, intervened with the shocking question that burned a hole through the wall of my impervious vanity for me to pass through and continue on my destined journey to wholeness and completeness.

I was sitting in my bedroom one evening, so forlorn and dejected that I had to put on Beethoven's Ode to Joy (his Ninth Symphony) to pick up my spirits, and (I can't be sure, but in my mind, I seem to think it happened just as Beethoven's Ode to Joy exploded in that bombastic crescendo that always, always brings me to tears of joy), I heard a voice in my mind ask me the question, **"Why do you lie?"**

Startled into awareness, I just stared, bewildered and dumfounded. I heard the voice as distinctly as someone sitting beside me, but it was in my own mind. It was a male voice, and I waited for it to say something more; but nothing more came, and I was beside myself.

One Rule to Live By

"What, me lie? How could I lie? I'm a truth seeker. I gave up everything to become a truth seeker; what do you mean, why do you lie?" I argued with myself, startled.

But I could not persuade myself, and that disembodied question burned into my soul and changed my life forever, because I now had a mental censor that kept me so honest that it changed every aspect of my behavior, no less than fledgling clinical psychologist Jordan Peterson's shocking realization that his life was a lie also, despite his belief in himself *(neither him nor I would ever have imagined we were so inauthentic);* and not until one comes face to face with the false self of their own ego/shadow personality will they find the way to their true self, for only in the transformation of one's false nature will one satisfy the longing in their soul for wholeness and completeness, which professor Jordan Peterson points to with the imperative of his *12 Rules for Life: An Antidote to Chaos* that I hope to bring to happy resolution in *One Rule to Live By: Be Good...*

19. All Paths Lead to the Sacred Self

"There is nothing but the self and God."

THE KEYS OF JESHUA
—*Glenda Green*

After I finished writing the previous chapter, "The Crossroad of Jordan Peterson's Life," I sat on my front deck and read the rest of *12 Rules for Life: An Antidote to Chaos* (I've been reading it slowly to savor the unique flavor of JBP's individuation process), and I could not believe how he brought his book to closure with the simple question in the Coda that he added at the end of his book to sum up where his call to be a hierophant for today's crazy world had taken him—right to the sacred sanctums of his inner self, exactly where Carl Jung's journey had taken him and mine took me.

"What will you write with your pen of light?" Peterson asks the reader, bringing climactic closure to the hierophantic message of his *12 Rules for Life: An Antidote to Chaos*; but, as ironic as this question was for me, I cannot answer it until I bring *One Rule to Live By: Be Good* to resolution; which, or course, will be entirely up to my muse.

My muse is my oracle, my inner guiding light, and I have learned to trust my oracle implicitly; this was my inspiration for the creative experiment that Jung called "active imagination" that I put to practice in my series of dialogues with St. Padre Pio who speaks for my oracle (my latest volume is *A Sign of Things to Come*), the same technique that Jordan Peterson used when he wrote with his Pen of Light. As he tells us in the Coda, this Pen of Light was "LED-equipped and beamed light out its tip, so that writing in the dark was made easier."

This novelty pen was a gift from his friend in California; and, being highly imaginative, he saw the symbolic implications of this special pen. "Since I had been given, of all things, a Pen of Light, which could write Illuminated Words in the darkness, I wanted to do the best thing I could do with it. So, I asked the appropriate question," Peterson said, and almost immediately his oracle answered his question: ***"Write down the words you want inscribed on your soul."*** And then he asked a series of thoughtful questions, and his oracle spoke again, using his special Pen of Light as his medium to bring his hierophantic message to resolution.

This was his way of engaging his transcendent function; a form of automatic writing, but not quite the same. It was something like what Neale Donald Walsh did when he wrote his *Conversations with God* books, letting go and letting God, as it were; but all it is really is a way of engaging one's creative unconscious, just another form of "active imagination."

I write all of my spiritual musings with my own Pen of Light—be it whatever pen I am using to jot down my ideas for spiritual musings, which I then complete on my word processor (I used to write my books in longhand, but I could never go back there again). I get an idea out of the blue, and then I engage my creative unconscious to work it out with me.

Sometimes it takes a lot of thought to work it out, and sometimes it just flows out of me with little or no rewriting, like my poem *What the Hell Is Going on Out There?* and the following spiritual musing that illustrates why one is called to the destined purpose of their inner journey, just as professor Peterson was called to be a hierophant for today's crazy world when he spoke truth to power in his courageous defence of free speech:

The Outer and Inner Journey

Talking with our new friend Sharon on our front deck the other evening as we sipped on a glass of wine, which she had brought over for dinner, she revealed that none of her friends had any inclination about her inner journey that she had been on for many years, and I replied: "That doesn't surprise me. Most people are caught up in their outer journey. But in time, they too will be called to their inner journey," and I made reference to our new neighbors who had just built their retirement home down the street and who had just left on a trip to the East Coast in their motor home because they were caught up in the outer journey of their life (they plan to travel in their motor home across Canada and the States for the next ten years, wintering in Florida with the occasional cruise vacation), and that's the subject of today's spiritual musing…

    Sharon cried when she read my twin soul book *Death, the Final Frontier,* because it confirmed her inner journey and satisfied her need to know why she was, and she read my twin soul book *The Merciful Law of Divine Synchronicity* and was brought to tears again, and I had to ask her why she cried.
    "Because I know why I am now," she said, a simple realization that took me most of my life to arrive at and many years to conceptualize in my writing, and all because I was called to the inner journey much earlier than most people (I was in high school when I was called), and I fulfilled my life's purpose; but what do I mean by the outer and inner journey?
    I don't know what relevance this may have just yet *(this is how my oracle works),* but yesterday I was nudged to watch Laurens van der Post's online documentary on C.G. Jung's life (I've read his book *Jung and the Story of Our Time* several times), and I was brought to tears at Jung's commitment to his inner journey, bringing to the world a new pathway that helps make sense of our purpose in life, a psychology of individuation that facilitates the natural process of man becoming what he is meant to be, and I also watched a YouTube video on the literary scholar professor Harold Bloom and was brought to tears again, but these were tears of sadness and not joy because professor Bloom's outer journey of teaching literature at Yale University for fifty-some years and writing more than forty books of literary criticism had not brought his inner journey to resolution as Jung's journey had brought him, and now I understand why my oracle brought these two remarkable men to my attention for today's

spiritual musing—*because they represent the two extremes of man's outer and inner journey.*

Three days before he died in the 86th year of his life, Carl Jung had a dream which confirmed that he had achieved "wholeness and singleness of self," but in the 87th year of his life professor Bloom was still wandering in the labyrinthine world of literature (epitomized by Shakespeare's world which Bloom described as "a breathtaking kind of nihilism more uncanny than anything Nietzsche apprehended"), because he was unable to come to a resolution for the purpose of his being; that's why he brought me to tears of sadness and not joy, and why I was so happy for our friend Sharon who cried with joy when my twin soul books brought some measure of resolution to her inner journey that she began thirty-six years ago with Jane Roberts book *Seth Speaks* (which I read 45 years ago; I have a sales receipt in the copy of my purchase at the Thunder Bay Bookshop, dated *Oct. 10, 1974*), which is why Sharon wrote in her Amazon review of my twin soul books, *"I can now see the sky through the trees and will go on."* I couldn't have asked for a better review.

I've quoted the following prescient words many times in my writing, but I can't help but quote them again because they speak to man's outer and inner journey: *"As each plant grows from a seed and becomes in the end an oak tree, so man must become what he is meant to be. He ought to get there, but most get stuck,"* said Carl Jung in an interview; but one may well ask, what is man meant to be?

"Why am I here?" Sharon asked, thus initiating her inner journey; and she read book after book after book hoping to find an answer to the question that everyone will ask one day when their outer journey can no longer satisfy the inherent longing in their soul to be what they are meant to be. *"Man must complete what Nature cannot finish,"* said the ancient alchemists, keepers of the sacred knowledge of the **secret way**; but why cannot the natural process of evolution satisfy soul's longing to be what we are meant to be?

Actually, it can satisfy our soul's longing to be what we are meant to be; but this is a mystery for another musing, which I happily bought to resolution in *Death, the Final Frontier* with my closing chapter "The Winning Run" that brought Sharon to tears, but only when man realizes that his outer journey cannot satisfy the longing in his soul for wholeness and completeness and is called to their inner journey.

"He's about five or ten years away from being called to his inner journey; unless, of course, he has a life-changing experience that precipitates the process," I said to Sharon, as we sipped on another glass of wine and talked about the inner and outer journey; I was making reference to our dog-walking neighbor whose wife had just taken an early retirement so they could enjoy the rest of their life together doing what they had dreamt and planned on doing when they were both retired.

"How do you know," Sharon asked, her eyes alight with curiosity.

"I saw it in his eyes," I replied, with an ironic smile. "One day, a few years from now, after they've had their surfeit of travel and the good life, he'll catch himself, perhaps in the middle of a barbecue, watching TV, or just talking with his wife over breakfast, and he'll stare into space with a blank look on his face and ask himself, *'Is this all there is to life?'* That's the call, Sharon; and as faint as it may be, it will be his call to the destined purpose of his inner journey…"

It takes a long time for life to make one ready for their inner journey to wholeness and completeness *(many lifetimes, in fact)*, and when one is ready they are called by life to a path that will help them resolve the paradoxical nature of their outer and inner self; this is why professor Jordan Peterson, who was stuck in academia, was called by life to speak truth to power, so he could continue on his inner journey by bringing his message of purpose and meaning through personal responsibility to a world that has lost its way. The world *beckoned,* and Jordan Peterson was *called.*

Why else would he have such a massive following, with millions of people viewing his online lectures and an exponentially expanding number of people tuning in to his podcasts and thousands, mostly young men, attending his international book tour talks? *A phenomenon, indeed!*

Why? Because as Jung said, like the acorn seed that must become an oak tree, so too are we born to become what we are meant to be; but most get stuck, and professor Jordan B. Peterson was called by life to help get the world unstuck. That's why 12 *Rules for Life: An Antidote to Chaos* has become a phenomenal bestseller, because by practicing these 12 rules for life one can get unstuck and continue on their destined journey to wholeness and completeness...

20. The Dilemma of Evolution

After I finished reading *12 Rules for Life: An Antidote to Chaos*, I was strongly nudged by my inner guiding principle to re-read Jess Stearn's book *The Search for a Soul: Taylor Caldwell's Psychic Lives*, which I finished reading in one day on my shaded front deck, getting much more out of it this time than I did the first time I read it more than thirty years ago.

It was a warm spring day in Georgian Bay, and I enjoyed reading on my front deck, but I had no idea why I was so strongly nudged to read Jess Stearn's book again until it dawned on me that my oracle wanted to enhance the paradigm of karma and reincarnation that *One Rule to Live By: Be Good* prepared one for, because all paths in life lead to this perspective, however many lifetimes it takes; and Jordan Peterson's *12 Rules for Life*, whose moral imperative was to help one resolve the paradoxical nature of their inner and outer self, can only make one ready for the **secret way** that will lead them to wholeness and completeness, because *12 Rules for Life: An Antidote to Chaos* can only take one so far on their destined journey through life, and no further.

This is the dilemma of evolution and the irony of Jordan Peterson's message. For all of his brilliance, passion, and good faith the good professor cannot provide a way to negotiate the rest of the way to wholeness and completeness *(I suspect he knows this intuitively, because there is only self-initiation into the mysteries of life)*, and after I read Stearn's book on Taylor Caldwell's past lives, I was called to re-read his book *Intimates Through Time: Edgar Cayce's Mysteries of Reincarnation*; and when I finished reading this book, I immediately began re-reading *Edgar Cayce's Story of Karma*, by his son Hugh Lynn Cayce, to remind myself of the bigger picture of why we are the way we are and why we do what we do, so I could expand the moral imperative of Peterson's message.

I had to read *12 Rules for Life* again to consolidate my impressions and make sure I had the facts right for this story, but every time I tried to get into it I was called away by Stearn's books, and only after I finished reading them did I see what my oracle was trying to tell me—that no matter how hard we try, we cannot deny the imperative of our inner nature to align ourselves with our destined purpose, which is to be true to who we are, just as I explored in my spiritual musing that was inspired by a movie that Penny and I saw last summer called *The Intern*, starring Anne Hathaway and Robert De Niro, and which I posted on my Spiritual Musings blog *August 28, 2017:*

Being the Tao

The idea for today's spiritual musing presupposes so much that I don't know if I can do it justice; but I have to try, or why else would I have been called by my muse to write it?

Upon reflection, I can see now how the idea came about; but it wasn't until I heard Jules (Anne Hathaway) say to her new intern Ben (Robert De Niro) in Nancy Meyers movie *The Intern,* **"How is it that you always manage to say the right thing, do the right thing, and be the right thing?"** that the words "BEING THE TAO" popped into my mind like a canon shot, because I had intuitively discerned that Jules Ostin's intern Ben Whittaker was *in* the Tao; and that's the subject of today's spiritual musing...

In the ancient Chinese teaching, Tao means the *way*, and the teaching of Taoism is all about living the *way;* but here's where we run into a problem because, as I wrote in my spiritual musing "An Old Chinese Proverb," defining the *way* of Tao is next to impossible to do. But because I *know* what the *way* of Tao is, I have to try; and I *know* what the *way* of Tao is because I was initiated into the sacred mystery of the *way* while on my own sacred journey to wholeness and completeness. This is why I said that this idea of BEING THE TAO presupposes so much that I may not be able to do it justice.

However, it behooves me to offer my personal definition of the *way,* which has been drawn from my own life of living the *way* consciously from the moment I awakened to the *way*: **the *way* is the redemptive wisdom of the teleological imperative of life**; and living one's life with purpose and meaning, regardless what path one is on, is living the imperative of the *way,* which initiates one into the sacred mystery of one's true self and the Tao. **In short, the *way* is the self-reconciling factor of life.**

But why did the phrase BEING THE TAO pop into my mind and not BEING IN THE TAO, which would seem to make more sense? This, I believe, is the central mystery of the *way* that I've been called upon to explore in today's spiritual musing—to draw the distinction between the two.

I've learned to have implicit trust in my muse (my creative unconscious), so I *know* that I've been called upon to elucidate the difference between BEING THE TAO and BEING IN THE TAO; and this difference speaks to the journey and the destination, because to *be* the Tao one must *become* the Tao, and that's what living the *way* is all about.

For clarity's sake, I'm going to simply refer to the Tao as the *way*, because my sidebar Merriam Webster dictionary defines way as: *a thoroughfare for travel or transportation from place to place; the course traveled from one place to another: route; a course (a series of actions or sequences of events leading in a direction or toward an objective)*, which implies that the *way* is a process that leads to a destination; but what destination does the *way* lead to?

That's the sacred mystery of the *way*, because the *way* leads to itself; that's why my muse popped the words BEING THE TAO into my mind instead of BEING IN THE TAO, because Jules Ostin's new intern Ben Whittaker *was* his own Tao, or *way*. And I knew this instinctively, because I too had become my own *way* in my self-initiation into the sacred mystery of the *way*; and being his own *way*, Ben Whittaker was BEING THE TAO.

This sounds like esoteric gobbledygook, but all it means is that seventy-year old intern Ben Whittaker was his own man; that's why his young boss Jules Ostin, founding owner of the hugely successful e-commerce business called "About the Fit," called him "cool." Ben Whittaker played the game of life, but he played the game by his own rules; that's what made him cool.

In my spiritual musing "The Essence of Cool," I quote David Brooks (columnist for the *New York Times* and author of *The Road to Character*): *"The cool person is stoical, emotionally controlled, never eager or needy, but instead mysterious, detached and self-possessed. The cool person is gracefully competent at something but doesn't need the world's applause to know his worth. That's because the cool person has found his or her own unique and authentic way of living with nonchalant intensity."*

That was Ben Whittaker to a tee, a self-possessed septuagenarian widower with a moral center; well-seasoned, balanced, and sensitive enough to care about people who come into his life. *"The cool person,"* said David Brooks, *"is guided by his or her own autonomous values, often on the outskirts of society,"* which was what fascinated me about the easy-going Ben Whittaker in Nancy Meyers deceptively simple, feel-good comedy *The Intern*.

The morning after Penny and I watched *The Intern*, I went online to read the reviews; and it didn't surprise me that every review missed the core message of the feel-good comedy which Ben Whittaker personified with easy-going aplomb, the message being the edifying principles of Tai Chi which are founded upon Taoism, the *way* to wholeness and completeness; that's what led me to see Nancy Meyers, the writer-director of *The Intern*, as the female Woody Allen of movie-making sans Woody Allen's moral vacuity, which was why Nancy Meyers had *The Intern* open with a scene of Ben Whittaker doing Tai Chi exercises in a park with a group of seniors, and why she brought *The Intern* to symbolic closure with another scene of Ben Whittaker doing his Tai Chi exercises in the park again, but this time with his young boss Jules Ostin joining him, thus implying that she was embracing the edifying philosophy of *Taoism* to help center herself in the *Tao* like her cool septuagenarian intern Ben Whittaker.

The premise of today's spiritual musing rests upon my perception that the seventy-year-old widower intern personified the principles of Tai Chi, and my feeling is that the script writer/director

Nancy Meyers succeeded brilliantly; otherwise my creative unconscious would not have picked up on it and inspired me with the words BEING THE TAO when Jules, albeit inebriated, said to her intern Ben: **"How is it that you always manage to say the right thing, do the right thing, and be the right thing?"** Which is nothing more, or less, than BEING THE TAO; which, in effect, simply means being one's own *way*.

And this is precisely how I saw professor Peterson's book *12 Rules for Life: An Antidote to Chaos*, as a Tai Chi exercise of the mind that helps one center oneself in the Tao, a way to consolidate the energies of one's life into a personal path, a guiding principle of 12 transformative rules that will give direction and purpose to one's life and help fill the hole in one's soul that religion, science, and politics have pathetically failed to do in today's crazy world of nihilism and confusion; but why the strong nudge to re-read some of my Edgar Cayce literature?

Was this where my oracle wanted *One Rule to Live By: Be Good* to go, to the frontiers of cognitive thought and into the deeper mysteries of soul's divine purpose in life, a subject that not even the Intellectual Dark Web would dare explore for fear of derision and ridicule?

The IDW has yet to resolve the issue of God, let alone the equally troublesome question of the self—epiphenomenon of the brain or not; but where else can one go to satisfy the longing in their soul for wholeness and completeness when they have reached the limits of cognitive reason?

Just listen to professor Peterson's lectures and interviews and watch his inquiring mind desperately trying to break through his wall of unknowing, a deeply nuanced thinker who takes his thoughts as far as his probing mind can possibly take them, frantically working his hands and fingers to assist his thinking like a metaphysical truth digger. It almost pains me watching him think.

One Rule to Live By

This is the irony of *12 Rules for Life: An Antidote to Chaos*; it brings one to the farthest reaches of existential thought, but no further. The rest of the way to one's true self has to be negotiated individually; not with cognitive thinking, but with personal commitment to a way of life that opens the door to the **secret way,** just as the practice of Tai Chi opened the door to the *way* for Ben Whittaker in Nancy Meyer's movie *The Intern*. And this is why I was called to write *One Rule to Live By: Be Good*, because when all is said and done, this is the only rule that one needs to complete the rest of the journey to wholeness and completeness...

21. Expanding the Existential Paradigm

When I first read Jess Stearn's book *The Search for a Soul: Taylor Caldwell's Psychic Lives,* the remarkable story of the historical novelist's past lives that she was regressed to under hypnosis, I knew that one day I would have my own past-life regressions, which I did when Penny and I moved to Georgian Bay fifteen years ago, and I got the answers that I was looking for to my haunting questions: why I was born into my family, why I had a sexual attraction for older women, and why I felt an inexplicable familiarity with the **secret way** in Gurdjieff's teaching which serendipity introduced me to in my second year of philosophy studies at university; and as I "worked" on myself with Gurdjieff's teaching, I reconnected with the **secret way** that I had lived in several of my past lifetimes, the first time as a student of Pythagoras, and the second time as a mendicant Sufi in ancient Persia, and I finally managed to satisfy the longing in my soul for wholeness and completeness in my current lifetime that the natural way of evolution through karma and reincarnation cannot realize.

This is why my oracle wanted me to re-read my Edgar Cayce literature, because no one—*and I mean no one!*—can satisfy the longing in their soul for wholeness and completeness until they expand the existential paradigm of their life and embrace *(and if not embrace, at least entertain)* the idea of a way out of the existential dilemma of the human condition which keeps soul trapped in the endless cycle of karma and reincarnation; this is why I'm so moved by professor Peterson's commitment to share his message with the world, because his *12 Rules for Life: An Antidote to Chaos* will consolidate one's energies and make one ready for the final stage of soul's evolution through life, which I intimated in a spiritual musing that I was called to write last summer:

One Rule to Live By

The Circumference of Our Life

It was something that I read two or three weeks ago, which I haven't been able to trace yet, but I think it was a Sufi saying that was quoted by a new poet that I was researching online, and it went something like this: *to walk the path one must first realize that one's own life is the path.* But wherever I came upon this saying (for the life of me, I cannot trace its source), it set free the idea for today's spiritual musing.

As I wrote in my spiritual musing "The Outer and Inner Journey," when one is ready for the inner journey, they will be called by *the omniscient guiding principle of life* to look for the path to their true self. This is the mystery that has taken my whole life to resolve, a resolution which came to me only after I had journeyed through the world of many teachings, all of which served their purpose of bringing me closer to my own path; and that's the irony of the **secret way of life**.

The **secret way of life** is what Jesus called the *way*. The *way* is life itself (which is why Jesus had so many metaphorical expressions for the *way*), and a path is an individualized expression of the *way* of life, like the teachings of Jesus, Buddha, Lao Tzu, Rumi, John Doe or Mary Jane; this is why the Sufis say that there are as many paths to God as there are souls. But this is all very abstruse and difficult to understand, and it behooves me to explain the logic of the *way*. But how?

Once again then, into the breach…

"Where are you?" Penny Lynn asked me this morning, noticing my far-away look as I paused to talk with her when she put her book down for our usual morning chat.

"Somewhere between here and there," I replied.

"Where's that?" she asked.

"Somewhere between the resolve and unresolved. I'm working on a new spiritual musing, but I don't have a point of entry. I've got the inspiration, but I haven't quite apprehended it yet. That's what John Keats meant when he wrote in his essay 'A Defense of

Poetry' that 'poets are the hierophants of an unapprehended inspiration.' I can see the idea of my spiritual musing, but until I apprehend it it's not mine."

For reasons which I can never fathom but which I know are choreographed by *the omniscient guiding principle of life*, in our little chat about this and that Penny responded with a *non sequitur* to something our friend Sharon had said to her friend Jennifer the other night when they were talking on the phone; Sharron said she didn't have anything more to talk about and bid her friend goodnight, and knowing what I knew about Sharon, who has been living the inner journey for the past thirty-six years, and her friend Jennifer who is stuck in the outer journey of her life and has little to no awareness of the inner journey (or doesn't want to know for fear of the commitment to the moral imperative of the inner journey), I replied to Penny's *non sequitur*: "That doesn't surprise me. What do they have to talk about when Jennifer's world is so small? The circumference of Jennifer's life is limited to the material world, Sharon has expanded her horizons beyond the material world; so it doesn't surprise me that Jennifer would exhausts Sharon's interest. It's all about expanding the circumference of our life, sweetheart; that's what makes life interesting—"

And the moment I said this, I *apprehended* my inspiration and thanked Penny for her *non sequitur,* which I knew was inspired by *the omniscient guiding principle of life* to give me the entry point that I needed for today's spiritual musing...

I could look it up in half a dozen books in my expansive library and find references from renowned spiritual teachers, poets and mystics to confirm my own realization that life is the *way*, but that would only clutter today's spiritual musing with pedantic references; but I can't help myself, I have to quote at least one remarkable person whose resolute commitment to the *way* brought me to tears.

"But one thing you must know: the one thing I have learned is that one must live this life. This life is the way, the long sought-after way to the unfathomable, which we call divine. There is no other way, all other ways are false paths," said Carl Jung in *The Red Book,* the

chronical of his self-initiation into the sacred mysteries of the *way*; and he spent the rest of his long and productive life working the sacred mysteries of the *way* into his psychology of individuation to help man realize his true self. But Carl Jung was called to the *way* because his outer life could take him no further on his journey to wholeness and completeness.

"*At this time, in the fortieth year of my life, I had achieved everything that I had wished for myself. I had achieved honor, power, wealth, knowledge, and every human happiness. Then my desire for the increase of these trappings ceased, the desire ebbed from me and horror came over me...My soul, where are you? Do you hear me? I speak, I call you—are you there? I have returned, I am here again. I have shaken the dust of all the lands from my feet, and I have come to you, I am with you. After years of long wandering, I have come to you again...*" confessed Jung in *The Red Book*, thus beginning his quest for his lost soul which he had forfeited to the material world to satisfy the dreams and aspirations of his outer life—as does everyone, for such is the natural process of evolution; and this is the mystery of the *way* that calls for elucidation.

How I came upon the sacred knowledge of the *way* doesn't really matter for today's spiritual musing; I've written about this in *The Summoning of Noman*, *The Pearl of Great Price* and my book of poetry, *Not My Circus, Not My Monkeys*, so I *know* that the life one lives, whether it be a life of art, music, literature, politics, religion, science, prostitution, carpentry, academics, or whatever, is the *way* of life, albeit the *way* of life lived unconscious of the imperative of the *way*. But the unconscious *way* of life can only take one so far in their journey to wholeness and completeness, and then one is called to the inner journey and one must live their path consciously, which will initiate one deeper into the sacred mysteries of the *way* to help them complete what Nature cannot finish and realize wholeness and completeness.

This is the core mystery of the *way*, then: through natural evolution we evolve unconsciously to our true self, and when natural evolution has made us ready to live the *way* consciously, we are called by life to find our own path and awaken to the *way*; so, the life we choose to live determines the circumference of our life, the parameters of our interests, passions, and dreams. But regardless how far we expand the circumference of our life, the natural *way* of life will never be enough to satisfy the longing in our soul for wholeness and completeness, just as Jung came to realize; but then what?

What does one do? Where does one turn? Does one live their life in quiet desperation, as Thoreau suggested about the vast majority of mankind? Or does one take up arms against a sea of troubles and get sucked into the *enantiodromiac* vortex of life's never-ending process of evolution, the tragic conundrum of the natural dynamic of karma and reincarnation? Or does one heed life's sacred call to the *way* and embark upon the inner journey to wholeness and completeness as Jung did, as I did, and every soul that embraces their destiny when life has made them ready? The choice is ours to make, life after life after life...

And this is why I sent professor Peterson copies of *The Lion that Swallowed Hemingway* and *The Pearl of Great Price* to read before he became a public figure. I *heard* him banging on the door to the esoteric third and final stage of evolution, and my heart went out to him; and three years later I sent him *My Writing Life* and *The Merciful Law of Divine Synchronicity*, because his passionate defense of free speech *compelled* me to send him these books for encouragement on his own remarkable Solzhenitsyn-inspired journey through life that unexpectedly catapulted him onto the world stage with his *12 Rules for Life: An Antidote to Chaos* that's taking the world by storm.

And this is why my oracle called me to write *One Rule to Live By: Be Good*, because the imperative of my own individual *way* may just crack open the door to the inner journey of one's life and help them expand the paradigm of their existential life, as Ouspensky's book *In Search of the Miraculous* helped to expand mine; but I do so, of course, with all the presumption of one who has found the *way*, lives the *way*, and makes no apologies for the way...

22. The Hope of Jordan Peterson's Message

After I finished reading *12 Rules for Life: An Antidote to Chaos*, I went on YouTube and watched some new interviews that Jordan Peterson had done while on his international book tour, and I also listened to a few new podcasts on Jordan Peterson and his message, and I was finally beginning to understand why he posed such a perilous threat to both the extreme right and extreme left of the political spectrum; and then I watched the televised Munk Debate on political correctness, and that sealed his hierophantic message to our crazy modern world.

The Munk Debates were established in 2008 as a charitable initiative of the Aurea Foundation co-founders Peter and Melanie Munk. The semi-annual debates take place at the Roy Thompson Hall in Toronto; and on *Friday, May 18, 2018* the motion of the debate was on political correctness: *"Be it resolved, what you call political correctness, I call progress."*

Arguing for political correctness: Georgetown University professor of sociology Michael Eric Dyson. Dyson has written more than a dozen books on race, culture and politics in the United States; and he was joined by Michelle Goldberg, a journalist, *New York Times* columnist, and bestselling author who writes about identity, culture and politics. And speaking against political correctness: English actor, author, comedian and film director Stephen Fry (who with wit and charm argued well but who still annoyed me), and Jordan B. Peterson, professor of psychology at the University of Toronto, practicing clinical psychologist of twenty years, and bestselling author whom *The Spectator* called "one of the most important thinkers to emerge on the world stage in many years."

I listened to the debate with rapt attention, and the following day I went online to get the reaction to the debate; and it was the consensus that Peterson and Fry had won the debate, which was a forgone conclusion for me because Dyson and Goldberg's case was not only weakly stated, but also argued in odious bad faith because of their blatant prejudice.

But the impression I came away with from the whole un-Socratic argument—Dyson played the race card and called Jordan Peterson an "angry white man," and Goldberg distorted a Peterson interview to deliberately advance her case for political correctness, calling him a misogynist; bad-faith logic if ever I saw it, because I was familiar with the interview that she was referring to and she deliberately mischaracterized Peterson—essentially, but not quite the same reason why I dropped out of university, my growing distrust of the intellect to find a way out of the conundrum of man's existential predicament, which Michelle Goldberg personified with odious bad faith logic.

For a long time, I could not express why I felt compelled to drop out of university, but I trusted my gut feelings, however distressing, and I *had* to leave because philosophy had done all it could for me; and over the years I came to see why the mind can only take one so far on the journey to wholeness and completeness, regardless how brilliant one's logic may be (*Nietzsche can be terrifying, and Sartre and Camus seductively comforting*); because, as John Milton tells us in his epic poem *Paradise Lost*, "The mind is its own place, and in itself can make a Heaven of Hell, a Hell of Heaven," and not until one sees the mind for what it is will one find the *way* to complete the journey to wholeness and completeness. This was the inspiration for my spiritual musing on the three great lies of life that trap one's soul in the shadow worlds of the mind:

The Three Great Lies of Life

It could have been something that I heard on the radio, but more likely it was my chapter "Afterlife Interview with Plato" that I had just started working on for my new novel *Sundays with Sharon* that set free the idea for today's spiritual musing as I drove into Midland to pick up my weekend papers; from the depths of my unconscious, the idea sprouted, "The Three Great Lies of Life," and I had to pull over to jot the idea down in my new leather-bound notebook that was resting on the passenger seat of my car.

I had a faint idea of what the three great lies of life were, but I knew for certain that this was the idea that my muse gave to me in the shocking title of my yet-to-be apprehended spiritual musing, "The Three Great Lies of Life," but by the time I found a safe place to pull over to jot the idea down, which happened to be the entranceway to the Wyevale Fire Hall on County Road 6, the idea opened up and the three great lies of life were revealed to me: 1, Atheism; 2, Christianity; and 3, Buddhism; and along with this unexpected apprehension, I also saw why this idea was set free.

In the afterlife interview with Plato that I had recently seen on YouTube, the exceptionally gifted Australian psychic/medium Alison Allen channeled the spirit of the ancient Greek philosopher Plato, who gave a simple explanation for his strange allegory of the cave that his redoubtable teacher Socrates revealed in Plato's *Republic;* and it was Plato's explanation in his interview with Alison Allen that gestated the idea for my spiritual musing "The Three Great Lies of Life," and so fecundly that it sprouted no less than an hour after I started my chapter "Afterlife Interview with Plato" for my novel *Sundays with Sharon* .

In the now famous allegory of the cave, Socrates describes a group of people who lived chained to the wall of a cave all of their lives, facing a blank wall. These strange prisoners watch shadows projected on the wall from objects passing in front of a fire behind them, and they give names to these shadows. The shadows are the prisoners' reality. Socrates explains how the philosopher is like a prisoner who is freed from the cave and comes to understand that the shadows on the wall are not reality at all, for he can perceive the true form of reality rather than the manufactured reality that is the shadows seen on the wall by the prisoners.

The inmates of this strange place have no desire to leave their prison, for they know no better life; but some prisoners manage to break their bonds one day, and they discover that their reality was not what they thought it was. They discovered the sun, which Plato uses as an analogy for the fire that the prisoners cannot see behind them. Like the fire that cast light on the walls of the cave, the human condition is forever bound to the impressions that are received through the senses. Even if these interpretations are an absurd misrepresentation of reality, we cannot break free from the bonds of our human condition and free ourselves from the phenomenal state just as the prisoners could not free themselves from their chains.

If, however, we were to escape our bondage, we would find a world that we would not understand, because the sun is incomprehensible for someone who has never seen it. In other words, we would encounter another "realm," a place incomprehensible because, theoretically, it is the source of a higher reality than the one we have always known; it is the realm of pure fact, the reality and truth of life sans the shadows and reflections projected on the walls of our mind, a reality that Plato called pure Form; and the explanation he gave in his afterlife interview with Alison Allen, that *his allegory of the cave was an elaborate metaphor for the ego*, was the critical piece of information that I needed to set the idea of my spiritual musing free, because the ego is our personal view of life born of our upbringing, and no two egos are the same.

Each ego has a separate viewpoint on life; and according to the afterlife spirit of Plato, *our ego is our personal cave, the reality that we project upon the walls of our mind.* That's why my unconscious set free the idea of the three great lies of life to explore in a spiritual musing, because in my journey of self-discovery I had unshackled myself from the chains of my own ego and set myself free to see that Atheism, Christianity, and Buddhism were illusory shadows projected upon the walls of the mind.

It would be easy, but ultimately unconvincing, were I to say that my personal view on these three great lies of life was founded upon intuition and/or reason alone, but it's not; my understanding that these three great belief systems are illusory shadows on the walls of the mind was born of my quest for my true self, which I could only have done by unshackling myself from the chains of my own ego; and it was comforting to learn that the way to soul's freedom from its own ego was established long before I was born.

One Rule to Live By

"There is a doctrine uttered in secret that man is a prisoner who has no right to open the door of his prison and run away," said Socrates in Plato's *Phaedo*; and he went on to say, *"this is a great mystery which I do not quite understand."* But being the great ironist that he was, Socrates was much too clever to reveal the **secret way** openly; which is why he wisely couched the secret teaching of spiritual liberation in his edifying philosophy of virtuous living: *For I deem that the true disciple of philosophy is likely to be misunderstood by other men,"* he said in the *Phaedo; "they do not perceive that he is ever pursuing death and dying **(through virtuous living)**; and if this is true, why, having had the desire for death all his life long, should he repine at the arrival of that which he has always been pursuing and desiring?"*

This is why Socrates was not afraid to drink the hemlock that ended his life, a choice he made when he was tried and condemned by the Athenian court for his heretical beliefs that the ruling elite felt corrupted the youth of Athens; but not before revealing the secret of spiritual liberation in the redemptive logic of his teaching, the deceptively simple philosophy that by practicing the noble virtues one would purify their soul of ego's illusions and realize their true and immortal self.

Socrates's philosophy frees the soul from its prison by purifying the false consciousness of ego with the transformative power of virtuous living. *"And what is purification but the separation of the soul from the body, as I was saying before; the habit of the soul gathering and collecting herself into herself, out of all the courses of the body **(through virtuous living)**; the dwelling in her own place alone, as in another life, so also in this, as far as she can; the release of the soul from the chains of the body,"* said Socrates in the *Phaedo*; and a few centuries later, Jesus couched the same teaching of spiritual liberation in his own teaching: **" He that findeth his life shall lose it, and he that loseth his life for my sake shall find it."**

But as I came to see in my own quest for my true self, the secret teaching of spiritual liberation is everywhere to be found, because this teaching *is* life itself; it is the redemptive gnostic wisdom that we realize through personal experience from one lifetime to the next, which eventually awakens soul to the **secret way** that is inherent to all human experience. This is how I came to see through the three great lies of life.

My initiation into the **secret way** began with my past-life regression to the Body of God where all souls come from. I was an atom of God without self-consciousness. I had soul consciousness, but no self-consciousness; and in the same regression, I was sent into the world to evolve through life until I had constellated enough of the "I am" consciousness of the creative force of life (the Logos) to realize my own reflective self, which I did in my first primordial human lifetime as the alpha male of a group of ten or twelve cave-dwelling higher primates . I *actually* experienced the birth of my own "I" in this past-life regression, and from one lifetime to the next I evolved in my reflective self-consciousness until I had grown enough in self-awareness to take evolution into my own hands, which I did in my current lifetime with a teaching that was introduced to the western world by a man called Gurdjieff, a teaching of self-transformation that awakened me to the **secret way** that helped me complete what Nature could not finish, just as Jesus promised in his teaching: ***"Lest ye be born again thou shall not enter the kingdom of heaven."***

This was my experience, and upon the basis of this incredible experience I came to see that Atheism, Christianity, and Buddhism were the three great lies of life, because they all contend a misperception about the immortal "I am" soul of man—Atheism contending that our immortal soul does not exist; Christianity contending that our immortal soul is created at the moment of human conception and only lives one lifetime; and Buddhism contending that we do not even have an autonomous, individual soul.

This is why my creative unconscious sprouted the idea for today's spiritual musing, because I *know* through my own incredible journey of self-individuation *(beginning in the Body of God to the dawning of my reflective self-consciousness and finally to the birth of my immortal spiritual self)* that the belief systems of Atheism, Christianity, and Buddhism are founded upon a misperception of the "I am" soul of man; which is why Socrates had the cheek to say that the unexamined life was not worth living, because not until we see through the illusions of our own ego will we realize our true, eternal self.

One Rule to Live By

And this is the hope of Jordan Peterson's message, because his book *12 Rules for Life: An Antidote to Chaos* is his "unapprehended inspiration" of the salvific *way* of liberation from the prison of ego that keeps soul fettered to the shadow worlds of the mind, an inspiration that the good professor is desperately trying to apprehended with his probing intellect; and although he's as close as anyone can get with his brilliant mind to opening the door to the third and final stage of human evolution, the irony is that this door will never open without the right key to unlock it.

"The mind is the slayer of the real, let the disciple slay the slayer," said Madam Blavatsky in *The Voice of Silence*; but how in the hell does one do that? How can one slay their own mind? And would one even dare suggest this to an academically trained intellectual like professor Dr. Jordan B. Peterson who taught evolutionary psychology for thirty years at Harvard and the U of T and has twenty years of experience treating people in his clinical practice, "one of the most important thinkers to emerge on the world stage in many years"? *What a bloody presumption!*

Or is this just another one of those mystical metaphors for the kind of life that one should live in order to transform the consciousness of their false nature and realize their true self? And if so, isn't this what professor Peterson portends with his *12 Rules for Life: An Antidote to Chaos*?

As sweet as the irony may be, it brings tears to my eyes...

23. The Curse of Our Modern World

"Our birth is but a sleep and a forgetting..."
—*William Wordsworth*

The curse of our modern world is moral relativism, the nihilistic conviction that morality is relative, a "personal value judgement," as postmodernists contend; and it's this pernicious belief that's responsible for what Dr. Victor Frankl (*Man's Search for Meaning*) called the "existential vacuum" that plagues our crazy world. But why, if not for the erosion of our spiritual values?

I have neither the learning nor interest to explore how this came to be (that's what academics like professor Jordan Peterson attempt to do), my concern has always been to find an answer to the haunting question of my life, *who am I?* And having found the answer *(which is the same for everyone, because we are all divine sparks of God),* I can speak with the gnostic certainty of personal experience, and what I experienced flies in the face of postmodern thinking which, try as it may, cannot resolve the paradoxical riddle of man's dual nature; our *essential* and *existential* self, if you will.

It's not enough to simply dismiss the reality of our *essential* nature, because the longing in our soul for wholeness and completeness does not go away by denying the existence of our eternal self, it only makes it worse; because, like the mushrooms that keep forcing their way up through the solid asphalt of our driveway that cause me much consternation every spring, so does our inner self have to force its way up through the fixed attitudes of our mind until it finally breaks through into the light of common day where it can realize its divine nature.

I could quote Wordsworth's *Intimations of Immortality* to offer a poetic perspective on the state of man's existential predicament— "Our birth is but a sleep and a forgetting; /The Soul that rises with us, our life's Star, /Hath had elsewhere its setting, /And cometh from afar; /Not in entire forgetfulness, /And not in utter nakedness, /But trailing clouds of glory do we come /From God, who is our home..."—but what good would that do? Who would care but someone who is so desperate to satisfy the longing in their soul for wholeness and completeness that they will grasp any straw that offers some measure of hope and resolution. But that's what I see today, that's the cry I hear from impassioned seekers like professor Jordan Peterson who's pushing through the mindsets of our postmodern world of nihilism and confusion with the redemptive imperative of his message.

It was a terrible presumption to send him copies of my books that spell out the incredible journey of my own individuation process, and whether he has read them or not does not really matter to me because life is an individual journey of self-discovery *(I have yet to hear from him, nor do I expect to; especially now that he's on his global book tour that keeps expanding);* I felt *compelled* by my own imperative to send them to him, and I did. The law of the *way* obligated me, no less than it obligated him to stand up for free speech and give his message of hope to the world.

And then my oracle *beckoned* me to write One Rule to Live By: Be Good to span what has been called "Lessing's Ditch" (the great divide between the universal ideas of reason and the historical facts of life, which professor Peterson's *12 Rules for Life: An Antidote to Chaos* endeavors but cannot quite do) with the bridge of my own self-realization and the creative wisdom of the Logos that assists me as I write this story; a sacred bridge spanning the oppressive existential vacuum of postmodern nihilism to the undiscovered country of the soul, which I also do with every spiritual musing that I'm called to write, like the following spiritual musing on the bedeviling concept of moral relativism that has retarded soul's journey to wholeness and completeness:

The Stupidity of Moral Relativism

Long before I began writing my spiritual musings, I wanted to write an essay on what I've always felt to be the bad faith of moral relativism; but yesterday afternoon, I don't remember when exactly, I was gripped by the thought of writing a spiritual musing on moral relativism, but instead of focusing on the bad faith I should focus instead on the false premise of moral relativism, because it would be more reflective of the subjective/objective truth of morality that I realized in my own journey of self-discovery.

I say subjective/objective truth, because I had a singularly convincing experience that initiated me into the mystery of our essential nature, and it was because of this subjective experience that I came to realize the objective truth of our moral nature; and this is the premise of today's spiritual musing…

Let me begin by addressing the central issue of moral relativism, the obvious objection that is sure to arise from what I've called the objective truth of our moral nature, which can be expressed in the following question that is at the very heart of the nihilistic philosophy of moral relativism: *how can an objective truth come from a subjective experience?*

A fair question. But one could discuss this issue until the end of time, which is why I dropped out of university in my third year of philosophy studies to find my own way in life, because I saw no end to the dialectical discourse that philosophy gives rise to, and in my quest for an answer to the question that set me on my journey of self-discovery (*who am I?*), I came upon Gurdjieff's teaching of "work on oneself" that initiated me into the mystery of our essential nature that became the objective truth and moral compass of my life; and although I have written about this in *The Summoning of Noman* and *The Pearl of Great Price*, it behooves me to offer a Reader's Digest version of my experience for today's spiritual musing.

One Rule to Live By

The experience that initiated me into the sacred mystery of our essential nature presupposes the principle of reincarnation, about which I have neither the desire nor inclination to prove; because, whether one believes in it or not, reincarnation is central to the objective reality of our essential nature, our immortal soul which returns from lifetime to lifetime for the encoded purpose of realizing its full potential, like an acorn seed becoming an oak tree, and although this may appear to be a circular argument which brings us right back to the subjective uncertainty of moral relativism, the very nature of my singularly convincing experience confirms the objective truth of our moral mature and disclaims the false premise of moral relativism; this is why Gurdjieff said, *"There is only self-initiation into the mysteries of life."*

Which means, quite simply, that although my journey of self-discovery initiated me into the mystery of the objective truth of our moral nature, it is still a personal experience and the reason why I have called it a subjective/objective truth.

Here then is the experience that initiated me into the mystery of our essential nature and the objective truth of morality, an experience that will tax the credulity of most, if not all of my readers...

Following up on my belief in reincarnation, which was outside the inflexible paradigm of my Roman Catholic faith that I was born into and the source of years of personal conflict, I promised myself that one day I would explore my past lives like the historical novelist Taylor Caldwell did in Jess Stearn's book that became the inspiration for my own past-life regressions, *The Search for a Soul: Taylor Caldwell's Psychic Lives*; and my opportunity came when my life partner Penny Lynn and I relocated to Georgian Bay fourteen years ago, when by "chance" I met a woman who did past-life regressions which inspired my novel *Cathedral of My Past Lives* that I'm going to publish when I feel the time is right.

I planned to have ten past-life regressions, but I only had seven because seven regressions gave me more than enough information to answer the questions that haunted me about my current lifetime, questions like, *why did I feel so out of context in my family?*

Why did I have a sexual fascination for older women? What was it about Gurdjieff's teaching that compelled me to live it? And other questions about my life that I suspected were brought about by past-life experiences; and I was right.

I got the answers that I was looking for in my past lives, which cleared up why I felt the way I did growing up; but because I became a seeker at a very early age (in high school, actually; the spark combusting with Somerset Maugham's novel *The Razor's Edge* that I read in grade twelve), I became obsessed with finding an answer to the question *who am I?*

I cannot go into detail here, or anywhere else for that matter, but in the twenty-third year of my life I had a traumatizing sexual experience *(which was impelled by an irresistible sexual impulse of my rakish past-life personality in Paris, France in 17th Century; I was known as "le salaud de Paris," and I had enormous sexual power over women in the aristocratic courts of Paris, a sexual power that corrupted me morally, and every woman that I seduced and wanted to be seduced by me, especially the older, more mature women who challenged me; hence, my erotic fascination for older women)* that brutally shocked my conscience from its primordial slumber and catapulted me into my quest for my true self, because I *knew* that the person who did what he did that night was not the real me; it was me, but not me, and I had to find the real me or die trying. And so committed did I become to finding my true self that I was willing to pay whatever price was asked of me, which I wrote about in my memoir *The Pearl of Great Price*.

To my complete surprise (and my regressionist as well), in my fourth past-life regression I was regressed to the very genesis of my essential nature: I was an atom in the Body of God where all new souls come from, the great Ocean of Love and Mercy, as mystics refer to the ground of all Being. I was an atom of God with consciousness, but no self-consciousness; and in the same regression, I went back to my first primordial human lifetime where I had evolved up the ladder of evolution into a higher primate with group consciousness but no reflective self-consciousness, and then the miracle that solved the mystery of my reflective self-consciousness happened: I was the alpha male of a small group of ten or twelve cave-dwelling higher primates when I experienced the birth of a new "I" of God in the dawning of my reflective self-consciousness. It was a rudimentary, low-resolution sense of self-awareness, but I experienced my own identity for the very first time in my essential existence; and this changed my life forever.

From the moment the new "I" of God was born in me, I had a separate identity from my little group of early hominids and all of life's creatures, and because I now had an individual will, my separate existence initiated a personal karmic destiny that began the individuation process of my newborn self; and from lifetime to lifetime, I evolved in my reflective self-consciousness until my current lifetime when I was ready to end my cycle of karma and reincarnation and realize my divine nature, which I did with the help of Gurdjieff's teaching and the sayings and parables of Jesus that I wrote about in *The Pearl of Great Price*.

And from my regressions to some of my other past lives, I learned how I had brought my karmic self with me from one lifetime to the next, and I came to understand why I was so out of context with my family and why I grew to have an erotic fascination for older women *(my past life personality as "le salaud de Paris" possessed me that godforsaken night with a sexual lust I could not control)*, plus many other things about my life that I would never have understood without my past-life regressions; and as I wrote my novel *Cathedral of My Past Lives*, I connected the dots and realized that we all have a karmic destiny that we create by the choices we make in life, as well as a spiritual destiny that is encoded in the DNA of our essential nature to become spiritually realized souls of God, whole and complete unto ourself.

And I learned something else about our two destinies that solved the mystery of our paradoxical inner and outer nature, something that no one has ever been able to explain clearly: *we can only realize the encoded imperative of our spiritual destiny through the resolution of our personal karmic nature, which we can only do by taking evolution into our own hands to complete what Nature cannot finish by being karmically responsible for the choices we make*; and this was the objective truth that I discovered from the subjective reality of my past life regressions, because it finally dawned on me that the immutable law of corrective measures is an objective principle of life that governs all moral behavior, whether we are conscious of it or not, and this makes moral relativism stupid.

Nietzsche wrote, *"You have your way, I have mine. As for the right way, it does not exist."* But he was categorically wrong. The right way is implicit in all we do, and not until we learn to live our life with karmic responsibility will we be free of the curse of moral neutrality that blinds us to our essential nature; and learning the right way is what human evolution is all about.

Carl Jung was aware of the erosion of our spiritual values with the proliferation of our materialist scientific worldview, which he addressed in *Modern Man in Search of a Soul*:

"I am persuaded that what is today of vital interest in psychology among educated people will tomorrow be shared by everyone. I should like to draw attention to the following facts. During the past thirty years, people from all the civilized countries of the earth have consulted me. I have treated many hundreds of patients, the larger numbers being Protestants, a smaller number Jews, and not more than five or six believing Catholics. Among all my patients in the second half of life—that is to say, over thirty-five—there has not been one whose problem in the last resort was not that of finding a religious outlook on life. It is safe to say that every one of them fell ill because he had lost that which the living religions of every age have given to their followers, and none of them has been really healed who did not regain his religious outlook. This of course has nothing whatever to do with a particular creed or membership of a church" (*Modern Man in Search of a Soul*, C. G. Jung, p. 229).

And this, ironically, is professor Jordan Peterson's massive appeal today, especially to the wayward younger generation that has become uprooted and disconnected from the spiritual values that give life meaning and purpose; his lectures, podcasts, and immensely popular *12 Rules for Life: An Antidote to Chaos* and book tour talks have a way of burrowing through the shadow worlds of the mind and into one's soul, planting auspicious seeds of hope that promise a better future.

Dr. Norman Doidge, who wrote the Forward to his good friend's book, rendered professor Peterson's *12 rules for Life* into one foremost rule that has the power to cast out the wicked spirit of moral relativism that has scourged our modern world with nihilism and confusion and portends the objective truth of my spiritual musing "The Stupidity of Moral Relativism"— **"And the foremost rule is that you must take responsibility for your own life. Period."**

Now, if we only had a new paradigm to live by...

24. If J. Peterson is Dangerous, God Help Us!

I was surprised to see a photo of Jordan Peterson covering three quarters of the front page of the INSIGHT section of the *Toronto Star* (*Saturday, May 26, 2018*) to highlight a piece by Jordan Peterson's former colleague and friend Bernard Schiff (who claims to be responsible for hiring Peterson at the University of Toronto), Jordan Peterson in a three-piece suit in the midst of emphasizing a point with his arms in the air and a terrifying evangelical look on his face that reflected the gravity of his message, and the photo had the arresting headline: "**I was Jordan Peterson's strongest supporter. Now I think he's dangerous.**"

And if that wasn't enough to pull the reader into the article, at the bottom of Peterson's preacher-like image (cleverly chosen by the editor, I'm sure, to emphasize the editorial point of Peterson being evangelical in his message) was written: "**Former U of T colleague examines the bestselling author's increasingly controversial positions and concludes that the teacher has become a preacher—using fear to unleash 'dark desires.'**" *Wow!*

I dove into Schiff's opinion piece and read it through without highlighting anything as I often do when reading about Jordan Peterson (I did that in my second reading), just to see what kind of impression his former colleague and friend would have on me, and I was stunned.

I had to read it again to confirm my first impression, but from everything that I knew about professor Jordan Peterson from all of his lectures that I had seen on YouTube and podcasts and all the articles I read on him and his talks and interviews and his book *12 Rules for Life* that I had just finished closely reading, I could not believe how his former colleague and friend could possibly have drawn the conclusion that he was dangerous. *"If Jordan Peterson is dangerous, God help us!"* I said to myself; but I refused to read the Schiff piece again until I had some distance from it...

I have home delivery for my *Saturday* and *Sunday Toronto Star*, and I drive into Midland to pick up my weekend *Globe & Mail* and *National Post;* but I couldn't stop thinking of Bernard Schiff's article as I drove into Midland later in the day to pick up my papers, and I made some mental notes to check out when I read the article again, one point in particular which got under my skin—Schiff's comment about Pankaj Mishra's review in *The New York Review of Books* of Peterson's book *12 Rules for Life: An Antidote to Chaos* which stunk to high heaven.

Bernard Schiff called Mishra's review "a thoughtful and informed critique of *12 Rules for Life,*" which only confirmed his obvious bias and misperception of Jordan Peterson's message, claiming that Mishra's review was objective and fair; but I had to read Mishra's review again (*"Jordan Peterson and Fascist Mysticism"*), which I did, and it only re-enforced my initial impression that it was a hatchet job on Peterson's book, with a cheap shot on his character thrown in for good measure. But I had to read Schiff's piece once more to confirm my feelings about these disaffected men, one a former colleague and friend and the other a resentful critic with a very big axe to grind.

But when I got home from my morning jaunt into Midland (I often do some grocery shopping when I pick up my papers), instead of diving back into Schiff's article as I had intended, I went straight to Conrad Black's column in the *National Post* first because I can't resist what he has to say, regardless of what he's writing about; that's how much respect I have for his new perspective on life that was born of his *metanoic* change of heart after serving time in a Florida prison for fraud and obstruction of justice *(a humbling experience that transformed him);* and as serendipity would have it, Black's column was on the recent Munk Debate on political correctness.

It was as obvious to Conrad Black as it was to most viewers that Jordan Peterson and Stephen Fry had won the debate in their argument that political correctness has gone too far, and as always with his insightful editorials, Conrad Black left me smiling; a warm feeling of goodness that I always get whenever he calls a spade a spade, especially on indigenous affairs that few journalists, let alone politicians, have the moral courage to speak to. *(Black himself affirmed my observation in his editorial in the National Post, April 6, 2019, "What People are getting wrong about the entire silly SNC-Lavalin affair," when he wrote: "I appear to be among the very few people in this country who has mentioned this aspect of the controversy, which indicates the extreme reluctance of anyone to touch native affairs policy. That is an aversion the political class and the media will have to overcome, as it is a vital and delicate field in desperate need of reform.")* And that's the problem I have with some of professor Peterson's more caustic critics; they exhibit a deplorable lack of character in their own self-deceiving and resentful nature that they are unconsciously and/or consciously blind to.

But to confirm my impression of the biased Peterson critic, I re-read Bernard Schiff's opinion piece again, slowly and carefully and with my blue highlighter, and the thought that came to me with piercing clarity after reading the article for the third time was that professor Jordan Peterson's former colleague and friend wanted to have his cake and eat it too. *It was that simple!*

This is what disturbed Bernard Schiff and other resentful critics about Jordan Peterson's fundamental message that one cannot have their cake and eat it too, because that's a misperception that flies in the face of life and common sense, especially to anyone over forty.

It's a hollow claim for one to believe that they can have their cake and eat it too without the hard work and sacrifice that life demands of us, and for Bernard Schiff to call Jordan Peterson dangerous for spreading the message that you cannot have you're your cake and eat it too without hard work and sacrifice misses the whole point of Peterson's message.

All weekend long I watched videos on professor Peterson and read the latest reviews of his book and opinion pieces, and I could not get over the devastating effect that his message was having as he went from city to city (60 in all now, across North America, Europe and Australia) promoting his shadow-shocking, life-affirming book *12 Rules for Life: An Antidote to Chaos*; and my initial impression was confirmed that today's crazy world desperately needs someone to clear the way of all this soul-crushing nihilism and divisive identity politics and political correctness gone loony to help society transform and transcend itself, which religion, science, and politics have failed to do; and if his former colleague and friend Bernard Schiff tagged professor Peterson with the "messiah virus" and sees him as dangerous, he's only dangerous in the most ironic sense...

Professor Peterson was called to his destined purpose, just as everyone will be called when life has made them ready for their path to wholeness and completeness; like the celebrated American poet Adrianne Rich for example, who inspired the following spiritual musing that addresses the essential message of professor Peterson's *12 Rules for Life: An Antidote to Chaos*:

The Two Hands of Life

"Adventure most unto itself /The Soul condemned to be;
Attended by a Single Hound— /Its own Identity."
—*Emily Dickinson*

It happened on Country Road 6, another perfectly-timed coincidence that confirmed the reality of the moment, a conversation that we were having on our way to Midland to pick up my weekend papers and a few items for the Spanish Chicken and Rice recipe that Penny was making for dinner; I was telling her about the American poet Adrienne Rich who wrote something that inspired today's spiritual musing.

She wrote: "A life I didn't choose to live chose me." And this radically different life that chose the gifted young wife and mother of three was the life of a lesbian poet activist that David Zugar described in *Poet and Critic* magazine as "a life of prophetic intensity and 'visionary anger' bitterly unable to feel at home in a world 'that gives no room /to be what we dream of becoming.'"

"Robert Frost meets Emily Dickinson in Adrienne Rich," I said to Penny, as we drove into Midland; but I had to explain what I meant by my insight into the lesbian/activist poet's life.

This insight came to me the night before while watching an online video of a memorial tribute to Adrienne Rich shortly after her passing at the age of 82, the impression forming in my mind that she was a natural amalgam of the spirit of Robert Frost and Emily Dickinson, and I said to Penny, "I'm glad I'm not going to my grave angry. That's my gift to myself."

"What do you mean?" she asked, intrigued by my comment.

"My gift to myself is that I'm not going to die angry," I replied, with an ironic smile at the price I had to pay for my precious gift. "I've been doing some research on the poet Adrienne Rich, and I understand now why she was so angry at life. That's why I wrote *Old Whore Life: Exploring the Shadow Side of Karma*. I know her anger well, sweetheart. I was no less angry, if not a thousand times more; but I managed to resolve my anger. Adrienne Rich did not."

"How do you know she didn't?" Penny asked.

"Her poetry doesn't speak resolution. On the contrary, it speaks to the messy human condition, especially the life of women. That's why she became an outspoken feminist. But hers is a strange story. Her father was a Jewish doctor who taught at Johns Hopkins University, and her mother was a Christian concert pianist who gave up a career in music for her husband. Her father encouraged his daughter to read and write poetry, though; and she graduated with a degree in English from Radcliffe College. She married an economics professor when she graduated and had three children, but her marriage was so strained that she had to leave her husband. The same year she left her husband, he committed suicide; and a few years later, she moved in with her lesbian lover. Adrienne Rich experienced the whole gamut of a woman's life: gifted young poet, housewife, mother of three boys, and confirmed lesbian; not to mention being Jewish and Christian. She had a lot of issues to work through, that's what fueled her poetry with so much passion."

"We all have issues," Penny said, with a wry smile.

"True. But some of us have more karmic baggage than others. That's life. But it doesn't matter who we are, unless we learn to resolve the two sides of our nature we're always going to be in conflict with life. That's the human condition. That's what Adrienne Rich's poetry is all about—the messy human condition. "The war poetry wages against itself," she wrote in one of her poems. That's why she was so angry. Robert Frost said, 'Poetry grabs life by the throat.' Adrienne Rich grabs life by the throat with her poetry, just like Robert Frost; but she was also driven like Emily Dickinson to find her own identity. But you can't find your true identity until you resolve the two sides of your nature, and the only way to do that is to make our two selves into one, the inner like the outer neither male nor female with no hypocrisy—"

"The hands of life!" Penny exclaimed, excitedly.

"What hands of life?" I asked, confounded by her remark.

"Didn't you see them?" she said.

"No. What?"

"There were two gloves on the side of the road. One up and one down. The two hands of life, just like you were saying—"

Penny's not a great articulator, but she has amazing intuition. *"What a coincidence,"* I said, and smiled as I always do whenever synchronicity speaks to us; and I turned the car around and went back to confirm what Penny had just seen that symbolized what I was just explaining.

And there they were on the side of the road: two discarded white gloves, one facing up and the other facing down, just like the two sides of our nature—our conscious ego personality and our unconscious shadow self, confirming with symbolic certainty what I was saying about Robert Frost meeting Emily Dickinson in the angry visionary poet whose shadow lesbian life chose her to help resolve the bifurcated nature of her identity— and what an adventure it proved to be as Adrienne Rich explored the alluring country of her conflicted, transgendered soul with prophetic intensity and visionary anger.

And whether he knew it or not, that's the path that Jordan Peterson was called to when he spoke up for free speech, the path of a visionary hierophant compelled by his own imperative to point a way out of the nihilistic impasse of today's crazy world; is it any wonder that his message is getting through to our disillusioned young people looking for direction and purpose?

How many people today, especially alienated young men, feel as Adrianne Rich did, "bitterly unable to feel at home in a world 'that gives no room /to be what we dream of becoming'"? Isn't this Jordan Peterson's massive appeal? Aren't they flocking to his talks like wayward birds to the hoopoe because he explains with passionate intensity and good-faith logic why our world is so crazy?

I'm not a stupid person, but I had no idea what was going on out there; that's why my muse expressed my frustration in my poem *What the Hell Is Going on Out There?* My creative unconscious spoke the frustration of our crazy world, and professor Peterson was called to offer an explanation with his studied maps of meaning; but because his message cuts to the quick, the nefarious forces of the shadow side of life that keep society from transcending itself have rallied to take the good professor down— *"a mean, mad white man"* Michael Dyson called him in the Munk debate, and *"a prophet for profit"* said another resentful critic—as they always do whenever someone dares to step outside the suffocating box of compromised thought and points a way out of the paradigm of our crazy world of moral relativism, identity politics, and political correctness gone loony.

One Rule to Live By

I can't remember how many times young men have said *"I get it now!"* as they listened to professor Peterson's message, sudden epiphanies that awakened them to the stark reality that they cannot have their cake and eat it too without sacrifice and hard work, an intensely passionate message that his resentful critics call alt-right, toxic, transphobic, misogynistic, and dangerous.

What a crock! It's no wonder the good professor loses his patience, like he did when he called Pankaj Mishra a prick for writing *"Jordan Peterson and Fascist Mysticism"* for The New York Review of Books that skewered his 12 Rules for Life and besmirched his character; and, in all honesty, I really don't know how he manages to stay so cool when he's so brutally assaulted with malicious intent and bad-faith logic, like he was in the Cathy Newman interview and the hit piece by Nellie Bowles in the New York Times (*"Jordan Peterson, Custodian of the Patriarchy"*) that took professor Peterson's words out of context to make him look like a misogynist—pernicious, unfair, and downright evil; the very thing that professor Peterson was unveiling with his dragon-slaying message of hope.

Let's just hope then that the "messiah virus"—*the salvific imperative of the Logos that everyone who is called to a higher path can easily fall prey to*—does not infect the good professor the way his former colleague and friend Bernard Schiff fears it has. That would be disappointing.

But I seriously doubt it will, though; because anyone who stares into the face of their own false ego/shadow personality and commits to the authentic life develops a healthy respect for the Logos, and Dr. Jordan Peterson has more than enough Jungian wisdom to ward off the "messiah virus" that so easily afflicts the inflated ego hungry for more attention and adulation.

"All I want to do is help young people make a better life," he keeps iterating in his talks and interviews; and I take Jordan Peterson at his word...

25. Integrating the Sacred Back into Society

I went online the other evening to see if any new videos on Jordan Peterson had been posted, and I came upon a new podcast by *Rebel Wisdom* (*The Peterson Paradox, May 28, 2018*), hosted by David Fuller, who used to work for Channel 4 News and BBC; and he said something to Rafia Morgan, the newest member of the *Rebel Wisdom* team, that captured the imperative of Peterson's message. "For me," said David Fuller, "he symbolizes the potential reintegration of the sacred into a society that I think has really lost its way in this kind of materialism and has cut us off from a really deep part of ourselves—the religious, the mythological, the spiritual, all these sorts of ways that we used to make sense of the world and I think speak to something really deep in ourselves..."

I couldn't agree more. How, when, and why society began to compromise its spiritual values for the pleasure and security of the material life does not really matter to me (again, that's for academics like professor Peterson to work out, which he attempted to do with his ground-breaking book *Maps of Meaning: The Architecture of Belief*); what has always concerned me was the purpose of my existence, the same question that haunts every soul that has evolved as far as Nature can take them. But in today's crazy world, to even mention the word "soul" seems to violate some unwritten code; and this is why Jordan Peterson has such a massive appeal—because he's waking people up to their disconnection from the ground of Being and the spiritual values that will reconnect them with their *essential* self. But Jordan Peterson is far too wise to be specific about God, soul, and the afterlife; and like his hero C. G. Jung, the good professor has couched his hierophantic message of hope in the safe academic paradigm of evolutionary science and behavioral psychology, which he taught for many years at Harvard and U of

T. This is why he hesitates to openly admit that he believes in God, the immortal soul, and afterlife, which only adds to his mystique. The most that he will say about his belief in God, as he expressed on a panel for an Australian TV show, is: *"I act as if God exists, and I'm terrified that he might."* That's the wisdom of someone who has earned his cake through hard work and sacrifice *(not to mention personal suffering, given his and his daughter's health conditions)*, because he knows that reconnecting with the Logos is a personal responsibility, which he addressed in 12 *Rules for Life: An Antidote to Chaos*; but because reconnecting with the source of our essential being is a personal responsibility, we will all eventually come to see the Logos in our own individual way through life experience, like Wordsworth did when he awakened to the life principle of the Logos through his love of nature, as he tells us in his autobiographical poem, *The Prelude*:

To every natural form, rock, fruit, or flower,
Even the loose stones that cover the highway,
I gave a moral life: I saw them feel,
Or linked them to some feeling: the great mass
Lay bedded in some quickening soul, and all
That I beheld respired with inward meaning.

This is why life is an individual journey of self-discovery, despite how one comes to this enlightened perspective, whether through love of nature, art, poetry, medicine, professor Peterson's message, or Gurdjieff's teaching that awakened me to the moral imperative of the Logos (the **secret way** that Jung saw in his practice and recognized in the ancient teachings of the Tao); because when all is said and done, there really is only self-initiation into the mysteries of life, which I'm compelled by the creative imperative of this story to illustrate with a spiritual musing that I wrote on how my own *way* kept me connected with my *essential* self, and the Logos:

Orest Stocco

The Longings of Our Soul

It's curious, how life works; one day we find ourselves being pulled to a new interest, as though we need the knowledge of this new interest to satisfy some longing in our soul, and when we have explored this new interest, we find ourselves being pulled to another interest to satisfy another and perhaps deeper longing in our soul that beckons our attention.

This insight came to me yesterday as I listened to the Pulitzer Prize winning journalist/author Chris Hedges as he was interviewed by Bill Moyers. I came upon Chris Hedges by "chance" online, and his political perspective fascinated me so much that I had to explore what he had to say, as though his iconoclastic point of view revealed the deep dark shadow side of politics that I longed to know more about; and I watched half a dozen or so interviews of him speaking about one or another of his best-selling books—*The Empire of Illusion: The End of Literacy and the Triumph of Spectacle*, *Days of Destruction, and Days of Revolt* and others; and he was so articulate on the dark side of human nature (especially corporate America) that I couldn't stop watching, however depressing his worldview proved to be.

In the Bill Moyers interview, Hedges reveals that the dark shadow side of life has made him an angry man, but he is a good man who wants to do his part to help set the record straight; and he paid a heavy price for his journalistic integrity, like losing his job at *New York Times* for being too honest. But that's *his* calling, and he has the courage to walk his talk; which got me thinking about the longings in our soul that keep calling us to new interests. This, then, is the subject of today's spiritual musing…

In my novel *Healing with Padre Pio,* which was inspired by my new interest in spiritual healing that initiated ten spiritual healing sessions with a gifted psychic medium who channeled St. Padre Pio for my novel, he said to me, "**Life is all about growth and understanding,**" which to anyone over forty should be so obvious that it could almost be considered tautologous; but to what end?

One Rule to Live By

That's the question that everyone would like answered, and one remarkable man did just that.

C. G. Jung, one of the founding fathers of depth psychology (the other was Sigmund Freud, but Jung went much deeper than Freud with his discovery of the collective unconscious), said: *"As each plant grows from a seed and becomes in the end an oak tree, so man must become what he is meant to be. He ought to get there, but most get stuck."* Given this realization, which took me many years to affirm with my own journey of self-discovery, it appears that the teleological purpose of our life is to become what we are meant to be, complete unto ourselves like an acorn seed becoming an oak tree; but how can we become what we are meant to be if we do not satisfy the longings in our soul?

"He ought to get there, but most get stuck," said Jung, speaking to the natural process of individuating our own identity through life experience; and it seems to me that we get stuck when we don't take the initiative to satisfy the longings in our soul by exploring new interests that will help us to grow into the person we are meant to be and realize our destined purpose of wholeness and completeness.

"Nature will only evolve you so far, and no further," said Gurdjieff, an enigmatic mystic philosopher who introduced the western world to a radical teaching of self-transformation that I lived for years and wrote about in *Gurdjieff Was Wrong, But His Teaching Works*, and the only way to become the person we are meant to be is to take evolution into our own hands to complete what Nature cannot finish, and we take evolution into our own hands by taking the initiative to explore new interests; that's how we satisfy the longings in our soul to become what we are meant to be, our true self whole and complete.

I took the initiative many, many times; but sometimes taking the initiative to explore a new interest can cost one dearly, like the time I explored an offshoot Christian solar cult teaching that did irreparable damage to my eyesight by practicing the solar techniques of looking into the sun (mornings and evenings) whose rays were said to be imbued with the sacred Logos which one needed to nourish their spiritual body, a very dangerous teaching which one day I may have the courage to write about in a novel I'm going to call *The Sunworshipper;* but only if my oracle insists. Otherwise I don't think I'll ever write it.

Being a truth seeker, it was my nature to take the initiative wherever my new interests pulled me, like my interest in studying philosophy at university which serendipitously led to Gurdjieff's teaching of "work on oneself" that sparked my interest in the sayings and parables of Jesus, the mystical teachings of Sufism, Gnosticism, Buddhism, Taoism, Jung's psychology of individuation, and a New Age spiritual teaching that I lived for many years but which I finally outgrew to devote myself to writing, a fascinating journey of self-discovery that I wrote about in *The Summoning of Noman*, followed by *The Pearl of Great Price* that brought my journey of self-discovery to personal and literary resolution.

But the pull of an exciting new interest that went a long way to transforming my life was long distance running, which I did for seven and a half years on Highway 11 along the shoreline of Lake Helen in my hometown of Nipigon, Northwestern Ontario before I burnt out on a housing contract on the Lake Helen reserve near my hometown that was too big for me to handle, and try as I may, I was never able to get back into running again which I miss dearly to this very day, because it was the most satisfying way to resolve my daily stress and grow in the consciousness of the person I was meant to be; but I did keep a journal from *August 1, 1988* to *January 8, 1989* to capture the daily flavor of my running experience, which I called *Thoughts in Motion: Diary of a Holistic Runner,* so I know from personal experience that taking the initiative to explore new interests nourishes the longings in our soul, and I'm convinced that **the more we nourish the longings in our soul, the more we grow into the person we are meant to be**.

But one day we will all see that exploring new interests won't be enough to satisfy the deepest longing in our soul for wholeness and completeness, as I painfully learned when I desperately needed to satisfy my deepest longing and did irreparable damage to my eyesight with that offshoot Christian solar cult teaching that promised instant nourishment of the Logos with its solar techniques; and that's when the *omniscient guiding principle of life* calls us to complete what Nature cannot finish by teaching us how to live our life unselfishly, learning to give back to life instead of always taking, because this is the only way we can resolve the paradoxical consciousness of our *being* and *non-being* and transcend our primordial selfish nature that keeps us bound to our ego/shadow personality.

"He labors good on good to fix, and owes /To virtue every triumph that he knows," said William Wordsworth, whose poem *Character of the Happy Warrior* became my ideal, because in the end all paths in life lead to the simple virtue of goodness; but that's another spiritual musing for another day.

———

When he was asked by David Fuller in the *Rebel Wisdom* podcast what he thought of Jordan Peterson, Raphia Morgan, who was a co-founder of *Path of Love* and deeply involved in spiritual work, replied: "I think he's somebody who gets the bigger picture and can weave things that would address real life concerns for lots and lots of people," to which Fuller replied: "He's carrying more than his fair share of the burden. He's carrying a sort of flame for this reintegration of the sacred, for this great tradition, for all this stuff that has to be integrated for us to move forward. We have to get past this sort of naïve materialism, naïve scientism that someone like Sam Harris represents. It's like, religion is stupid, and everyone else is stupid who doesn't think like this. *Whoa.* Grow up. The arrogance. That is just ridiculous. And he's carrying this. He's the hero of the moment for this other way of looking at the world," and Raphia Morgan responded: "We need a bigger wisdom that is more inclusive and that is not giving up taking a stand. It's taking a stand for a higher wisdom that is more inclusive, that is willing to look at the right, that is willing to look at the left, that can find some kind of synthesis out of all that and stand on that and address the real issues and not just get lost in a kind of name-calling polarity that has been going on forever. It's just so tiring," and both Fuller and Morgan felt that Jordan Peterson was burning out because he had taken upon himself the burden of reintegrating the sacred back into the world which he didn't have to do alone, and they both felt he was dangerously polarizing in his message (hence their podcast, *"The Peterson Paradox")*; but again, if Jordan Peterson is getting dangerous, it's only in the most ironic sense, because he has to rally the redemptive spirit of the Logos to bring some measure of respectable order back into the chaos of our crazy world of moral relativism, identity politics, and power-crazed political correctness. That's why he was called to his destined purpose; and as much as I fear for what the shadow side of life will do to keep him from integrating the sacred Logos back into society, I have faith in his oracle...

26. A New Paradigm for Our Crazy World

> "There are more things in heaven and earth, Horatio,
> Than are dreamt of in your philosophy."
> —*William Shakespeare*

Being the kind of writer that I am with a gift for seeing both the beginning and the end of the ideas that I am given to explore in my writing (especially ideas for my spiritual musings that come to me like packaged truths), I had my suspicion where *One Rule to Live By: Be Good* was going; but I did not want to think about it, because I had to get there first.

I'm not quite there yet, but I'm getting closer. I have to read Jordan Peterson's *Maps of Meaning: The Architecture of Belief* before I work my way around the corner; but all the same, I can no longer hold back the creative imperative of *One Rule to Live By: Be Good*.

I know that we need a new paradigm for our crazy world to live by that will be large enough to include every facet of the human condition, a paradigm that will allow everyone to grow in their destined purpose to wholeness and completeness, but I also know that this new paradigm will only be embraced by those whom life has made ready; and this was the inspiration for the following spiritual musing that I dared (*it was foolhardy, I know; because it's so far out there it may damage the credibility of this story*) to post on my Spiritual Musings blog *Saturday, February 10, 2018*:

On the Cusp of a New Spiritual Awakening

This is a spiritual musing that I look forward to writing. I shouldn't, because it could easily come back to bite me; but I can't help myself, the call to write it is so strong that I *have* to write it.

The idea came to me this morning as I was reading my newly minted copy of *My Writing Life*, the sequel to *The Lion that Swallowed Hemingway,* while drinking my first cup of coffee. Just as I finished reading Chapter 29, "Hemingway's Brain," which I concluded with stinging irony that suicide might be genetically encoded (this was a satirical put-down of psychiatrist Dr. Andrew Farah's theory that Ernest Hemingway's suicide was induced by chronic traumatic encephalopathy from the nine blows to his head that Hemingway received over his life-packed life), because Dr. Farah's theory rested upon the unproven scientific theory that our personality is a by-product of our brain and can be affected by repeated blows to the head, which certainly can happen as extensive studies of football player head injuries have proven, but our personality is a fractal of the individuating consciousness of our essential self, which is not an epiphenomenon of the brain; our essential self is our true and immortal divine self, independent of our biology, and although our personality may certainly be affected by brain chemistry, our essential self imbues our personality with our evolving identity that is independent of our brain, and no sooner did I read the last line of "Hemingway's Brain" and the title of today's spiritual musing popped into my head— "On the Cusp of a New Spiritual Awakening." That's how ideas for my spiritual musings come to me, out of the "blue."

As I said, I look forward to writing today's spiritual musing despite how threatening it may be to conventional wisdom; but before I do, I have to watch a YouTube video again where the exceptionally gifted Australian psychic Alison Allan channels the higher self of well-known living people—Oprah Winfrey, Shirley MacLaine, Hillary Clinton, Donald Trump, Jim Carrey, George Clooney, Bill Murray and others, which proved to be not only shockingly mischievous, but absolutely visionary in its serendipitous discovery, because it opened the psychic door to the higher self of every living person, which was totally new to the phenomenon of channeling because psychic mediums only channelled the spirit of the dead, not the living.

Here's how it happened. Alison had written down a list of names (departed souls) for her to channel on the *Afterlife Interview* segment of the *Alison and Kari's Shiny Show* (as advertised on

One Rule to Live By

YouTube: *"Kari Mena, Energy Healer and Alison Allan, Medium, are two like-minded people who want to share the experience of the spirit world"),* and by mistake, Alison had written down Shirley MacLaine's name, but as she went over her list she realized that she wasn't dead yet; and when she discussed this with her co-host Kari, they were given the inspiration to try channeling the higher self of famous living people, and that's how they "chanced" upon what will undoubtedly be a new frontier of the spiritual awakening that's taking place in the world today, and which they even became aware of as Alison channeled the higher self of those famous people still living, because they both recognized that what they were doing was not unlike what the old pioneers did as they explored their new country (in Kari's case, the America west, and in Alison's case, the unexplored frontiers of Australia)—*only they were exploring the undiscovered far country of the soul!*

Of course, the materialistic scientific community pooh-poos this field of inquiry; but the social paradigm of personal meaning is shifting so quickly today—what with all the mind-expanding shows in the movie industry, television, Netflix, Prime Video and other social media networks with themes dealing with reincarnation (*Cloud Atlas,* starring Tom Hanks), recurring parallel lives (*Before I Fall,* modelled on *Groundhog Day* starring Bill Murray), and SF movies that extend human life beyond our five senses—that the recalcitrant soul-denying scientific community is beginning to cave, which books like *Proof of Heaven* by Dr. Eben Alexander, M.D. and *Many Lives, Many Masters* by Dr. Brian L. Weiss, M.D., written by established medical doctors who once held onto the theory that we do not have an autonomous self that exists independent of our physical body are proving, with more personal stories of OBEs (out of body experiences), NDEs (near-death experiences), and after-death memoirs like *My Life After Death: A Memoir From Heaven,* by Eric Mendhus, coming out every day; and, at the risk of sounding immodest, I can even cite my own parallel life story in my memoir *The Summoning of Noman* and my intensely personal novel *Healing with Padre Pio,* which was inspired by the spiritual healing experience that I had with the gifted psychic/medium who channeled the departed spirit of St. Padre Pio. The times are changing so rapidly that I can almost hear Bob Dylan's squeaky voice singing in my ear: *"For the times they are a-changin…"*

But old dogs die hard, and it will take some time for the higher frequency energy of this new spiritual awakening to break up the stifling consciousness of crystallized belief systems that keep social consciousness trapped in fixed mental attitudes, like the unproven scientific belief that our reflective self is a by-product of our brain, and there's nothing anyone can do about this because life is an individual journey of self-discovery, and not everyone can make the shift in their personal paradigm to this new awakening; but it's happening all the same, as adventurous souls like Alison and Kari are proving…

The Internet, a global computer network providing a variety of information and communication facilities, is here to stay, and however it evolves in this rapidly changing world it will continue to expand the horizons of man's thinking like nothing before. When Gutenberg invented the printing press in the mid 15th Century, it ushered in the modern period of human history, playing a key role in the development of the Renaissance, Reformation, the Age of Enlightenment, and the scientific revolution; and it laid the material basis for our modern knowledge-based economy and spread learning to the masses; but the Internet, a highly evolved technological version of the Gutenberg press, opens us up to a whole universe of learning, giving us instant information as it springs forth from the deep founts of human consciousness, like the serendipitous discovery that Alison and Kari made by daring to channel the higher spiritual self of famous people still living, and as surprised as I was in their discovery, so were the spirits that they channeled.

For the record, the Alison and Kari YouTube video that inspired the idea for today's spiritual musing is titled: *Shiny Show E6: Contacting Higher Selves of Famous People*, which is worth watching, if not for the information, which is mind-boggling, at least for the sheer entertainment, which is hilarious; and just to show how surprised these people were when the gifted Alison intruded into their spiritual space by calling upon their higher self, let me quote their exact words:

One Rule to Live By

The comedian and actor Jim Carrey's higher self was called first, and Jim Carrey, one of the fractals (personalities) of his higher self's multiple fractals, responded to what Alison and Keri were doing: "How naughty this is," he said, annoyed but somewhat amused; and Alison got the distinct impression that Jim Carrey compared what they were doing to making love with the neighbor's wife...

When Alison called Oprah Winfrey's higher self, Keri, being the annoying little brat that she is, asked Oprah if she would plug her *Shiny Show*, and Oprah replied: "Baby steps, baby steps." And just as she was leaving, because she didn't want to reveal any more than she had to and only appeared to Alison out of courtesy, she said to the girls that she was going to be one hell of an interview when she crossed over, if the *Shiny Show* was still around, that is...

And then Alison called Shirley MacLaine's higher self (whose books I had read and loved, my favourite being *Sage-ing While Age-ing* with *The Camino* a close second), and Shirley MacLaine, being her characteristic feisty self, said: "What the hell do you think you're doing? This is ridiculous. Good fun, but ridiculous. You're busting the chops of all the rules by doing this; and it's fun, but—it's funny, but it's naughty." And when Keri asked her how she felt about how the world had finally embraced her spiritual views (on reincarnation and UFOs), Shirley MacLaine replied: "It's about bloody time..."

And then Keri asked Alison to call the heartthrob actor George Clooney's higher self, and he simply said, "Seriously girls? Come on? Moving on, girls," and he left...

Steven King's higher self was called next, and the famous author crossed his arms and furrowed his brow and gave the girls a studied look, and said: "There's a book in this..."

And then the celebrated scientist Stephen Hawking's higher self was called, who didn't mind appearing, and Alison asked him a question that had been on her mind ever since she read his book *A Brief History of Time*. Stephen Hawkins was born 300 years to the day that the famous Galileo Galilei died, and Alison felt that he was the reincarnation of Galileo, which he confirmed; then Keri asked him about his theory that there was no God, and he replied, "It's just a game...just because you say there is no God does not change the fact that there is a God," and he told the girls that he would be back in the not too distant future...

After Stephen Hawking, the actor William Shatner's higher self was called, and the first thing Captain Kirk said to the girls was, "To boldly go where no-one has gone before, ladies," a reference to that famous line from his Star Trek show. And then he added, *"Wait till you get over here. This is the real Star Trek..."*

And then Keri asked Alison to call up the actor of the SF *Matrix* series, Samuel L. Jackson's higher self, and he said to them: "Whatcha you girls doing now? What the hell you doing? Just because you can do it doesn't mean you should." And Keri asked if they were breaking some spiritual law with their playful foray into the far country of the soul, and Jackson replied: "You're breaking some big spiritual butt. You're opening doors that are never going to close, girls. Once the word is out there, every f—r is going to be doing it..."

And then, to my absolute delight, Alison called up the three candidates that were running for the American presidency, Hillary Clinton, Donald Trump, and Bernie Sanders, and they all confirmed what Stephen Hawking said, that it was all just a game; but Donald Trump said something that puzzled the girls: "All is not what it seems, ladies. Don't be fooled by what's in the brochures..."

Donald Trump won the presidency and has been stirring the pot ever since, shaking up the American political system like no other president before him, which is probably the best thing that could have happened to American politics; but that could be a whole musing in itself, if ever I am called to write it. Suffice to say, there's an electrifying spiritual awakening taking place today, and I'm happy to be part of this new phase of human evolution, however bizarre it may appear to be.

This is why Jordan Peterson was called to write *12 Rules for Life: An Antidote to Chaos* and I was called to write *One Rule to Live By: Be Good;* the good professor to satisfy our need to know what the hell is going on out there and provide a roadmap for all wayward souls looking for direction and purpose to satisfy the longing in their soul for wholeness and completeness that religion, science, and politics cannot satisfy, and me to provide an expansive new paradigm for this crazy world of moral relativism, identity politics, and radical political correctness gone loony that professor Peterson's *12 Rules for Life* will prepare one for, a comprehensive paradigm that embraces all dimensions of human nature, including the redemptive laws of karma and reincarnation—*an unbelievably presumptuous proposition, I know; but I really am a servant of my muse...*

27. Jordan Peterson's Most Important Rule

If I heard it once, I heard it three or four times; when asked by interviewers on his book tour which one of his 12 rules for life he thought was most important, professor Peterson always replied, with a thoughtful look that conveyed the gravity of his choice, that it would have to be *Rule 8: Tell the truth—or, at least, don't lie,* closely followed by *Rule 7: Pursue what is meaningful (not what is expedient),* and I totally comply with his choice, because telling the truth keeps our false shadow self from growing into the monstrous beast that it can become, like it did in my high school hero and literary mentor Ernest "Papa" Hemingway who sacrificed *everyone* on the sacred altar of his art. "He's a pathological liar and the cruelest man I know, and I have known some very cruel men," said his third wife, the journalist/author Martha Gellhorn, who refused to submit to her husband.

This is why I sent the good professor my book *The Lion that Swallowed Hemingway* ("lion" symbolizes his ravenous shadow) before he came into public prominence, and my sequel *My Writing Life* three years later when he was catapulted onto the world stage with his overnight bestseller *12 Rules for Life: An Antidote to Chaos,* because I wanted to share with him my own insights into the shadow-possessed personality, which he was very familiar with given his Jungian studies and clinical practice and in-depth research into the Soviet system and Nazi regime; and I also sent him *The Pearl of Great Price* and *The Merciful Law of Divine Synchronicity,* because they tell the story of how I integrated my shadow self with my ego personality and became one self whole and complete.

This, of course, is next-to-impossible to do when one's ego personality is so thoroughly imbued with one's false shadow self that one cannot tell the one from the other, which is why it's impossible to break free of the human predicament in one lifetime alone; but how can one break free of their false shadow self when the consciousness of their own nothingness denies the divine imperative of the transformative process of karma and reincarnation?

It's only because I *know* this that I can tolerate the unconscious bad faith of some of Jordan Peterson's most cynical critics, like Channel 4 News's Cathy Newman. But as disappointing as Cathy Newman was, none of Peterson's critics annoyed me more than the fiendishly devious Philip Dodd in the podcast *Jordan Peterson & Philip Dodd on Free Thinking BBC May 2018*. This man was so evil in his intent to paint Jordan Peterson a "Fascist mystic" that I had to hold myself back from screaming; that's how much I detest the bad faith of the shadow-possessed personality.

But was Philip Dodd aware of himself? Was he aware of his own false nature as the good professor and I and all good people listening were?

No, he wasn't. He was being true to himself; but, sadly, it was his false self that he was being true to. And it was this perception that inspired the following spiritual musing that will take me around the corner and begin the process of bringing my story home:

A Very Big Thought

"The good is the purest energy of God. Be good, do good, and you will satisfy your longing for God."
—*Pythagoras*

I have a very big thought that's taken hold of me, and I fear being called to work it out in a spiritual musing. I don't want to go there, because if I do I'll be pulled into the deepest end of the pool, and that terrifies me no less than when I'm called to write a poem that sends chills up my spine, like my poem "Soul of a Liar" that captures the true spirit of the shadow personality—

Soul of a Liar

It's not true, what they say about you,
it's a lie like all the other lies that they say
about everyone they talk about, because
nothing they say can be trusted, —

Why is that?

They mean well, but they continue to lie
despite their good intentions, and they
never stop lying even when they
know that they are lying, —

Why is that?

They lie best when they tell the truth,
which is the mystery of the liar's nature,
and not until they can no longer suffer
what they are will they stop lying, —

Why is that?

    The central concept of this poem, which my muse worked out for me to apprehend the soul of a liar, was revealed in the paradoxical sentence: "They lie best when they tell the truth." My insight pinned the devil down and forced it to yield its power, an insight that I could not quite articulate until I wrote this poem, thus confirming Zen poet Jane Hirshfield's contention that poetry does our thinking for us.
    I've always known that a shadow-possessed personality cannot be trusted, and by shadow-possessed I mean a person like my high school hero and literary mentor Ernest "Papa" Hemingway whose menacing shadow took over his ego and drove him into deep depression and suicide (his third wife Martha Gellhorn called him "the biggest liar since Munchausen," and all his friends knew he could not be trusted), which I explored in *The Lion that Swallowed Hemingway* and my sequel *My Writing Life*; but I could never quite give my gnostic awareness of the shadow-possessed personality the literary clarity it deserved (as far as poetry can be clear, that is) until I worked it out in "Soul of a Liar," and this is what I've been called

upon to do in this spiritual musing with my big thought on the gnostic way of life that has taken hold of me.

My big thought presupposes my life's quest for my true self, and because my journey of self-discovery was born of my own life-experiences which I creatively worked out in more than twenty books into the quintessential gnostic truth of my life, I fear that by giving literary clarity to my very big thought I may jolt the reader into a perspective they may not be ready to apprehend; but I am a servant of my muse.

It seems then that the quintessential gnostic truth of my life is what I've been called upon to explore in today's spiritual musing, despite my trepidations; but where's my point of entry? What gate will open to let me into the deep mystery of this simple gnostic truth?

No sooner did I ask this question and a quote from Albert Einstein popped into my mind, *"Everything should be made as simple as possible, but not simpler,"* and I *know* beyond a shadow of doubt that this is my entry into the quintessential gnostic truth of my life; because, after years of inspired reading, studying, and living and writing about the **secret way of life,** I'm left with the simple gnostic truth that **the ultimate purpose and meaning of life is to simply be a good person, because being a good person embodies all ways in life, both secular and spiritual, into one's destined purpose of wholeness and completeness.**

There, I've said it; now all I have to do is unpack it. And that's where trepidation sets in, because the simplicity of this gnostic truth can burn a hole in one's mind like a laser beam of pure intention that cuts through all the precious vanities of one's life and set soul free from all the delusions of one's ego/shadow personality, and this no one wants to do for fear of self-negation (***"For whosoever will save his life shall lose it: and whosoever will lose his life for my sake shall find it."*** said Jesus); hence my apprehension. But why? Why must one fear being a good person? What is it about being good that terrifies people? Why would there be a saying in the streets, quoted so often it makes me sick, "No good deed goes unpunished"?

No sooner did I ask this and Saint Augustine popped into my mind with his famous supplication, *"Lord, make me chaste, but not yet."* But just to make sure that I remembered the quotation correctly,

I Googled St. Augustine and learned that the original Latin translation of his famous saying was, **"Make me good, god, but not yet."** Which is even better yet, because the original Latin translation gives synchronous confirmation to the theme of today's musing, which can be rendered into one simple question: **why be good?**

Why was St. Augustine torn between being good and not being good? What was this dilemma that tortured his soul? He did not want to sacrifice his concupiscence (*he loved sex too much*), but to be good he had to tame his lustful beast of desire; that's why he was torn in two, and he suffered unbearable emotional and mental anguish and soul-wrenching torment: hence his famous memoir, *Confessions*.

St. Augustine's *Confessions* is one of the most moving pieces of literature the world has ever seen, and to be honest I cannot bear reading it. His abject sycophancy to God turns my stomach. Which is why I walked away from my Roman Catholic faith to become a seeker at such an early age; I could not prostrate myself in abject submission to the God of Christianity like St. Augustine did, and I had to find my own way to my true self. And after years of living the secret teachings of the way that I first discovered in Gurdjieff's teaching through Ouspensky's book *In Search of the Miraculous,* my own eclectic path eventually wrought out the gnostic way of life by the self-reconciling virtue of simply being a good person.

But this does not preclude any other way, either secular or spiritual, to one's destined purpose of wholeness and completeness, because all ways lead to one's true self eventually; and what my big thought is trying to tell me is this: **all ways in life lead to the simple way of being a good person, because goodness engages the transformative process of reconciling one's ego/shadow personality with one's soul, which is the only way to wholeness and completeness.**

I would never have arrived at this simple gnostic truth had I not had the experiences to support it, but it's to the nature of these experiences that brings my gnostic truth into question, because my experiences were so far outside the scope of normal human experience that no one would believe me if I revealed them; but I have revealed them in my books *Gurdjieff Was Wrong, But His*

One Rule to Live By

Teaching Works and *The Pearl of Great Price,* and it behooves me to reveal them here to support the premise of today's spiritual musing.

I had four unbelievable experiences in my quest for my true self that connected the dots and solved the riddle of the meaning and purpose of our existence. 1: I had a totally unexpected and spontaneous experience in the early stages of my quest of going back through time where I experienced the inception of life on Planet Earth when Soul, the *I Am* consciousness of God, animated the amino acids, the first building blocks of life that were formed when gaseous vapors from the lifeless planet rose up into the air and mixed with gaseous vapors in the sky, thereby initiating the life-process in the world *(giving credence to the Intelligent Design theory of evolution, Soul being the omniscient guiding principle of life).* 2: Years later, I had a past-life regression to the infinite Body of God where all souls come from. I was an atom of God with no reflective self-consciousness, an embryonic soul waiting to be born in the world. 3: In the same regression, I was sent into the world to process the vital life force, the un-self-realized *I Am* consciousness of Soul, into a new "I" of God through natural evolution, and I experienced the birth of my own reflective self-consciousness in my first primordial human lifetime as the alpha male of a small group of cave-dwelling higher primates; and from lifetime to lifetime, I continued to evolve in my reflective self-consciousness until I was ready to take evolution into my own hands to complete what Nature could not finish *(explaining once and for all where our self came from).* And finally, 4: In my current lifetime, I found the **secret way of life** first in the teachings of Gurdjieff and then in the sayings and parables of Jesus, and I transformed the consciousness of my ego/shadow personality and *became* my true self, thus completing what Nature could not finish *(thereby fulfilling soul's destined purpose of wholeness and completeness).*

These experiences informed me that we are all atoms of God, sparks of divine consciousness as the poets say, souls encoded with God's DNA; and we are all destined to realize a separate and distinct identity, a new "I" of God, which we do with teleological imperative through natural evolution from one lifetime to the next until we are ready to take evolution into our own hands and complete what natural evolution through karma and reincarnation cannot finish. This is the meaning and purpose of our existence.

Every soul will eventually come to see that Nature cannot complete the process of self-realization, and one must take evolution into their own hands to fulfill their destined purpose of becoming what they are meant to be, which after years of living the **secret way of life** led me to see that being a good person will complete what Nature cannot finish, because **goodness is the sum of all virtues which transforms our ego/shadow personality and makes our inner and outer self into one self, whole and complete**; but to explain the individuation process goes beyond the scope of today's spiritual musing, and if I'm called to expound upon the transformative power of goodness, I will happily do so, but again with trepidation.

———

Wouldn't you know it, then; this is why I was called to write *One Rule to Live By: Be Good*. This unbelievable but true story of my own individuation process, inspired by professor Jordan Peterson's call to become a hierophant for today's crazy world, was born of my own creative imperative, initiated by my angry poem *What the Hell Is Going on Out There?*, and it doesn't really matter that my story was set free by professor Peterson's call to destiny with his defense of free speech that impelled him to share his own individual *way* in *12 Rules for Life: An Antidote to Chaos* that unexpectedly gave him a global platform to provide an answer to my angry poem, when one is called by life, one is called by whatever means necessary to fulfill their destined purpose to wholeness and completeness. So, I'm very grateful for the good professor's inspiration; but I would have written a book not unlike this regardless *(all roads lead to Rome)*, because my oracle always has its way with me…

28. Jordan Peterson and the Authentic Life

> "One man who stopped lying could bring down a tyranny."
> —Aleksandr Solzhenitsyn

It's much more difficult to live the authentic life than people think, as I painfully learned in my own journey of self-discovery, a terrifying truth that I spent the best part of my writing life trying to conceptualize and articulate; and here I am again faced with the same dilemma of man's irreconcilable nature, because I will never bring One Rule to Live By: Be Good to resolution until I demystify the mystery of being true to oneself, because **one can be true to oneself and not know that they are being true to their false self.**

I never knew that I was being true to my false self until I heard a voice in my mind ask me the question that alerted me to my false nature, *"Why do you lie?"* And Jordan Peterson thought that he was being true to himself until he had the shocking realization that his life was a lie also, which began his own long and difficult journey to authenticity; but how long must one suffer the oppressive weight of their own self-delusions before they wake up to their false nature?

That's the moral of Aleksandr Solzhenitsyn's monumental work *The Gulag Archipelago* in which he explores his own complicity in the Soviet system that led to the unbearable suffering and deaths of millions of innocent people, his willful capitulation to the lie of the utopian dream of socialism, one innocuous lie at a time until he got swallowed whole by the Great Lie of Socialism and was himself imprisoned by the system that he himself helped make possible; and as he examined his own conscience and listened to the stories of hundreds of inmates in the Gulag, he finally saw through the Great Lie of the Soviet system and had to share his truth with the world, which he did with his books on the Soviet Gulag that garnered him the

Nobel Prize in Literature in 1970, "for the ethical force with which he has pursued the indefensible tradition of Russian literature."

This is why Jordan Peterson found in Aleksandr Solzhenitsyn a hero to model his own life; and it was the ongoing soul-making suffering of the Russian people that Svetlana Alexievich recorded in her own writing that also garnered her the Nobel Prize in Literature in 2015 and which, to my total surprise and wonder, inspired one of my favourite spiritual musings:

The Tremor of Eternity

> "Suffering is a special kind of knowledge."
> —*Svetlana Alexievich*

Svetlana Alexievich, "historian of the soul," won the Nobel Prize for Literature in 2015 for her "polyphonic writing, a monument to suffering and courage in our time," as the Nobel citation put it; but I could not finish reading her last book *Second Hand Time, The Last of the Soviets*. It was too Dostoevskian in its existential density, and I had to put it aside.

That was last year. This year I picked up the *September 2017* issue of *The Atlantic* magazine in Barrie (the day of my auto accident, which put a damper on my browsing in Chapters) and noticed an article on Svetlana Alexievich which was prompted by the English translation of the book that launched her career, *The Unwomanly Face of War*. The article was written by Nina Khrushcheva, granddaughter of the Soviet Premier Nikita Khrushchev's son, and I read something that sparked the idea for today's spiritual musing:

"Her goal was not modest: to listen to "specific human beings, living in a specific time and taking part in specific events," while remaining ever alert to "the eternally human in them. The tremor of eternity. That which is in human beings at all times."

One Rule to Live By

Svetlana Alexievich's books transcend journalism. By the magic of creative effort, Svetlana managed to distill "the eternally human" out of the story of every person that she interviewed for her oral history of the Soviet people, and the question that I want to explore in today's spiritual musing is this: what is this "tremor of eternity" in the human soul?

Coincidence or not (I believe it was a meaningful coincidence, because whenever I get an idea for a spiritual musing *the merciful law of divine synchronicity* kicks in to flesh in my musing), I just happened to select the movie *Fences* on Netflix for Penny and I to watch the other evening, starring Denzel Washington and Viola Davis, and the existential density of this unbearably poignant story brought to mind Svetlana's ambitious literary goal of recording the story of "specific human beings, living in a specific time and taking part in specific events," and I could feel "the tremor of eternity" in the lives of the black people in the movie *Fences,* specific lives oppressed in their own specific way no less than the lives of people under Soviet rule that Svetlana recorded in the oral histories of her books.

The existential density of the movie *Fences* strongly suggested to me that it had been adapted from a play, so I did a Google search and learned that the screenplay was written by the playwright August Wilson who had adapted it from his Pulitzer Prize-winning play *Fences,* just as I suspected; but that didn't help me resolve the question of "the tremor of eternity" that I saw in the soul of his characters, and I had to ponder deeply.

I *knew* with intuitive certainty that this "tremor of eternity" had to do with existential suffering brought about by the oppressive conditions of one's life, whether it be the life of the Soviet people living under socialism or the life of black people in Pittsburgh, Pennsylvania; and I went back to the article in *The Atlantic* and found confirmation in Svetlana's own words, which reflect the wisdom that she accrued from recording thousands of stories from specific people living in a specific time and taking part in specific events:

"Sometimes I come home after these meetings with the thought that suffering is solitude. Total isolation. At other times, it seems to me that suffering is a special kind of knowledge. There is something in human life that is impossible to convey and preserve in any other way, especially among us. That is how the world is made; that is how we are made."

"That's it," I exclaimed to myself, not with the excitement of a mind-shattering epiphany, but with the quiet calm of unsurprising coincidental confirmation.

Svetlana had intuited one of the deepest mysteries of the human condition, that the human soul is made through pain and suffering—an insight much too deep for tears, as the poet Wordsworth would say; which was why she found it "impossible to convey." But Svetlana did her creative best, which the Nobel Prize committee recognized as "a new kind of literary genre," describing her work as a "history of emotions…a history of the soul."

"To me the meanest flower that blows can give /Thoughts that do often lie too deep for tears," said William Wordsworth in his poem "Intimations of Immortality," but these were thoughts born of the joyous anguish of life and not the anguishing pain of suffering like that of the oppressed Soviet people in Svetlana books, or of the oppressed black people in *Fences;* which confirmed my gnostic understanding of the growth and individuation of the human soul through the *enantiodromiac* process of natural evolution.

This is the core idea of today's spiritual musing, then; but like Svetlana Alexievich, I find it impossible to convey the sacred mystery of this idea, and I have to abandon to my creative unconscious to bring today's spiritual musing to satisfactory resolution...

I pondered deeply. What did Svetlana Alexievich mean by calling suffering "a special kind of knowledge"? Listening to thousands of people tell their personal story of suffering for her oral history of the Soviet people who were conditioned by the inflexible ideology of socialism, she felt "the tremor of eternity" in each person's soul, "that which is human in all of us," which was why she was called a historian of the soul in the Nobel Prize citation.

And as I watched the movie *Fences*, I also felt "the tremor of eternity" in the soul of Troy Maxson (Denzel Washington) and his wife Rose (Viola Davis), and I *knew* with gnostic certainty that the "tremor of eternity" that I felt in their anguished soul was that "special kind of knowledge" that was created out of the *enantiodromiac* process of soul-making; but this is such a deep concept to explain that I have to defer to my twin soul books, *Death, the Final Frontier* and *The Merciful Law of Divine Synchronicity*, which tell the story of how I came to see in my own journey of self-discovery that **human suffering is Nature's way of satisfying the longing in our soul to be all that we are meant to be.**

"That is how we are made," she said. This is the mystery that Svetlana Alexievich caught a glimpse of as she listened to the Soviet people tell the story of their personal suffering and which I caught a glimpse of in the movie *Fences* as I watched Troy Maxson and his wife Rose suffer the existential anguish of their marriage and life circumstances, a glimpse into the sacred mystery of suffering that has puzzled the world since the dawn of man; but without suffering, where would we be?

Would we have that "tremor of eternity" in our soul? Would we even be aware of our immortal nature that Wordsworth caught a glimpse of in his poem "Intimations of Immortality" and Svetlana Alexievich caught a glimpse of in the suffering of the Soviet people and which I saw more and more clearly in Troy Maxson and his wife Rose in the movie *Fences*?

Through suffering, we grow in that "special kind of knowledge" that nourishes the longing in our soul to be all that we are meant to be; but is there any other way to grow in our immortal nature other than through the existential pain and suffering of the human condition?

The ancient alchemists *knew* that Nature will only evolve us so far, and then we have to take evolution into our own hands to complete what Nature cannot finish; this is the mystery that Svetlana Alexievich confronted in her quest to record the oral history of the Soviet People and which Troy Maxson and his wife Rose were up against, and this is the mystery that I sought to resolve in my lifelong journey of self-discovery.

I felt the "tremor of eternity" in the soul of the Soviet people that Svetlana Alexievich creatively recorded in her oral histories, and I felt the "tremor of eternity" in the soul of Troy Maxson and his wife

Rose in the movie *Fences* as I watched them suffer in their existential anguish, but I also *knew* with gnostic certainty through my own journey of self-discovery that there was a way out of our existential suffering; but that's a subject for another spiritual musing, if I'm ever called upon to write it.

Aleksandr Solzhenitsyn's legacy to the Russian people and to the whole world began when he examined his conscience and realized that his own lies contributed to the Great Lie of the Soviet System, and dismantling his own life-lie was the inspiration for professor Peterson's own journey to authenticity, which is why *Rule 8: Always tell the truth—or, at least, don't lie,* is his favorite rule in his shadow-dismantling book *12 Rules for Life: An Antidote to Chaos,* because always telling the truth and not lying transforms one's life-lie and goes a long way to making one whole; and by consequence, society as well. This is why professor Peterson's message to the younger generation can be so harsh, because dismantling one's life-lie is the first step on one's journey to authenticity; and unless one takes this first step, one will never know which self they are being true to...

29. No Ordinary Psychologist

> There is a tide in the affairs of men.
> Which, taken at the flood, leads on to fortune;
> Omitted, all the voyage of their life
> Is bound in shallows and in miseries.
> On such a full sea are we now afloat,
> And we must take the current when it serves,
> Or lose our ventures.
>
> —William Shakespeare

    I never quite appreciated what the venerable Capuchin monk, who suffered the holy wounds of Jesus for fifty years before dying and to whom thousands of healing miracles have been attributed, said to me during one of my spiritual healing sessions with the gifted psychic medium who channeled him for my novel *Healing with Padre Pio*, perhaps because I was much too modest, or naive, but when he told me that my writing will **"open the door to a new way of perceiving, a new way of thinking and understanding,"** I did not make the connection with something else that he said to me: **"You have transcended yourself and your community."** By community, he meant both the New Age spiritual community that I belonged to at the time but subsequently left shortly after writing my novel, and also the entire human community; but I've written more than half a dozen books since I wrote *Healing with Padre Pio*, and I understand what he means now.

    If natural evolution can only take us so far in the consciousness of our individuating self, as ancient wisdom would have us believe and which I confirmed with my own journey of self-discovery, where does one turn when the natural process of self-individuation through karma and reincarnation can take them no further? This was the angry question that my poem *What the Hell Is Going on Out There?* shouted from the depths of the my soul and the collective psyche of the world—

> Hierophants of the world,
> I've lost all faith in religion, science,
> and politics, but not in the better nature
> of my fellow man, so please tell me:
> *what the hell is going on out there?*

This was my *cri de coeur*; but it was also a plea from the collective psyche of the world, because religion, science, and politics have failed to provide a way out of the existential dilemma of the human condition that has become hopelessly confused from the blind and treacherous ethos of moral relativism that sick little Friedrich Nietzsche's Zarathustra proliferated with his God-is-dead philosophy—*grotesque child of Darwin's scientific theory of evolution which took God out of the equation of the human condition and sanctioned the crippling doctrine of atheism*—and no one knows what to do to save the world from imploding; but the Universe heard my plea, and along came a U of T professor of psychology and clinical therapist who refused to disabuse his conscience and took a defiant stand for free speech that was compromised by a morally obtuse amendment to the Canadian Human Rights Act, Bill C-16, and Jordan Peterson was catapulted onto the world stage with the overnight success of his shadow-shocking, soul-saving book *12 Rules for Life: An Antidote to Chaos* where he was given a global platform to answer the angry question of my poem.

There have been plenty of articles written on Jordan Peterson since he stepped onto the world stage, some wickedly intent on destroying him for the serious threat he poses to postmodern neo-Marxist nihilism, identity politics, and political correctness gone loony, like Nellie Bowles's hit piece in *The New York Times (May 18, 2018: "Jordan Peterson, Custodian of the Patriarchy")*; but the more he was heard by good and decent people genuinely concerned with the conditions of our crazy world, the more the imperative of his message appealed to them, especially to wayward young men, and many people have come to his defense; like Heather R. Higgins, an American businesswoman, political commentator, and non-profit sector executive who wrote an insightful editorial on Jordan Peterson for *The Hill* (May 30, 2018): *"How philosopher Jordan Peterson will change the world."*

Heady stuff, to be sure; but professor Peterson has been put through the wringer many times since he stepped up to the plate, and he is wise enough to not let praise and adulation go to his head, and Heather Higgins hits home with her keen and honest perspective on the intrepid hierophant who was driven from the earliest age by a fiercely obsessive *daemonic* spirit to understand "the general social and political insanity and evil of the world." Higgins writes:

> "The first reason that Peterson had such impact is that this is no ordinary psychologist or professor, staying in his narrow lane. Peterson not only is extraordinarily intelligent, but also widely learned. Listening to him is like wrapping your mind with a Paul Johnson history (*I cannot help but laugh at the remarkable coincidence, but I just happen to be re-reading Paul Johnson's book* Intellectuals, *a brilliant exposé on the hypocrisy of intellectuals who left their mark on the world: Jean-Jacque Rousseau, Shelley, Karl Marx, Henrick Ibsen, Tolstoy, Hemingway, Bertolt Brecht, Bertrand Russell, Jean-Paul Sartre, Edmund Wilson, Victor Gollancz, and Lillian Hellman*), an interdisciplinary, intercultural, time-traveling tapestry of transcendent themes and truths — where evolutionary biology, history, literature, philosophy, psychology, music, art, religions, culture and myth are all interwoven...for many individuals, he reconnects them with responsibility for their lives, giving them agency and purpose — and not just for themselves, but in the effect they will then have on the world around them. **Peterson is very insistent that each individual decision moves the entire world closer to either heaven or a bottomless hell. Because those aren't just theoretical places we may go to after we die, but apt descriptions of the worlds we create around us** (bold italics mine) ... But those who like orthodoxies that would limit the speech, ideas, and freedoms of others in order to enforce a social construction of their own should be afraid. Like the boy who had the courage to tell the emperor he had no clothes, or like Aleksandr Solzhenitsyn, whose

lone voice of truth helped topple a totalitarian empire, when this too crumbles, Jordan Peterson will be seen as the courageous catalyst that exposed the lies and made us a wiser people."

Bravo, Heather Higgins! But just what is this "impact" that Jordan Peterson is having with the moral imperative of his message? What's Jordan Peterson doing that's so effective?

Not an easy question to answer. Ironically, not even the good professor knows why he has attracted millions of viewers to his YouTube lectures and other platform and thousands of people to his book tour talks (which has now expanded from 60 to 100 cities, and which I'm sure will include even more cities as his message inflicts more souls with the immortal wonder of his message) and why his *12 Rules for Life: An Antidote to Chaos* has sold over a million copies and counting, which shot his *Maps of Meaning: The Architecture of Belief* to the Amazon bestseller list; but I believe I know the answer, and it has to do with what St. Padre Pio said about my writing **"opening the door to a new way of perceiving, a new way of thinking and understanding,"** which all boils down to what Emily Dickinson discerned to be our soul's greatest need, it's own identity, and which I explored in another one of my favorite spiritual musings long before I was called to write this story:

The Satisfaction of Doing,
and the Mystery of Soul-Making

Nothing pleases me more than that special feeling of goodness that comes from a satisfying piece of writing, like the spiritual musing that I was called to write on the natural process of soul-making through suffering, "The Tremor of Eternity," which revealed much more about the human soul than I could have wished for; but why was it so satisfying? That's the subject of today's spiritual musing…

Once I am blessed with an idea for a spiritual musing (or a poem or story), I never know where I'm going to find my point of entry. It may come unannounced through associative thinking, or unexpectedly in conversation, watching TV, or reading the weekend papers or a magazine; but more often than not, it takes me by surprise with serendipitous delight, like it did this morning when I came upon something that Virginia Woolf said in Lyndall Gordon's biography *Virginia Woolf, A Writer's Life*: "I have some restless searcher in me…Why is there not a discovery in life? Something one can lay one's hands on & say 'This is it?' I have a great & astonishing sense of something there."

This "great & astonishing sense of something there" that Virginia Woolf sensed was that same "tremor of eternity" that Svetlana Alexievich sensed in her oral histories of the Soviet people, the same secret that Ernest Hemingway sensed in Cezanne's paintings and sought to discover through his own writing, a secret that Hemingway felt only the poets had the gift of discerning, as John Keats did when he caught a glimpse of it in a letter to his brother that he titled "The Vale of Soul-Making."

"There may be intelligences or sparks of divinity in millions," wrote Keats, *"but they are not souls till they acquire identities, till each one is personally itself. Intelligences are atoms of perception—they know and they see and they are pure; in short, they are God. How then are Souls to be made? How then are these sparks which are God to have identity given unto them—so as even to possess a bliss peculiar to each one by individual existence? How but by the medium of a world like this?"*

When Virginia Woolf analysed the writer's life in a draft of her experimental novel *The Waves,* she remarked that there was "a certain inevitable disparity" between the public and private self, "between the outer & the inner." "The outer facts are there," writes her biographer Lyndall Gordon, "but only as a prop for the unfolding creative side." Which brought to mind Emily Dickinson's cryptic poem—

The props assist the house
Until the house is built,
And then the props withdraw—
And adequate, erect,
The house supports itself;

Ceasing to recollect
The augur and the carpenter.
Just such a retrospect
Hath the perfected life,
A past of plank and nail,
And slowness, —then the scaffolds drop—
Affirming it a soul.

A poetic description of conscious soul-making through life experience, and a light much too bright for the common eye! In her experimental novel *The Waves*, Virginia Woolf broke down what she knew of human nature into six ways, so as to analyse the composite and fuse her six characters into one ideal human specimen; but she failed, because she could not affirm her composite creation a soul.

As Lyndall Gordon tells us in her biography: "After *The Waves* was published she wrote to G. L. Lowes Dickinson: 'The six characters were supposed to be one. I'm getting old myself—I shall be fifty next year; and I come to feel more and more how difficult it is to collect myself into one Virginia," which brought to mind the Socratic principle of realizing one's true self through a life of virtue, of which he believed goodness to be the most noble, a principle that Socrates spelled out in Plato's Dialogue the *Phaedo*: *"And what is purification but the separation of the soul from the body, as I was saying before; the habit of soul gathering and collecting herself into herself, out of all the courses of the body **(by living a life of virtue)**; the dwelling in her own place alone, as in another life, so also, in this, as far as she can; the release of the soul from the chains of the body."* Which leads one to wonder, where was the moral factor in Virginia Woolf's experimental novel of self-integration? Was there even room for virtue in her arrogant, self-obsessed life?

Virginia Woolf failed to discover "it," that "great & astonishing sense of something there" that Socrates couched in his philosophy and which Cezanne and Hemingway sensed in art and Svetlana Alexievich sensed in the "tremor of eternity" in the human soul that in my quest for my true self I discovered to be the natural *enantiodromiac* dynamic of life that individuates the dual consciousness of our *being* and *non-being* (Woolf's "unfolding creative side" that Keats discerned to be the secret of soul-making through life experience); but Emily Dickinson ferreted out the **secret**

One Rule to Live By

way of life and shared it in her "letter to the world," which the world failed to discern. Even the eminent literary scholar professor Harold Bloom, who taught literature for more than half a century at Yale University, got headaches trying to decode the secret in Dickinson's poetry; but wise to the cruel ways of the world, Dickinson wrote—

Tell all the truth, but tell it slant,
Success in circuit lies,
Too bright for our infirm delight
The truth's superb surprise;

As lightening to the children eased
With explanation kind,
The truth must dazzle gradually
Or every man be blind.

That was my dilemma. And then I read Rumi. *"Tell it unveiled, the naked truth! The declaration's better than the secret,"* declared the mystic poet, and unabashedly I told the story of my quest for wholeness and completeness in my twin soul books *Death, the Final Frontier* and *The Merciful Law of Divine Synchronicity*, and I've been writing about the secret of soul-making in my spiritual musing for years, to the chagrin of my puzzled readers; so, what is this mysterious secret, and just how does it relate to that special feeling of goodness that I experienced writing my spiritual musing "The Tremor of Eternity"?

It's all about soul-making. That's what Svetlana Alexievich sensed in the "tremor of eternity" in the oppressed soul of the Soviet people. That's the purpose and meaning of life, the alchemy of soul-making through individual life experience; and not until one learns the art of *conscious* soul-making will one resolve the longing in their soul for wholeness and completeness.

Socrates couldn't help himself and couched the secret in his philosophy, but which ultimately got him tried and condemned for sedition and heresy by the aristocratic elite because they felt he was corrupting the youth of Athens; and Emily Dickinson concealed the secret in her poetry; and Rumi declared the secret in every ecstatic verse that poured out of him; and I resolved the mystery that haunted Virginia Woolf and Cezanne and Hemingway and professor Bloom and every soul destined to satisfy the deepest longing in their soul to be all they are meant to be, which Emily Dickinson spelled out in her riddling poem—

Adventure most unto itself
The Soul condemned to be;
Attended by a Single Hound—
Its own Identity.

We are all condemned to become ourselves, whole and complete—the "circumference" of our life, as Emily Dickinson defined the fullness of our being; but because the natural law of *enantiodromia* will not allow the evolutionary process of life to complete what we are meant to be, how then do we satisfy the deepest longing in our soul for wholeness and completeness?

This was my challenge when I set out on my quest for my true self more than half a century ago, and when I finally resolved the mystery it amused me to see that life *itself* was the solution to our existential dilemma that stumped the great creative thinkers of the world like Tolstoy, Dostoevsky, Nietzsche, Kierkegaard, Jean-Paul Sartre, and Albert Camus, to name but a select few; but I had to step so far outside the paradigm of man's *enantiodromiac* conundrum that I doubt anyone will believe me when I tell them that **the only way out of our paradoxical predicament is to simply be a good person.**

That's it. No messiah, guru, or Master. No religion. No philosophy. No science. No politics. Just being a good person resolves the paradox of our dual nature, because being a good person is the sum of all ways in life and makes our two selves into one. That's why I felt such a satisfying feeling of goodness when I wrote "The Tremor of Eternity," because when I brought my spiritual musing to resolution, I tasted the fruit of my own life-tree, and it was good. Bitter-sweet, to be sure; but all the more satisfying.

This is professor Jordan Peterson's inexplicable appeal. His hierophantic message of hope has taken the best of religion, science, and politics and rendered the wisdom of the ages into the simple shocking truth that there are no free rides in life. *"Sort yourself out, bucko,"* he admonishes the wayward young men who come to his book tour talks by the thousands, and then he lays his *Rule 6* on them: *"Set your house in perfect order before you criticize the world."*

Or, to quote from the *Book of Ecclesiastes*, the Preacher sums up the essential wisdom of Jordan Peterson's core message: *"...of making many books there is no end; and much study is a weariness of the flesh. Let us hear the conclusion of the whole matter: Fear God, and keep his commandments: for this is the whole duty of man. For God shall bring every work into judgement, with every secret thing, whether it be good, or whether it be evil."*

In short, life is all about soul-making; and soul-making is a personal responsibility, which is all the good professor is really saying....

30. A Little Corner of Joyful Plenitude

Sunday, June 10, 2018. Sitting on our shaded front deck. Sunny, warm, with the faintest of breezes to freshen the air, birds chirping and splashing in our bird bath in the shade of the maple tree, Penny sipping on a glass of red wine and I gently nursing a glass of sherry, just talking and smiling and laughing, enjoying each other like a newly retired couple (Penny is still working) *sans* the fear of the dreaded phone call that always seemed to come at the most inopportune time from one of our tenants renting a unit in our triplex in my hometown of Nipigon in Northwestern Ontario where Penny and I lived before moving to Georgian Bay fifteen years ago, and Penny said, "I'm glad we didn't go out today. This is much better."

    I had suggested we take a drive into Meaford, browse through *Factory Outlet* where we often find something to purchase, and then go out for a fish and chip dinner, but I was also glad we stayed home; and I had to express my joy, *"Isn't it wonderful? No more dreaded phone calls!"*

    We had just closed the deal on the sale of our triplex on *Tuesday, May 15,* two days after Penny's birthday, and she said: "It hasn't sunk in yet. I keep waiting for the dreaded phone call."

    I laughed. "It's like a ghost that keeps hanging around. But it's getting fainter and fainter by the day, like the life has been sucked out of it. Well, it can't haunt us any longer. Doesn't it feel wonderful to be free of all that hassle? Don't get me wrong, sweetheart. If it wasn't for our triplex, we wouldn't have our beautiful home here in Georgian Bay; but good God, it feels good not to be burdened with that responsibility anymore!"

    Penny smiled. Her face looked twenty years younger. "It's moments like this that nourish our soul," I said, full of love for the woman I had abandoned for my besotting lover in our past lifetime together in Genoa, Italy; but we found each other again in this lifetime, and I was almost but not quite free of my karmic obligation for breaking her heart the way I did in Italy, and it felt good. "You know, Penny Lynn," I said, taking in the moment, "we've carved out a nice little corner of joyful plenitude here, and it's all been worth it. I wouldn't trade this moment for the world."

I had gone into Midland earlier to pick up my *Sunday Star*, and I decided to drive to *No Frills* to pick up some pork and beef burgers to barbeque, which was the only grocery store that carried pork and beef burgers; but instead, I bought a package of Sirloin burgers that were on sale, and Penny went into the house to prepare a pasta salad to go with our burgers.

"How about corn?" she asked. I had also picked up four cobs of corn.

"Not for me. A burger and pasta salad will be plenty," I said, and went back to my reading.

Besides the *Toronto Star*, I had three books on the deck with me, reading a chapter from one and then another; my second reading of *12 Rules for Life*; *Great Short Works of Fyodor Dostoevsky*; and *On Pluto,* by retired journalist Greg O'Brien, whose account of his descent into Alzheimer's (inspired by Lisa Genova's novel *Still Alice*) was very hard reading; but I had to read it for my novel *Sundays with Sharon* that got interrupted when I got called to write *One Rule to Live By: Be Good*, and I was reading Dostoevsky to delve deeper into Jordan Peterson's psyche, because this Russian writer, whom Peterson can't stop praising, had an enormous influence on his thinking, even more than Nietzsche whom he referred to so often that I *had* to order some of Nietzsche's other books; but I couldn't stop thinking about what I had said to Penny earlier, how we had carved out a nice little corner of joyful plenitude for ourselves in our lovely new home in Tiny Township, Georgian Bay after our past and current life history that we were karmically fated to work out together.

I've written about our past life experience as man and wife in Genoa, Italy in my novel *Cathedral of My Past Lives*, but I haven't published it yet, and I honestly don't know when I'll get back to it because my muse keeps calling me to write other books, like *One Rule to Live By: Be Good* that beckoned me like a love-starved siren *(what dangers await me, I cannot say)*; but as I got back into *12 Rules for Life*, I couldn't help thinking of a spiritual musing I had written that was inspired by the Shirley MacLaine movie *The Last Word* that Penny and I had seen last summer, and I made the connection with Jordan Peterson's book because his *12 Rules for Life* prepares one for the final journey of one's life, the inner journey that Shirley MacLaine was on most of her life:

Still Ahead of Her Time

"So far I like this lifetime the best."
—*Shirley MacLaine*

In *Stupidity Is Not a Gift of God*, I wrote a spiritual musing called "A Cheap Shot at Shirley MacLaine," because I wanted to come to the defense of her belief in reincarnation which was ridiculed by the brilliant writer Ken Wilber whose Buddhist belief in reincarnation negated the "kooky" actress/writer's perspective, which I happened to share (we both believe in the autonomous, individual self; Buddhism doesn't); and upon reading a review of MacLaine's recent movie *The Last Word* in last weekend's *National Post* (*Saturday, March 11, 2017*), which Penny and I went to see in Barrie this weekend, I was strongly nudged to write another spiritual musing on Shirley MacLaine because of my admiration for her unflagging courage, a feisty independent thinker not afraid to speak her mind just like the role of Harriet Lauler that she played in the comedy-drama *The Last Word*.

Harriet/MacLaine (the role was written for Shirley) is a feisty eight-one-year-old retired very successful advertising executive whose failed attempt at suicide led her to re-examine her life, which by happy coincidence was sparked by the obit pages of the newspaper that she was using to sop up the wine she had spilled onto her dining room table in her second attempt at suicide as she was about to wash down another handful of Clonazepam before she accidentally tipped over her glass of wine.

In her attempt at suicide, the ER doctor questions whether taking a handful of Clonazepam with a bottle of red wine was really an accident, and Harriet, true to her brazen, take-no-prisoners personality, snapped back, "Yes, I was sleepy and I was thirsty." But as she read the obituaries in the newspaper she was using to sop up the wine she had spilled, she got a shocking glimpse into how she might be remembered when she died, which snapped her back into executive control mode; and taking charge of her life like she was accustomed to, she marched over to *The Bristol Gazette* office building and demanded the publisher to have their obit staff writer work out her obituary by interviewing the 100 people on the list she had drawn up because she wanted to see what they would have to say about her when she died.

Anne, the young obit writer (played by Amanda Seyfried), accepted her assignment with strong reservations (after meeting Harriet, Anne said, "She puts the bitch in obituary"); and she interviewed everyone on the list that she could get hold of and wrote up a draft of Harriet's obituary, but it proved unsatisfactory to the feisty Harriet Lauler.

Harriet didn't want to be remembered that way, so she embarked upon what proved to be the last adventure of her life—refashioning her image so she would be remembered for who she really was and not the person everyone took her to be, assigning Anne to rewrite her obituary in the process, and the result is an entertaining comedy-drama that called for several Kleenex tissues…

I've read most of Shirley MacLaine's books and seen many of her movies, and true to my conviction that a writer does not choose the books they write nor does an actor choose the roles they play, rather they choose the writer and the actor, I can't help but marvel at Shirley MacLaine's inordinately successful career as an actor/writer, because I believe she chose her current lifetime to expand the paradigm of social consciousness with her "kooky" view of the world that she realized while looking for herself.

"The truth is that no matter where I went, I was always looking for myself. The journey into myself as I evaluated my beliefs and values, whether living at home or in far-flung corners of the world, has been the most important journey of all. That journey is what led to my search to understand the true meaning of spirituality. I was learning that I was truly creating everything. I was learning to understand the character I had created as myself in the theater of life," said Shirley MacLaine in her tell-it-as-I-have-lived-it memoir *I'm Over All That and Other Confessions.*

Driven by the imperative of her essential nature to realize what C. G. Jung called "wholeness and singleness of self," at the age of eighty-two she may not have realized her goal to her satisfaction, but Shirley MacLaine is still true to her calling to find herself; which was why I had to see *The Last Word,* because the title of her latest movie (she was one of the executive producers) spoke to what I believe to be her most sagacious view on life and which Harriet/MacLaine passed on to the young staff writer who wrote up Harriet's new obituary which we get to hear at her funeral because Harriet Lauler does die of congenital heart failure, thus bringing *The Last Word* to a sad but satisfying closure.

The essence of Harriet/MacLaine's wisdom that she passed on to the young obit writer who kept a notebook of personal essays in her dream of becoming a real writer one day and who by the end of the movie is completely won over by the feisty octogenarian who challenged Anne's life premise, was for her to be true to herself, something that sounds like an shopworn cliché but which holds as much truth today as it did when Polonius uttered those famous words of advice to his son Laertes in Shakespeare's play *Hamlet*: **"This above all to thine own self be true, /And it must follow, as the night the day, /Thou canst not then be false to any man."**

That sums up Shirley MacLaine, a woman who risked her professional reputation for her belief in reincarnation and UFOs which labelled her "kooky" but which only confirmed that she was decades ahead of her time; and in her role as the uncompromising Harriet Lauler, I think Shirley MacLaine gets the last word, confirming my belief that the movie *The Last Word* chose her to play the role of Harriet Lauler and not her the role, and I honestly think I can hear Shirley MacLaine laughing.

There's not much about Jordan Peterson that bothers me, I too think he's "a deeply, deeply good man" with a mission to fulfill— *"What shall I do when the great crowd beckons?"* his Pen of Light asks; and his soul replies, *"Stand tall and utter my broken truths."* But in one of the many interviews that I saw of him, his casual dismissal of the New Age movement did rankle me a little. Not enough to taint my impression of the hierophant who was called by life to answer the angry question of my poem *What the Hell Is Going on Out There?*, but enough for me to comment.

Despite some of the obvious flakey elements of the New Age movement, which Oprah claimed Shirley MacLaine helped launch by being so open about her belief in past lives and UFOs *(but which she refused to take credit for)*, the New Age movement helped to open the way for our final journey through life that Dr. Peterson never seriously entertained because it would have risked his reputation as a professor of psychology and clinical therapist; and if he did take his thought processes that far, which I don't think he did for propriety's sake, he might have embarked upon a different path altogether. As it is, I *know* that he has been called to the final journey of his life—*because the great crowd did beckon him to stand tall and utter his broken truths to the world*, which he is doing with inexhaustible fervor on his ever-expanding global book tour.

But, as he tells us in *12 Rules for Life*, he's yet to cross the great divide, which may be why he never responded to the books I sent him that spell out how I found my way through the eye of the needle and crossed the great divide to satisfy the longing in my soul for wholeness and completeness; but I'm only guessing.

He could have thought that I was just another flake like "kooky" Shirley MacLaine, or maybe he was just too busy to even bother, especially now that he's so popular.

I don't doubt that the good professor skirted around the edges of the New Age movement, because he's such a deep and passionate thinker he would have had to look into it purely for academic reasons; but not until one has been thoroughly "cooked" by life, as the Sufis say, will one be called to step out of their recurring cycle of karma and reincarnation and into the final stage of divine reconciliation, as "kooky" Shirley MacLaine was called and shared with the world with her incredible life story, which is why I admire her for being so forthright about her quest for her true self.

And that's what I find so ironic about Jordan Peterson, because I *know* he's ready to step outside his safe academic paradigm of evolution and into the final stage of self-fulfillment, like our hero G. G. Jung did, which he brilliantly worked out in his psychology of individuation. For whatever personal reason, Dr. Jordan Peterson cannot make this commitment. He's got one foot in and one foot out, and that's what's excited the phenomenal interest in the hierophantic message of his *12 Rules for Life: An Antidote to Chaos* that he's delivering to spiritually famished crowds around the world with a post-haste imperative that could easily be mistaken for messianic fervor...

31. Nietzsche, Dostoevsky, and Solzhenitsyn

In Chapter 18 of my most intimate memoir *The Pearl of Great Price*, "The Dust on a Butterfly's Wings," I wrote: "Stories bear the truth of the human condition, and the human condition is the story of our becoming; but not until we solve the riddle of our becoming will literature resolve the issue of the human condition. This makes literature endlessly fascinating, because every writer speaks to their place in the *enantiodromiac* process of man's becoming, which Jung called "individuation," and in their stories they stake out the geography of man's soul, whether it be the happy country of one's *being*, the unhappy country of one's *non-being*, or that miserable place of being stuck between two countries—the no-man's land of one's soul." The writers Nietzsche, Dostoevsky, and Solzhenitsyn staked out the geography of their soul in their writing, and with such passionate intensity that their work will resonate throughout the ages; this is why the young seeker Jordan Peterson was attracted to their writing, because he too was staking out the geography of his own soul.

In *Maps of Meaning: The Architecture of Belief*, he recalls his youthful crises of faith, concluding that religion was for the ignorant, weak, and superstitious. "I stopped attending church and joined the modern world," he wrote, and he turned to socialism and became active in the New Democratic Party of Canada and got his first degree in political science where he sought an explanation for "the general social and political insanity and evil of the world."

But socialism came out cravenly wanting. This was the Cold War era, and student Peterson was preoccupied by the possibility of nuclear annihilation, which *literally* gave him nightmares, and he concluded that the question was a psychological one; so, he sought psychological answers and earned a PhD from McGill University and became a clinical psychologist and a professor of psychology, first at Harvard and then at the University of Toronto.

In his quest for an answer to "the general social and political insanity and evil of the world," he discovered Nietzsche, Dostoevsky, and Solzhenitsyn—and G. G. Jung, of course, who became his guiding light and abiding hero (*Jung's intelligence was "bloody terrifying,"* said Peterson); and he studied these authors with such commitment that one could almost call it pathological. I know that feeling well from my own need to find an answer to my haunting question, *who am I?* Like he said, he was "obsessed" in his quest for an answer to his question; but why did these authors have such an attraction for the budding professor and clinical psychologist? What set them apart from the rest of the literary world? What was *their* truth that set young Jordan Peterson's soul on fire?

The answer can be found in the sacred mystery of story, the archetypal imperative of one's soul that seeks out meaning and wholeness through individual life experience, just as I pointed to in a spiritual musing that I posted on my Spiritual Musings blog *November 11, 2017*, because every person's story bears witness to the sacred mystery of their own *becoming*:

The Power of Story

The idea for today's spiritual musing hovered above my head like a heavy rain cloud waiting for the right atmospheric conditions to set its refreshing life-giving moisture free, and the right conditions came with the natural daily addition of more thoughts and insights that added to the specific gravity of the idea of my spiritual musing, the simple idea of story.

Penny and I were having coffee in my writing room early one morning, as we always do, and she put the book she was reading down and said to me, "This is boring. I'm tired of reading this kind of stuff. I'd rather read a good story instead—"

One Rule to Live By

She was reading Robert Moss's book, *The Boy Who Died and Came Back, Adventures of a Dream Archaeologist in the Multiverse*, an autobiographical account of his near-death and dream experiences which I had read, along with four or five of Robert Moss's other books, my favorite being *Conscious Dreaming*.

"Why?" I asked, intrigued by the abruptness of her comment, as though she had just had her fill of that kind of literature. "Why would you prefer a good story instead?"

"Because I get more out of a good story than this stuff. I don't know what it is, but I just can't read these kinds of books any more. I like your writing. It doesn't bore me like this stuff, but I'd rather read your stories instead. I get much more out of a good story."

That did it. The cloud burst and the idea for today's spiritual musing on story possessed me with a *daemonic* imperative, and I *had* to explore it…

I had just finished writing *My Writing Life, Reflections on My High School Hero and Literary Mentor Ernest "Papa" Hemingway*, an unexpected sequel to *The Lion that Swallowed Hemingway*, unexpected because the call to write this sequel came with a surprise Christmas gift of an *Indigo Hemingway Notebook* from Penny's sister which called me back to creative writing that I kept putting off for one reason or another, like my book of short stories *Sparkles in the Mist*, my novel *The Waking Dream* (in which Carl Jung actually came to me in a dream to talk about "the alpha and omega of the self" and also to discuss my book *The Way of Soul*, which was published on the inner planes because Jung was holding it in his hands but was not yet published out here), my novel *An Atheist, An Agnostic, and Me*, an allegorical novel called *The Gadfly*, my novel *St. Paul's Conceit* (my sequel to *Jesus Wears Dockers*), and several other works that were still waiting to be re-worked and polished; so Penny's comment hit home, because I could no longer hold back what I had come to realize about story upon completing my new memoir *My Writing Life*.

I love Hemingway more for his short stories than his novels, but story is story, and a short story simply concentrates the teleological imperative of the human condition much more succinctly than a novel; that's why I was called back to my high school hero and literary mentor with my sequel to *The Lion that Swallowed Hemingway*, because I could no longer put off writing the stories that have been calling me for years. But not until Penny's comment about her preference for reading a good story over those other kinds of books, of which my library shelves are burdened, did I finally get the message; and before I jump in with both feet and commit to creative writing, I have to explore the power of story in today's musing…

    I tried one more time to draw Penny out, but she could not express why she got more satisfaction out of reading a good story than from those other kinds of books that Robert Moss and Carolyn Myss and Neale Donald Walsh and Thomas Moore and Gary Zukav and Dr. Wayne Dyer and Deepak Chopra and kindred inner-directed truth-seeking people have written, and I have no choice but to abandon to my muse to explore the allure of story in today's spiritual musing; but I fear this may be a dangerous spiritual musing.

    A dangerous spiritual musing dares to say the unsayable, and I hate being called to explore an idea that I know with intuitive certainty will take me beyond the edge of thought, because it will defy logic; but such is the nature of story, whose aesthetic imperative is to nourish the soul and resolve the paradox of man's dual nature. That's the danger, because how can one expect anyone to believe that man is simultaneously both real and false, that he is and is not what he is, a walking, talking paradoxical creature?

    It took me a lifetime to resolve the paradoxical nature of the dual consciousness of man, the *being* and *non-being* of our individuating reflective self, which has been the central theme of all my writing; but it wasn't until Penny, in her exasperation with Robert Moss's *The Boy Who Died and Came Back*, blurted out that she got more out of reading a good story than those other kinds of books did it dawn on me why; and as simple as it may be, she got more out of reading a good story because **story has the power to resolve the paradoxical nature of man's dual self that those other kinds of books can only point to.**

    That's a big statement. Big enough to explore in a whole book, which curiously enough I've already done in books like *The Lion that Swallowed Hemingway, Gurdjieff Was Wrong, But His Teaching*

One Rule to Live By

Works, and especially in my book *The Pearl of Great Price*; so, I need not explore it in today's musing. My point is to explain what Penny meant by saying that she got more out of reading a good story than she did out of those other kinds of books; so, just what is it about story that satisfies this longing in one's soul for—*what?* Just what is it exactly that a good story satisfies, if not personal resolution of one's paradoxical nature?

That's the epiphany that came to me when Penny said she got more out of reading a good story than those other kinds of books that she now found boring; but just what did she mean by those other kinds of books, anyway? And why cannot they satisfy that longing in one's soul for resolution of one's real and false nature, soul's longing for meaning and wholeness? What's missing in those other kinds of books?

I've been reading those other kinds of books my whole life, ever since I was called to find my true self by Somerset Maugham's novel *The Razor's Edge* more than half a century ago, and if I were to define what Penny meant by those other kinds of books I'd have to say inner-directed books, books that address the author's own journey of self-discovery, books like *The Seven Storey Mountain* by the Trappist monk Thomas Merton, Shirley MacLaine's *Sage-ing While Age-ing*, Victor Frankl's remarkable *Man's Search for Meaning*, C. G. Jung's even more remarkable "*confrontation with the unconscious*" that he chronicled in *The Red Book* and teases us with in his remarkable memoir *Memories, Dreams, Reflections,* and the incredible personal memoir *Proof of Heaven,* by Doctor Eben Alexander.

The marketplace is flooded with those other kinds of books, with new ones coming out every time someone feels compelled to tell their "amazing" story of self-discovery, which often translate into self-help books of spiritual awakening, each person's story being but another path to one's true self little realizing that all ways lead to Rome eventually (I'm still waiting for Shirley MacLaine's next book just to see how far her journey of self-discovery has taken her); and that's the gist of today's spiritual musing—the simple truth that **every person's own life is the way to the resolution of one's dual nature,**

one's personal path to wholeness and completeness. That's the power of story that Penny intuited…

"But they all serve their purpose," I replied to her, coming to the defense of all those other kinds of books which, incidentally, I love to read. "Those books point to the *way*, each according to the author's personal journey of self-discovery; like Moss's book *The Boy Who Died and Came Back*. But I guess when you've read enough of these books, they can get boring," I added, assenting to Penny's literary ennui.

"Well they bore me now. My next book's going to be a good story," she said, and when she finished reading Moss's book (Penny is stubborn and will finish every book she starts, including Joyce's *Ulysses* which she called "a conglomeration of words") she came into my writing room for our morning coffee with June Callwood's *Twelve Weeks In Spring*, ("…*the inspiring story of how a group of people came together to help a friend, and in doing so discovered their own unexpected strength and humanity*"), which she found on one of my shelves and which, ironically, bridged those other kinds of books to what Penny called a good story with the heart-wrenching story of sixty-eight year old Margaret Fraser's death by cancer which she did not have to face alone because her writer friend June Callwood and a group of friends helped see her through to the end; but I have not shared this irony with Penny yet. I'll wait until she finishes reading *Twelve Weeks in Spring* first; then I can share with her why a good story can be so satisfying.

The irony of course is that life itself is the *way* to one's real self; and by *way*, I mean the natural individuation process of man's paradoxical real and false nature—which makes every story, whether it be biographical or fictional, one's personal *way* to wholeness and completeness, the only difference being that a good story satisfies soul's longing for resolution much more than those other kinds of books that only point to resolution, because **a good story nourishes the reader with "meaning," that special energy that soul needs for growth and self-fulfillment.** That's why when I pressed Penny again to explain why she got more out of reading a good story than those other kinds of books, she thought for a moment and then replied (and the emphasis is mine): **"A good story pulls me in, and I experience the story as I'm reading it. Those other kinds of books don't do that for me. They only scratch the surface."**

"That's because a good story is about *becoming*, which is the divine imperative of man's existence," I responded. "You experience your own *becoming* as you're reading a good story, and this nourishes your soul's longing for meaning and wholeness. This is why you find good stories more satisfying."

"Much more satisfying than those other kinds of books," Penny said, with a note of triumph in her voice, thus bringing closure to today's spiritual musing.

So, without going into detail; suffice to say that Jordan Peterson's fascination with Nietzsche, Dostoevsky, and Solzhenitsyn can be found in the unique individual story of these heroic souls, their own personal way to resolving the dual consciousness of their paradoxical nature, the *being* and *non-being* of their reflective self-consciousness, because their commitment to self-resolution was all-or-nothing for them, just as mine was when I vowed to find my true self or die trying, and just as Jordan Peterson's was in his own obsessive quest for an answer to "the general social and political insanity and evil of the world," But just what was it about Nietzsche, Dostoevsky, and Solzhenitsyn that touched the soul of so many readers, especially budding clinical psychologist Jordan Peterson? What made their personal story so different that they influenced world thinking?

Nietzsche unleashed the archetypal spirit of nihilism with his death-of-God philosophy in his most biblical book, *Thus Spoke Zarathustra*, a terrifying intellectual justification for the spiritually vacuous ethos of moral relativism; Dostoevsky opened the gates of hell with his do-or-die inquiry into good and evil, especially with his most famous novel *Crime and Punishment* that terrorized the soul with the premise that if God did not exist everything was possible; and Solzhenitsyn dared to point the finger at himself for the evil of the world, a moral responsibility that helped bring down the Soviet empire, beginning with his novel *One Day in the Life of Ivan Denisovich* and ending with his monumental *The Gulag Archipelago*, which pointed to the sacred individual self and spiritual liberation through moral accountability; this is why their writing will resonate throughout history, because they speak to the haunting mystery of the purpose and meaning of our existence.

But still, that doesn't explain the power of their personal story; and the only way I can ever explain why young seeker and budding psychologist Jordan Peterson was so fascinated with Nietzsche, Dostoevsky, and Solzhenitsyn would be to explain the *enantiodromiac* process of our becoming; or, what Jesus referred to as the making of our two selves into one.

Gurdjieff had a saying that reflects the premise of his teaching: *"Happy is the man who has a chair to sit on, happy is a man who has no chair to sit on; but woe to the man who stands between two chairs."* This is a working metaphor. "Chair" stands for man's soul, and Gurdjieff is saying that a man who is born with a soul is happy (because he doesn't have to go through the torment of creating it); a man who has no soul is happy also (because he is blissfully unaware of the torment he will have to go through to create it); but a man who stands between two chairs is in the throes of creating his own soul, and this is the worst kind of suffering that one will ever experience in this world, to which I bear witness with my story *Gurdjieff Was Wrong, But His Teaching Work,* and even more poignantly in my most intimate memoir *The Pearl of Great Price.* This is how I gave birth to the meanest saying of my life, *"The shortest way to God is through hell."* So, the question is this: where do Nietzsche, Dostoevsky, and Solzhenitsyn stand in Gurdjieff's metaphor of the soul?

Gurdjieff was categorically wrong in his premise that not everyone is born with an immortal soul but can create one if they know how *(which he did; this is why he attracted so many followers, especially writers and artists, myself included; I stood in terror between the two chairs of my being and non-being and Gurdjieff's teaching saved me)*; but I've already explored this in *Gurdjieff Was Wrong, But His Teaching Works*. Suffice to say that his metaphor holds true regardless, because making the two selves of our *being* and *non-being* into one self is what the final journey through life is all about; and Nietzsche, Dostoevsky, and Solzhenitsyn were called to the final journey of their life, the journey to wholeness and completeness, and their story speaks to their journey of self-discovery—Nietzsche's story, which speaks with Zarathustrian bombast to the desolate geography of man's *non-being* but which ultimately drove him insane because he got stuck in his *non-being* and failed to resolve the paradox of his real and false self, leading the world down the garden path with his paralytic philosophy of eternal recurrence; Dostoevsky's story, which speaks with creative genius to his unbearable anguish of standing between two chairs and in the treacherous throes of making his two selves into one, a monumentally heroic effort that he never got to resolve before dying, but inspiring the world with his efforts that he poured into his stories, like his iconic novel The Brothers Karamazov; and Solzhenitsyn's story, which speaks to the most heroic effort of the three writers, because he came closest to resolving the paradox of his *being* and *non-being* by assuming moral responsibility for his own evil that helped support the totalitarian regime responsible for the death of millions of people. Three great writers that spoke to soul's journey through life, each endeavoring to resolve the existential predicament of the human condition and leaving their heroic legacy to the world. That's why western-boy Jordan Peterson, who's stuck in the tumultuous throes of creating his own soul, stands tall between his two chairs like Gary Cooper in High Noon, was so fascinated with the creative genius of Nietzsche, Dostoevsky, and Solzhenitsyn; they provided him with a road map for his own journey of self-discovery, which he shared with the world in his own epic story *Maps of Meaning:*

The Architecture of Belief first, and then with his reader-friendly, but tendentious soul-making *12 Rules for Life: An Antidote to Chaos* that continues to take the world by storm...

32. Dr. Peterson's Jungian Gift to the World

> "I have, I believe, known many of those the world considered great,
> but Carl Gustave Jung is almost the only one
> of whose greatness I am certain."
>
> *Jung and the Story of Our Time*
> —Laurens van der Post

 I *knew* from day one why professor Peterson was called by life to answer the angry question of my poem *What the Hell Is Going on Out There?*, which spoke for me and the collective unconscious of society, but I had to let my muse work it out as I wrote *One Rule to Live By: Be Good* and make conscious what I had intuited; and the more I got into my story, the more it became clear to me that there was a void in the soul of man that religion, science and politics could not fill, and professor Peterson was called to help fill this void with his studied maps of meaning, and so desperate was the void in man's soul to be filled with meaning that his book *12 Rules for Life: An Antidote to Chaos* became an overnight sensation, with thousands of wayward young men flocking to his book tour lectures to hear his soul-piercing hierophantic message of hope, like his talk in Sydney, Australia where it took four and a half hours for Jordan Peterson to sign his book for the audience.

 But I had to wonder, what was it about his fiery message that attracted so many young men to his book tour talks? And as I wondered, a spiritual musing that I had posted on my blog *Saturday, July 15, 2017* came to mind, and I *knew* why—**because the imperative of Jordan Peterson's message inflicted these young men with an immortal wound of wonder:**

Wounded with Wonder

Orest Stocco

Three years ago I wrote *The Lion that Swallowed Hemingway*, a literary memoir that I thought would bring resolution to my lifelong fascination with Ernest Hemingway who called me to writing in high school; but apparently I wasn't done with him yet, because on *March 1, 2017* I was called to write a sequel, which I completed three months and one week later on *June 7, 2017,* a very private journal called *My Writing Life, Reflections on My High School Hero and Literary Mentor Ernest "Papa" Hemingway,* and now I'd like to write a spiritual musing on my unique literary experience…

In *A Woman Looking at Men Looking at Women*, the novelist/essayist Siri Hustvedt explores the question of where authors get their ideas in an essay called "Why One Story and Not Another?" And the conclusion she came to, as tentative as it may be because it seems to her that nothing is ever conclusive when it comes to the body-psyche relationship, was that "there are clearly unconscious processes that precede the idea, that are at work before it becomes conscious, work that is done subliminally in a way that resembles both remembering and dreaming," further adding: "I argue that a core bodily, affective, timeless self is the ground of the narrative, temporal self, of autobiographical memory, and of fiction and that the secret of creativity lies not in the so-called higher cognitive processes, but in the dreamlike configurations of emotional meanings that take place unconsciously" (*A Woman Looking at Men Looking at Women,* by Siri Hustvedt, pp. 388-9). And I don't disagree with her reasoning, but with qualifications.

But why one story and not another? Why was I called to write *The Lion that Swallowed Hemingway* and then a sequel three years later? Why did the idea for my literary memoirs come to me when they did, and with such a compelling need to write them?

"Every good novel is written because it has to be written. The need to tell it is compelling," writes Siri Hustvedt; but this can be said of any genre, be it novels, short stories, poetry, plays, memoirs, or personal essays like my spiritual musings: when an idea comes to me, depending upon the urgency of the need to give it expression, the compulsion is determined, and my compulsion to write *The Lion that Swallowed Hemingway* possessed me with such *daemonic* intensity that I HAD to write it just to get it out of my system, just as I was compelled to write the sequel *My Writing Life*.

But why? Why was I possessed by the idea to write these books? Siri Hustvedt is a novelist and essayist with cross-disciplinary interests, and her compulsion to write possesses her as it does every writer who is called to their art; and herein lies the mystery—in the *call* to one's life-path, whether it be writing, art, or whatever life-path, which speaks to the individual imperative of one's destined purpose…

Over coffee the other morning, Penny and I got into a discussion on this mystery of being called to one's life-path, because it was my conviction (drawn from years of being possessed by ideas that had to be given expression through novels, short stories, poetry, memoirs, and spiritual musings, not to mention the countless books that I felt *compelled* to read in my quest to find my true self that spoke to this issue) that to be called is to be ready to begin the journey of self-reconciliation, and to Penny's disconcertment, I said to her: "Not everyone is called to their life-path. I was called to writing in high school by Hemingway, but my call to writing was supplanted by a higher calling to become a seeker when I read Maugham's novel *The Razor's Edge* in grade twelve; but I was ready to be called. Not everyone is ready—"

"I don't agree," Penny jumped in, contending that every person is on their own path no less than any writer, artist, doctor, or whatever the discipline; and I spent the next twenty minutes of our coffee time before she had to get ready for work explaining that a call to one's life-path presupposes many lifetimes of experience in one's calling. "It took many lifetimes for Mozart to become Mozart, and the same with Albert Einstein. Reincarnational memory and genetics work together. This is the mystery of being called," I explained, which just happened to be the preoccupying theme of *My Writing Life* that I had just completed; but Penny still couldn't see it, which is why I was called to write today's spiritual musing…

My fascination with Ernest Hemingway called me to writing in the early grades of high school, but in grade twelve our English teacher assigned our class to read Maugham's novel *The Razor's*

Edge, and so moved was I by Maugham's hero Larry Darrell's quest for the meaning and purpose of life that I was inflicted with what professor Harold Bloom called an "immortal wound" which set my soul on fire, a wound of wonder that supplanted my call to writing and launched me on my quest for my true self; and I devoted my best and most creative energies to my quest until I found "the most precious treasure in the world," which I finally wrote about several years ago in my most intimate memoir, *The Pearl of Great Price.*

Despite my call to find my true self, I never gave up on writing, and whatever energies I had left over from earning my daily living (I started my own contract painting business after I left university where my quest had taken me), plus desperately seeking my true self (the "pearl of great price") by "working" on myself daily with Gurdjieff's teaching, and all the reading that I was called to do, I spent on writing; and my fascination with Hemingway grew in proportion to what he taught me about the craft. He was my high school hero because he called me to writing, and he became my literary mentor because I never stopped learning from him; but my quest for my true self initiated me into the sacred mysteries of the **secret way of life** that parted the veil that shrouds poetry and literature, and my two callings became one purpose.

So I owed a debt to Hemingway who called me to writing, and I owed a debt to Somerset Maugham whose novel *The Razor's Edge* inflicted me with an immortal wound of wonder; and though I thought I had resolved my obligation to my high school hero and literary mentor with *The Lion that Swallowed Hemingway* (in which I did my level best to shed light on his paradoxical personality), I wasn't done with him yet, nor had I even addressed my debt to Somerset Maugham for writing *The Razor's Edge* that set my soul on fire; that's why I was called back to Hemingway when I received an *Indigo Hemingway Notebook* for Christmas from Penny's sister three years after I had written *The Lion that Swallowed Hemingway,* and I HAD to write *My Writing Life* to resolve my debt to these two great writers who affected the course of my life.

I would never have parted the veil that shrouds poetry and literature had I not found my true self, but the quest for the "pearl of great price" opens up pathways to one's destined purpose; and in my journey of self-discovery, so many pathways opened up to me that I finally came to see the archetypal pattern of every soul's journey through life, which is to realize one's own individual identity.

Jesus called this final stage of soul's journey through life being born again, but this is much too abstruse for today's scientifically-minded world, and the only way to convey the gnostic wisdom of the **secret way of life** would be through what Jung called "the process of individuation," the natural course of soul's evolution to wholeness and completeness, as Emily Dickinson intuited in one of her poems—

> Adventure most unto itself
> The Soul condemned to be;
> Attended by a Single Hound—
> Its own Identity.

Somerset Maugham's novel launched me on my quest for my true self; and in my quest, I discovered the **secret way** to the most precious treasure in the world, the **secret way of self-reconciliation**. Jesus called it making our two selves into one, our inner and outer self that psychologists call our *essence* and *personality*, philosophers call our *being* and *non-being*, and mystics and poets call our *real* and *false self*, which was a price much too dear for the shadow-afflicted Ernest "Papa" Hemingway to pay, and way beyond the reach of William Somerset Maugham who did not even believe in God or the immortal soul and afterlife; that's why I had to write a sequel to *The Lion that Swallowed Hemingway*. I had to thank them both by telling the incredible story of my successful journey of self-discovery to show my gratitude for the influence they both had on me with the tragic story of their own unresolved journey through life.

This is the mystery that shrouds poetry and literature, the incomprehensible journey of self-discovery that we are all **condemned** to complete by the archetypal imperative of our *essential* nature, a journey that takes us through one lifetime to the next until we are made ready by life to take evolution into our own hands and complete what Nature cannot finish; only then will we be called to the path that will initiate us into the sacred mystery of our own individual identity...

I finally got Penny to see that a call to one's path is a call to one's own life, but a life that has evolved in its *essential* nature through karma and reincarnation and is ready to begin its journey of self-reconciliation; and it doesn't matter what path one is called to— be it religion, art, medicine, psychology, politics or whatever; that's the path that one has earned over the course of many lifetimes of natural evolution, the path of self-reconciliation that Socrates referred to as "soul gathering and collecting herself into herself."

"As each plant grows from a seed and becomes in the end an oak tree, so man must become what he is meant to be. He ought to get there, but most get stuck," said Jung, and we all get stuck despite our best efforts. Hemingway got so stuck in his shadow-afflicted personality that he blew his brains out with his favorite shotgun because he lost his reason for living *(he had to have life on his own terms or not at all!),* and Somerset Maugham got so mired in the soul-denying hedonism of his ego-driven personality that he got tired of life altogether and just wanted to fade away into oblivion; but I prefer Emily Dickinson's poetic perspective over Jung's metaphor of the acorn seed, because it's closer to the mark, and a little more hopeful.

We are all **condemned** to become our true self, said the prescient poet (an assurance that Jung can only promise with his psychology of individuation), and getting there is what life is all about. That's what I tried to say in *The Lion that Swallowed Hemingway,* and what I tried to bring to resolution in my sequel, *My Writing Life,* thus satisfying my call to write these two very personal memoirs.

And that's why my oracle *beckoned* me to send professor Peterson my four memoirs that personally delineated the **secret way of self-reconciliation**, *The Lion that Swallowed Hemingway* and *The Pearl of Great Price* three years before he became a public figure, and *My Writing Life* and *The Merciful Law of Divine Synchronicity* when he was unexpectedly catapulted onto the world stage with his overnight bestseller *12 Rules for Life: An*

Antidote to Chaos; but explaining why he has attracted so many followers, predominantly young men looking for meaning and purpose (Peterson is uneasy about calling them "followers," but he can't come up with another word that would make him risk-free of being labelled "prophet" or "guru"—or "Pied Piper" even, which he smiles at but hates) is next to impossible to do, because who has the omniscience to factor in all the variables? Peterson is a mixed bag of tricks; but, essentially, he wants to make the world a better place.

But I know from my own journey of self-discovery that a message that sets one's soul on fire with an immortal wound of wonder has to bear the Logos, the redemptive power of Holy Spirit that Jesus called the *way* but which I simple refer to as *the omniscient guiding principle of life*; and Jordan Peterson's message, which he spells out with vernacular ease in his *12 Rules for Life: An Antidote to Chaos*, is so fraught with the Logos that it has the redemptive power to connect one with their destined purpose of becoming what they are meant to be—just as Jung intuited in his own journey of self-discovery; and this is Dr. Peterson's Jungian gift to the world, the gift of reconnecting one with their life story, their inner path to wholeness and completeness in what they are meant to be...

In *Jung and the Story of Our Time*, Jung's respected and admiring friend Laurens van der Post reveals what I believe to be one of Jung's most important discoveries, if not *the* most important discovery of his long and unbelievably productive career as a healer of souls (Claire Dunne called her biography *Carl Jung: Wounded Healer of the Soul*, because Jung had to suffer the cleansing fire of making the dual natures of his inner and outer self into one for the "wholeness and singleness of self" that he finally achieved), Jung's remarkable discovery that every person has their own personal story to wholeness and completeness that can be so interrupted that they end up needing help, as Jung discovered in the Burgholzli mental hospital in Zurich where he began his career:

> "Jung came to the conclusion that *every human being had a story, or to put it in its most evolved form, a myth of its own*...Jung said that he learned from the start how in every disturbance of the personality, even in its most extreme psychotic form of schizophrenia, or dementia praecox as it was then called, one could discern the elements of a personal story. *That story was the personality's most precious possession, whether it knew that or not,* and the person could only be cured—or healed, as he put it...by the psychiatrist getting hold of the story. That was the secret key to unlock the door which barred reality in all its dimensions within and without from entering the personality and transforming it. More, he held that *the story not only contained an account of the peculiar hurt, rejection, or trauma, as other men were hastening to call it, but the potential of wholesome development of the personality*. The arrest of the personality in one profound unconscious timeless moment of itself called psychosis, he would tell me, occurred because the development of the person's own story had been interrupted, however varied, individual, and numerous the cause of the interruption. All movement of the spirit and sense of beginning and end had been taken away from it and the story...suddenly stood still" (*Jung and the Story of Our Time*, by Laurens van der Post, pp.118, 119, 120; bold italics mine).

Out of his ten-year internship at the Burgholzli mental hospital under the tutelage of Dr. Bleuler, to whom he was greatly indebted "for the encouragement he gave him as a young man and for the example he set of total respect for his vocation as a psychiatrist," Jung grew in his compassionate understanding and deep respect for the archetypal story that ensouled every person, like the case of "a comparatively young woman" who had been sent to the asylum as "insane beyond redemption." But after considerable effort, Jung got her to tell him one of her dreams.

"From that moment on, the dreaming process in her and the interchange between them accelerated and intensified," wrote Laurens van der Post. She progressed so well that Jung was prepared to let her back out into the world to resume her life story, which had been interrupted for reasons we may never know. And on the morning of her release, Dr. Jung asked her, "Did you by any chance dream again last night?"

"Yes, I did," she answered; paused, and then added, "And it's no use badgering me, because for once I'm not going to tell you what it was."

"I cannot tell you how moved I was," Jung told his friend Laurens van der Post. "I could have wept with joy because you see at last the dream, the story, was her own again. And at once I discharged her."

Dr. Jordan Peterson is a clinical psychologist with twenty years of experience helping clients reconnect with their story that got interrupted—a betrayal that led to a bitter divorce; intolerable working conditions beset with radical political correctness; crippling depression; agoraphobia; a devouring mother who could not let go of her daughter; whatever trauma brought them to him, Dr. Peterson did his honor best to help them reconnect with the imperative of their interrupted story to personal wholeness, just as he had learned from the "wounded healer" who beckoned the budding psychologist to take up "the study of comparative mythological material" that connected him with his own story and "cured" him of his apocalyptic nightmares (a cure he tells us in *Maps of Meaning* that was "purchased at the price of complete and often painful transformation"); that's why his hierophantic message has inflicted the souls of countless followers with an immortal wound of wonder that set their soul on fire, like the young man who waited in line for four hours in Sydney, Australia just to meet the "great man" who changed his life by following his online lectures for three years before meeting him to sign his book *12 Rules for Life: An Antidote to Chaos*.

"I had to look him in the eyes and thank him for what he did for me," said the young man from Brisbane, who finally secured a ticket to his sold-out second lecture in Sydney; and he was only one out of the countless grateful benefactors that our modern day hierophant reconnected with the imperative of their inner self with his no-nonsense message of self-reconciliation by taking responsibility, both moral and practical, for their own life—*a providential, Solzhenitsynian-inspired imperative that makes the good professor so proud that he literally chokes up with tears whenever young men tell him how he has helped them get their life together...*

33. Message from the Woodpecker

> "Synchronistic events urge upon us a view of the world as a unified field in which one's own experiences and actions are fundamentally connected to the experiences and actions of others."
>
> *Synchronicity and the Stories of Our Lives*
> —Robert H. Hopcke

When something out of the ordinary happens in our day, it means that life is trying to get our attention. Life uses the anomalous experience to tell us something we need to know to further and deepen our understanding of whatever it is that needs our attention (this is why I call the symbolic language of life *the omniscient guiding principle of life*), like the odd experience I had the other morning when I was working on my chapter "Dr. Peterson's Jungian Gift to the World"—*I needed to see the deeper implications of my chapter that my creative unconscious made manifest.*

It's not uncommon for me to hear a woodpecker pecking on a tree in our front yard, as I just did this morning when I began this chapter; but the other morning the pecking was so different and persistent that I had to look out my window to see what it was all about.

I looked at the usual trees, but I couldn't spot where the pecking was coming from; and then, to my surprise and wonder, I saw a large woodpecker with a red patch on its head perched on the window ledge of the driver's door of our Honda Civic parked in our driveway just below my writing room above our double garage, hanging on as if for dear life but so fascinated by the image it saw of itself in the car door mirror and its reflection in the car window that it was fixated on what it saw, and it pecked the mirror out of position (as Penny learned later when she got into the car to go to work); and I stared at the woodpecker glancing from the mirror to the window, back and forth, pecking at its own image and not pecking, totally bewildered.

"*If that isn't a symbol, nothing is!*" I said to myself, and broke into a mirthful chuckle; and I watched the woodpecker as its neck frantically turned from mirror to window, pecking and staring at its reflection until it got fed up and flew off onto the trunk of the nearest tree, which happened to be the big oak that shades our front deck where I do a lot of reading, and then it flew off.

I have a book by Steven D. Farmer, PhD, a shamanic practitioner, ordained minister, licensed psychotherapist, and former college professor with over thirty years experience as a professional healer and teacher, and whenever Penny and I have an anomalous experience with one of nature's creatures we check out his book to see what the symbolic meaning of their appearance might mean; so, I took out *Animal Spirit Guides* and looked up woodpecker:

"If WOODPECKER shows up, it means: ***A storm is brewing, either literally or metaphorically; but have faith, as you are protected no matter what***. It's a good time to do some drumming and/or rattling, whether on your own or with a group of friends. ***You're entering into a time of abundance and plenty.*** Go to a place of Nature and lie on your back *on the ground, breathe slowly and steadily, and see if you can feel Mother Earth's heartbeat.* ***Pay particular attention to your own cycles and rhythms and do your best to honor them by aligning yourself with them, rather than being contrary to them***" (*Animal Spirit Guides,* by Steven D. Farmer, Ph. D., p. 405, bold italics mine).

I shared my experience with Penny when she came into my room for her morning coffee; and as we talked, we set free what the language of life was trying to tell me with its message from the woodpecker. (*I'm amazed at how often our morning conversations have connected dots that I would never have seen, proving for me over and over again the miracle of the Logos in honest conversation!)* "It has to be telling me something about the chapter I'm working on," I said, baffled by the message.

"What's your chapter about?" Penny asked.

"Essentially, it's about how Jordan Peterson's message has connected thousands of his young followers with their own life story. Peterson is following in Jung's footsteps, because Jung was the first to discover that we all have a life story that drives us to become what we are meant to be; but most of us get stuck. Jung helped people get unstuck, and that's what Jordan Peterson is doing with his message to the world. That's why he was called by life."

"How does one get stuck?" Penny asked, cutting to the quick.

"Debilitating life traumas, like losing one's job or a bitter divorce. But basically, too much shadow," I answered, with no need to explain further because she was more than familiar with my work (Penny edits and proofs and formats my books for publication on Lulu). "That's the problem with our crazy world today, too much shadow—*THAT'S IT!*" I exclaimed, suddenly catching the meaning of the woodpecker's message.

"What?" Penny asked, startled by my epiphany.

"*That's the message! The woodpecker was puzzled by its own reflection!*" I said, totally awakened to the message now. "The woodpecker didn't know that its reflection was him—or her, as the case may be; and neither does the world know its own reflection. That's what Carl Jung brought to our attention, and now Jordan Peterson is doing the same with his message to the world. I've got a quote in one of my synchronicity books that speaks to this, which I can look up later; but do you remember the spiritual musing that I wrote on the bread maker we got from Tony last summer?"

"Wasn't that something?" Penny said, with a big smile. "Why?"

"That's just how life works for us, sweetheart," I replied, with a chuckle. "When we need something, life comes to our assistance. We needed a new bread maker, and life provided. And don't forget the inner voice that told you to go to the casino; not once, but two or three times. We needed money for unexpected expenses, and life provided. God, life is mysterious. Well, I couldn't see the deeper implications of the chapter I was working on, so life sent me a woodpecker to inform me. That's why it behaved so strangely."

"What was the woodpecker's message?" Penny, in all her innocence, asked.

"It's all about self-reconciliation," I replied; but I didn't want to explain further until I had finished writing my chapter on Dr. Peterson's Jungian gift to the world, because my high school hero and literary mentor had taught me to never talk about something you're going to write about because it will lose its magic, like a butterfly losing the dust on its wings.

But just to make the point about how *the merciful law of divine synchronicity* works in our life (and everyone's life for that matter, even if they aren't aware of it), let me quote the spiritual musing that I wrote on our remarkable new bread maker coincidence that I posted on my Spiritual Musings blog Saturday, September 30, 2017:

The Bread Maker Coincidence, and Sharon's Comeuppance

In our house, we call her Sharon. She's Murphy's nasty sister, the Murphy of "Murphy's Law." As I joked with our neighbors one day when they walked over with a glass of wine to join us on our deck, "If you think Murphy's bad, wait until you meet his sister Sharon. She's ten times worse than her brother."

Murphy's Law states that if anything can go wrong, it will; and to make the point with our neighbors that our life had really been thrown off kilter the past few weeks, starting with the stupid accident I got into with our Honda Civic, which I explored in my spiritual musing "The Old Trickster," I had to kick Murphy's Law up a notch; that's how his nasty sister Sharon came into being.

Well, Sharon struck again this past week, following in her brother footsteps, starting with the leak in Goober's new tank. Goober is our goldfish, which we brought with us when Penny and I moved to Georgian Bay fourteen years ago, so Goober is old as goldfish go; and Penny got Goober a new tank a few months ago at Walmart in Wasaga Beach, regretting that she did not get the larger tank which was only a few dollars more; and then our bread maker died the other day when I put on dough for pizza; and the following morning our coffee maker sputtered in that familiar way that coffee makers do when they're about to give up the ghost; so, we had to replace all three items, and Penny and I went shopping Sunday in Midland after we treated ourselves to a late breakfast at *Captain Ken's* in Penetanguishene.

Penny had gone on Amazon to check out bread makers, so she had a good idea of what she wanted; but there wasn't much selection at *Canadian Tire* in Midland, and what they did have were too pricey for our budget; so, we went to Walmart and came home with a larger tank for Goober and new coffee maker but no bread maker, and Penny decided to order one from Amazon. But when we got home, Murphy's nasty sister stepped in when the garage door wouldn't open when I pressed the remote control affixed to the sun visor of the car. I tried several times, and when I went in to check I saw that the screws holding the bracket attached to the automatic door-opening track had ripped loose and had to be re-screwed, which I had done twice already, and this final indignity was like a slap in the face; but strangely enough, this set into motion *the merciful law of divine synchronicity*, and Sharon's comeuppance…

I love coincidences. I look forward to them every day, and I'm always tickled with joy when they happen because you cannot plan a coincidence. Like Murphy's Law and his nasty sister Sharon's Revenge, coincidences have a mind of their own, and they only happen for a good reason; and that's what I'd like to explore in today's spiritual musing.

Because I've been engaged with the synchronicity principle most of my life, which was fully realized when *the merciful law of divine synchronicity* brought me to a street in Tiny Township, Georgian Bay, named after me, STOCCO CIRCLE *(my surname is Stocco; and finding a building lot on this street proved to be the most remarkable coincidence of my entire life, which I hope to write about in a story whose ironic title my muse has already provided, "We May be Tiny, But We're Not Small")* where Penny and I built our new home fourteen years ago, I'm not surprised when the dots for a new spiritual musing begin to connect, because that's how the synchronicity principle works in the service of soul's imperative for wholeness and completeness, and something that Zen poet Jane Hirshfield said about her relationship to poetry in Bill Moyers book *Fooling with Words, A Celebration of Poets and Their Craft,* caught my attention the other morning when I felt "nudged" to read Moyers book again; and as I always do when something speaks to me, I highlighted the passage: **"Sometimes I think that poems use us in order to think, to do their own work,"** said Jane Hirshfield. **"You know, most of the time I feel as if I am in the service of the poem—a poem isn't something I make, it's something I serve."**

And herein lies the mystery of the synchronicity principle that Jane Hirshfield failed to see, that not only is she in the service of her poetry, but that the spirit of poetry, what I call "it" in the poem I wrote that she inspired, serves her no less than she serves the spirit of poetry, *the omniscient guiding principle of life* that serves every soul in their destined journey through life—

JANE, ZEN, AND POETRY

She almost has "it" but does not quite
know it; another experience, another
poem, another nanometer closer to "it."
Something she said gave her away:
"Most of the time I feel as if I am
in service of the poem," but not until
she sees that "it" is in equal service
to her will she have "it" and be
whole and complete.

One Rule to Live By

Being a writer *compelled* to write, I *know* what Jane Hirshfield meant by saying that sometimes she feels like she is in the service of her poems, because when I'm called to write a poem I often do not know what the poem wants to say, thus affirming Hirshfield's insight that our poems do our thinking for us (as do my spiritual musings, but with less mystifying imagery); but what is the poet serving if not one's own destined purpose to wholeness and completeness?

A poem shines a light upon one's path, making one's way easier because it brings one's outer journey into harmony with one's destined purpose to wholeness and completeness, and **coincidences are life's way of confirming the natural harmonization process of inevitable self-reconciliation**; but what does this have to do with Murphy's Law and Sharon's Revenge?

Aye, there's the rub; because life has a way of throwing a monkey wrench into the gears of our life. But how can we expect our life to run smoothly all the time when there are built-in faults and obsolescence into the human condition?

If something can go wrong, it will; and our bread maker had to wear out eventually, as did our coffee maker, so why be surprised when they do? We didn't expect our fish tank to spring a leak so soon after our purchase, though; but the fatigue-factor built into everything eventually catches up to us, and our tank sprung a leak because the fault was in the assembly, thus affirming Murphy's Law that if anything can go wrong, it will. And our bread and coffee makers had a limited life span, so there shouldn't have been any surprise there either. But because these items gave up their ghost in such close temporal proximity to each other (the superstition of three "bad" things happening in a row), we attach some kind of nefarious meaning to their occurrence. But there's nothing sinister about built-in defects and obsolescence; that's just the way life is.

And as to our garage door, the final indignity, I should have seen it coming because I knew that the metal of the door was too thin for the screws to hold indefinitely (a manufacturing fault), which was why I decided that this time I would fasten a ¾ 6 x 12 inch piece of plywood to the door to fasten the screws that held the bracket attached to the automatic track; but I didn't have a piece of plywood, and I was going to walk over to my neighbor Tony's place later because I knew he would have it, as well as the screws; *and that's when the remarkable coincidence with the bread maker happened...*

Penny went for a walk around STOCCO CIRCLE after we brought our new fish tank and coffee maker and other sundries into the house, and I sat on the front deck to read my *Sunday Star* just to pause and catch my breath; but when Penny came back from her walk, she said: "Tony's home. He's out in his garage."

"I'll go over and see if he has a piece of plywood and some screws," I said, and Penny went into the house. But unbeknown to me, while I was talking with Tony in his garage Penny had gone online to select and order a new bread maker from Amazon.

I rode my bike to Tony's and saw him standing by his work bench studying something that was making a funny but familiar sound. I greeted Tony and asked what he was doing, and he told me he was trying to figure out what that unit he was studying was.

"That's a bread maker," I said, "and it's supposed to work like that." Tony had the unit plugged in but thought that it was malfunctioning because the little paddle that kneaded the bread dough wasn't revolving as he thought it should; it pulsed, revolving interruptedly.

Tony was cleaning out his garage and back-yard shed and old lawn chairs and other collectables from under his back deck that had been there for years and loading everything onto his trailer and then he was going to make a trip to the dump, that's why he was checking out that appliance which just happened to be a perfectly good bread maker that an Italian lady for whom he had done a small job had given to him a few years ago, and he was going to throw it away because he didn't know what to do with it.

"It works just fine, Tony," I said. "Maybe Maria can use it?"

A widow also, Maria was Tony's second life companion (his first was an alcoholic and didn't' work out); but Maria was old fashioned, and she kneaded her dough by hand, that's why Tony offered it to me, and I was strongly "nudged" to leave my bike and carry the bread maker over to our house after quickly telling Tony why I had come over. He did have a piece of plywood and screws, but

One Rule to Live By

I wanted to surprise Penny first with the remarkable coincidence of the bread maker that Tony had just given me.

Penny was in her office upstairs, and as soon as I walked into the house, I shouted up to her: "Have you ordered the break maker yet?"

"I'm just about to," she said.

"Well don't!" I shouted. *"Come on down here. I got a bread maker from Tony!"*

Penny couldn't believe the coincidence. She had just taken her Master card out and was about to order the new bread maker when I shouted up to her not to, and after giving the bread maker (which was a higher end model called *Bread Chef*) a thorough cleaning, she put on a batch of dough to make fresh buns for dinner; and while she was doing that, I went back to Tony's and explained my garage door problem, and being such a good neighbor Tony walked over with me and sized up the problem, and together we got the automatic garage door opener working properly (plus another little job), and then we sat on the front deck and had a nice cold beer, and that's how Sharon got her comeuppance.

As ironic as it may be, in the woodpecker's message I saw how the archetypal shadow of our crazy modern world of nihilism and confusion was getting its comeuppance with professor Jordan Peterson's no-nonsense message of self-reconciliation that he was called upon by life to give to the world through his global bestseller *12 Rules for Life: An Antidote to Chaos* and book tour talks throughout North America, Europe, and Australia, which sparked such an interest in his ponderous tome *Maps of Meaning: The Architecture of Belief* that it spiked up to the Amazon bestseller list; and when the woodpecker's message finally sunk in, something that I had read in David Richo's book, *The Power of Coincidence: How Life Shows Us What We Need to Know*, came to mind, and I went to the assigned shelf for my synchronicity books in my writing room to look it up:

> "Perhaps all is happening in life just as we intend. Then suddenly we meet someone, or find out something, or have an accident, or hit bottom and our world spins in a new direction that ultimately makes all the difference. ***Those unexpected events beyond our control are the forces of synchronicity that make us who we are—and who we were meant to be.***
> "Synchronicity is a mind-boggling and sometimes eerie rendezvous between the world and our inner selves. ***Something happens in the external world and it fits exactly with what we need right now, showing that our human nature and mother nature are two sides of the same coin.*** In nature, each season produces just the conditions that the ecology and the earth require for its evolutionary growth. Likewise, in ***our human story, we keep finding just what we require so we can evolve as psychologically healthy and spiritually aware beings. Synchronicity comes to us as an assisting force in this evolution. We are helped in finding ourselves and we help others find themselves.*** Thus, synchronicity contributes to the joyous fulfillment of our personal destiny in an always luminous world that longs for more light" (*The Power of Coincidence*, by David Richo, Ph.D., p. 2, bold italics mind).

Was it a coincidence that professor Peterson stepped up to the plate to defend free speech and was instantly catapulted onto the world stage with his book *12 Rules for Life: An Antidote to Chaos,* and was he called by life to answer the angry question of my poem that I wrote the year before which spoke for myself and the collective unconscious of the world?

"What the hell is going on out there?" I asked, and professor Peterson provided an answer that satisfied my desperate need to know, and not only my need to know, but the collective need of the world to know what the hell was going on out there; hence the overwhelming attention that he was getting with his book and talks and online lectures, because, as my oracle informed me in my spiritual musing, __coincidences are life's way of confirming the natural harmonization process of inevitable self-reconciliation,__ and it had to be one of the most meaningful coincidences I had ever witnessed for professor

Peterson's book to be called *Maps of Meaning: The Architecture of Belief*, which provided maps of meaning for an answer to the angry question of my *inspired* poem.

But professor Peterson stirred the pot with his hierophantic message of self-reconciliation in his shadow-shocking, character-building overnight bestseller, and a wicked intellectual storm was brewing in social consciousness, beginning with the Cathy Newman interview, and it's not about to stop. I've just learned that his 60-city book tour has expanded to include more cities, and his talks are really stirring the pot of social consciousness, which speaks to the message the woodpecker gave me with its strange behavior; and as difficult as it may be to believe, here's what I believe is happening with the Jordan Peterson phenomenon that's taking the world by storm.

My poem shouted loud and clear that religion, science and politics have failed to satisfy our need to know what the hell was going on in the world, and so unbearable was our need to know that the oracle of life *had* to provide an answer, just as David Richo intuited: **"Something happens in the external world and it fits exactly with what we need right now, showing that our human nature and mother nature are two sides of the same coin."**

So, along came professor Jordan Peterson to satisfy our desperate need to know what the hell was going on out there with his profoundly studied maps of meaning that he brilliantly rendered into his reader-friendly overnight bestseller *12 Rules for Life: An Antidote to Chaos*; but what is it that the world so desperately needed to know? That's the puzzling question.

Every seed must become what it's meant to be, said Carl Jung; but one doesn't need Jung to see the obvious. A tomato seed cannot become an oak tree, and neither can an apple seed become a donkey; every seed must be true to its own nature, and this is the mystery that Jordan Peterson's message speaks to—the divine seed of our *essential* nature that is sown in this world to grow and evolve in its own identity; which is why the core of

Peterson's message is the sanctity of the individual self that has been so wickedly abused by the soul-sucking nihilistic forces of our crazy modern world that life *had* to step in to redress the spiritually oppressive imbalance.

"As each plant grows from a seed and becomes in the end an oak tree, so man must become what he is meant to be. He ought to get there, but most get stuck," said Jung (I know, I keep quoting this; but it does sum up the essential wisdom of the individuation process); but why do most of us get stuck? That's the real issue of the human predicament. Must take pause...

Drawing upon the gnostic wisdom of *Ecclesiastes*, imagine a great river of individual souls flowing through life and then coming upon a dam that impedes its flow (*"Vanity of vanities, saith the Preacher, vanity of vanities; all is vanity. What profit hath a man of all his labor which he taketh under the sun?"*), and the river backs up and backs up and creates an immense ocean of frustrated souls longing to continue on their way to wholeness and completeness but cannot because the impenetrable dam of the collective vanity of the world holds them back, and religion, science and politics cannot open the floodgates and let them free to continue on their destined journey; and as metaphorical as this may be, this is the sad reality of the human predicament.

But some exceptional souls do manage to get free and continue on their destined journey, great souls like Carl Gustav Jung; and in their compassion for humanity, these great souls inform us on how to continue our own destined journey to wholeness and completeness. And as presumptuous as it may seem, I *know* that professor Jordan Peterson also found a way to continue on his destined journey, and in his compassion for his fellow man he was also *compelled* by his own imperative to share the gnostic wisdom of his own individual *way*, the same wisdom of self-reconciliation that all cultures throughout history have been teaching in their myths and secret teachings that professor

One Rule to Live By

Peterson ferreted out in his *Maps of Meaning* that he rendered into *12 Rules for Life,* and what we have to reconcile is our *existential* outer self with our *essential* inner self, because this is the only way we can become what we are meant to be; but we can never reconcile our outer self with our inner self until we become aware of our own shadow, the repressed dark side of our ego personality.

The woodpecker saw its own reflection in our car mirror and window, but it didn't know that it was its own reflection that it saw; and the message that the oracle of life gave me with the woodpecker's odd behavior was that our crazy modern world can see its archetypal false shadow self everywhere (the *Toronto Star* Washington bureau chief Daniel Dale fact-checked president Trump's tweets and utterances and found 1,075 falsehoods in the first 365 days of his administration, proof positive of Trump's false shadow self) but cannot recognize its own false self. That's why Jung said that it takes great moral courage to see our own shadow; which is what keeps us from getting past the impervious dam of our own vanity on our destined journey to wholeness and completeness.

And this is what the oracle of life was telling me with the woodpecker's strange behavior. We can see our shadow like the woodpecker saw its own reflection, but we don't know that it's our own false self that we're looking at just like the woodpecker did not know that it was seeing its own reflection in the car mirror and window—*the mote in the other person's eye, said Jesus.*

That's why Aleksandr Solzhenitsyn became professor Peterson's hero, because he had the moral courage and spiritual fortitude to look at his own life-lie and do something about it, as did Jordan Peterson who chronicled his own experience in *Maps of Meaning* which he distilled into *12 Rules for Life* that's taking the world by storm and slated to be translated into 40 languages.

Solzhenitsyn chronicled his experience in the Soviet Gulag and garnered the Nobel Prize for Literature, which helped bring down the Soviet empire that was founded upon the Great Lie of a utopian fantasy; and not unlike his Russian hero, professor Peterson's iconoclastic message of hope through responsible self-reconciliation poses such a threat to the archetypal shadow self of our crazy modern world of moral relativism, identity politics, and political correctness gone loony that he's created a firestorm of soul-wrenching self-reflection with his disarming country-boy honesty and uncanny scholarly wisdom, and the world has taken notice. And if the second part of the woodpecker's message augurs true, according to the shamanic wisdom of *Animal Spirit Guides*, we will be "entering into a time of abundance and plenty." I sincerely hope so...

34. Taking a Hiatus from Writing this Summer

> "The most essential gift for a good writer is a built-in, shockproof shit detector."
> —Ernest Hemingway

"Set your house in perfect order before you criticize the world," said professor Peterson in *Rule 6* of his *12 Rules for Life: An Antidote to Chaos*, and though I may not have my metaphorical house in as perfect order as I long for it to be, I work on myself daily; but I do have house-responsibilities that I have neglected for years, starting with painting the house which I began last summer but never got to finish, and some health issues to attend to (dental work, losing some weight, and, despite my heart condition, try to get into better shape). And I have a stack of books that I have to read before I can bring this story home; so, I'm going to take a hiatus from writing this summer and just do some editing and tightening, and probably write the odd musing now and then, because when my oracle calls for a spiritual musing I *have* to write it. They expand the horizons of my individual *way*. And as for criticizing the world, I'll leave that for my muse to work out...

Penny went to work yesterday morning (she's a Hallmark rep), and after she did her work at her Collingwood stores, she was "nudged" to go the Georgian Downs casino in Innisfil, just south of Barrie. Three separate times, Penny heard a voice within speak to her. *"Go to the casino,"* it said, and she went and won over three thousand dollars twice and nine hundred another time; but now she only gets strong "nudges" every now and then, and she never tells me when she goes.

The casino gods were good to her once again, and she came home with another win (eight hundred dollars this time) which totally surprised me, because last week she was also "nudged" to go to the casino and won enough for the purchase of a new mattress and box spring for our spare bedroom that she kept putting off. Out of curiosity, she had gone online to see which stores in Barrie offered the best deal, and she settled on *Mike the Mattress Guy*, which, coincidentally, was on Mapleview Drive on her way to the Georgian Downs casino in Innisfil.

"*Hi Mike,*" she said, with a wave of her hand on her way to the casino. "*Maybe I'll see you on the way back.*" Which she did, and they delivered the mattress and box spring two days later, with no delivery charges; so, it came as another surprise when she pulled into the driveway yesterday afternoon with another I-can't-believe-it smile on her face.

"I got you some gravity money," she said, and handed me four hundred dollars. "Half for you and half for me," she added, with a beaming smile. And then she went to the car and came back with a box of books that I had ordered from Amazon. "I said to myself on the way home, wouldn't it be nice if O's books came in today?" she said (O is my nickname). "They weren't supposed to come in till tomorrow, but I thought I'd check the mailbox just to see. Now you have your gravity money and new books to read. It's been a good day for the O and Penny Lynn, wouldn't you say?"

"Our little corner of joyful plenitude just keeps getting better and better," I said, with a tear in my eye; and I got up and kissed her.

"Gravity money" is a concept I came up with twenty-some years ago, drawn from my belief in "The Matthew Principle" (taken from Christ's Parable of the Sower, Matthew. 13: 12: "*For whosoever hath, to him shall be given; and he shall have more abundance...*"), which can simply be expressed as **like attracts like,** or **much gathers more,** and I make a point of carrying three or four hundred dollars of gravity money in my wallet, not just for emergencies, but because I believe in the spiritual law of attraction (*The Secret*, a best-selling book by Rhonda Byrne that was also made into a movie, was based on the law of attraction);

and, coincidentally, Penny had just asked me the day before she was "nudged" to go to the casino again how my gravity money was holding out, and I told her that I had to dig into my gravity money the last few times I went into Midland to pick up my weekend papers and groceries. I had overspent our weekly grocery money and had to dip into my gravity money; and, as "luck" would have it, yesterday Penny replenished my gravity money when she came home from the casino because I was down to forty dollars. *Go figure!*

But I did distill her experiences of going to the casino for my book of poetry, *Not My Circus, Not My Monkeys*, a riddling poem *a la* Emily Dickinson, just to pique my readers' curiosity with how the omniscient guiding principle of the **secret way of life** works in our life:

God Within

Flat, existential plane
of life and limb,
toiling, toiling, toiling
for profit unseen.
One day a voice speaks
from within:
"Go to the casino,"
and all the profit
that she wins
goes to life and limb,
and the voice confirms
God within.

Professor Peterson's *Maps of Meaning: The Architecture of Belief* (over 500 larger-than-normal pages and in smaller type) had arrived the week before from Amazon.ca, which was where I had to order it from because Amazon.com did not have it, and I was well into it already (it's not the easy read that *12 Rules for Life* is and it demands close attention), and the box from Amazon.com that Penny brought home along with her casino winnings contained the books that I felt compelled to read this summer because I had to digest the authors that had such a powerful influence on Jordan Peterson's journey of self-discovery: *The Will to Power,* by Friedrich Nietzsche. *Basic Writings of Nietzsche,* edited and translated by Walter Kaufman, which included: *The Birth of Tragedy, Seventy-five Aphorisms from Five Volumes, Beyond Good and Evil, On the Genealogy of Morals; The Case of Wagner,* and *Ecce Homo;* Fyodor Dostoevsky's novels *Demons* and *The Idiot,* plus *Great Short Works of Fyodor Dostoevsky,* which included: *Notes from Underground, The Gambler, A Disgraceful Affair; The Eternal Husband, The Double, White Nights, A Gentle Creature,* and *The Dream of a Ridiculous Man;* a collection of stories called *Great Short Works of Leo Tolstoy,* which included: *The Death of Ivan Ilych, The Cossack,; Family Happiness, The Devil, The Kreutzer Sonata, Master and Man, Father Sergius, Hadji Murad,* and *Alyosha the Pot*; and of course, *The Gulag Archipelago,* abridged version, authorized by the author Aleksandr Solzhenitsyn; plus a book strongly recommended by professor Peterson which I did not have in my personal library on C. G. Jung: *The Origins and History of Consciousness,* by Erich Neuman, with a forward by Jung. An impossible amount of reading for one summer, but I hope to read what I can just to be true to my mentor's literary credo that credits his iceberg theory with leaving out of a story only what the writer knows from experience, which gives the story it's emotional impact. As Hemingway explained his iceberg theory of writing to George Plimpton for the *Paris Review,* speaking about his novel *The Old Man and the Sea*:

> "I've seen the marlin mate and know about that. So I leave that out. I've seen a school (or pod) of more than fifty sperm whales in that same stretch of water and once harpooned one nearly sixty feet in length and lost him. So I left that out. All the stories I know from the fishing village I leave out. But the knowledge is what makes the underwater part of the iceberg." (*Ernest Hemingway on Writing,* edited by Larry W. Phillips, *from* GEORGE

One Rule to Live By

PLIMPTON, "An interview with Ernest Hemingway, *The Paris Review 18*, Spring 1958).

I've already read something by all of these authors (except for Eric Neuman), but not enough to give my Peterson-inspired story *One Rule to Live By: Be Good* all the literary gravitas that it deserves for maximum emotional impact on the reader—*as if the incredible story of my own journey of self-discovery doesn't have enough existential (and spiritual) density!*

But reading more Tolstoy, Nietzsche, Dostoevsky, and Solzhenitsyn will deepen my consciousness of the unbearable anguish of their existential predicament (and Jordan Peterson's, whose plight in the "creation" of his own soul moves me to tears, both of joy and sadness), which will then be "implied," as Hemingway believed, in *One Rule to Live By: Be Good* and speak more impactfully to the resolution of the existential predicament of our crazy modern world that professor Peterson has addressed with beguiling honesty in *12 Rules for Life: An Antidote to Chaos.*

But if I don't finish reading all of these books before I get back to *One Rule to Live By: Be Good* in the fall *(which I seriously doubt)*, I'll finish reading them whenever I can. After all, who's to say just how much gnostic gravitas a book needs to win a reader's confidence?

Until the leaves turn color, then...

35. The Great Choreographer of Life

We're into September and the leaves are beginning to turn color, but we're back from our little getaway in Northwestern, Ontario where we visited Penny's family and old friends, and my muse beckons; so, I'm going to jump right into my story with a divinely choreographed experience that I had in the Lakehead, because it bears direct relevance to *One Rule to Live By: Be Good* that will help bring the imperative of Jordan Peterson's *12 Rules for Life: An Antidote to Chaos*, which can only take one so far on their journey to wholeness and completeness, to resolution.

I did an enormous amount of reading this summer. Not as much as I had hoped, but I managed to read professor Peterson's ponderous *Maps of Meaning* and enough Tolstoy, Nietzsche, Dostoevsky, and Solzhenitsyn to get into their psyche (as well as a few chapters of Erich Neumann's book); and this gave me a much greater appreciation for Jordan Peterson's obsession with these authors.

I had to read the Preface to *Maps of Meaning; The Architecture of Belief* twice before I caught the gist of Peterson's evolving thesis (**"Personal interest—subjective meaning—reveals itself at the juncture of explored and unexplored territory, and is indicative of participation in the process that ensures continued healthy individual and societal adaptation,"** he wrote in his Preface, a thematic overview of his "maps of meaning" that he rendered into *12 Rules for Life: An Antidote to Chaos*), and it wasn't until I plodded through the first and was well into the second chapter that I finally caught the logic of his thinking, a scholarly but creative dialectic that espouses the wisdom of evolutionary biology, neuroscience, mythology, psychology, religion, philosophy, literature, and his own life experience; and from then on it was like reading a mystery thriller, because with every chapter professor Peterson "mapped" out the polyphonic meaning of the human condition with the brilliance of a Sherlock Holmes, connecting disparate clues to create a picture large enough and clear enough to justify the presumptuous title of his book, and when he brought *Maps of Meaning; The Architecture of Belief* to resolution (as far as he could take it, that is) with a quotation from the *Gnostic Gospel of Thomas*, which contains some of the most secret sayings of Jesus, I *knew* precisely why I had been called to write *One Rule to Live By: Be Good*, because the secret sayings of Jesus were the "key" to solving the final mystery of the human condition. **"Whoever finds the interpretation of these sayings will not taste death,"** said Jesus in the *Gospel of Thomas*, which is what the good professor leaves us with—*the sacred mystery of realizing our essential, divine nature!*

Not only did *Maps of Meaning; The Architecture of Belief* explain the wisdom of his reader-friendly shadow-dismantling, soul-making second book *12 Rules for Life: An Antidote to Chaos*, it answered my nagging question: why was I *compelled* to send him *The Lion that Swallowed Hemingway* and *The Pearl of Great Price* three years before he came into public prominence, and *My Writing Life* and *The Merciful Law of Divine Synchronicity* shortly after he stepped onto the world stage with his overnight bestseller *12 Rules for Life: An Antidote to Chaos*?

I had no choice, really; because I was no less beholding to the same divine imperative that compelled the Sufi poet Jalal ad-Din Rumi to do his own oracle's bidding *("Tell it unveiled, the naked truth! The declaration's better than the secret")*, because where Jordan Peterson's journey of self-discovery left off, my story began; and professor Peterson *had* to hear what I had to say, because I was obligated by the law of the *way*, as is every soul that passes through the eye of the needle...

Not long after I experienced my spiritual rebirth in my mother's kitchen that summer day while she was kneading bread dough on the kitchen table, I had another momentous experience which engendered one of the most remarkable coincidences of my life, or anyone's life for that matter.

In a dream one night, I met the spiritual teacher of an ancient spiritual teaching that I had just begun studying. I didn't want to call him my Spiritual Master because I had a very bad taste in my mouth for Spiritual Masters after my experience with an offshoot Christian solar cult teaching that did irreparable damage to my eyesight, so I said to him, "What do I call you?"

He smiled; then he put his arm around my shoulder and slowly turned me around, and as I turned, I found myself staring into the Face of God. So overwhelming was God's love that I could not contain myself and exclaimed, twice in rapid succession as if I couldn't get it out fast enough, "I LOVE YOU GOD! I LOVE YOU GOD!" And I woke up in a daze of absolute wonder.

It took two years before I made the connection between my question to my teacher on the inner and the answer that he gave me by letting me look into the Face of God, and I smiled when I made the connection that he was a God-realized soul, and looking into the Face of God was his answer to my question "What do I call you?" Which gave me a gnostic understanding of what Jesus meant when he said, "I and my Father are one." That was my initiation into the mystery of Jesus.

But time fades all memories; and ten or twelve years after I had this experience, I began to doubt that it had actually happened. And that's when I experienced the remarkable coincidence that symbolically confirmed my ineffable experience of looking into the Face of God.

It was Sunday morning, a bright, crisp sunny spring day, and I went for my usual weekend run along the shoreline of Lake Helen on Highway 11, several miles from home. I parked my car where I often parked it, across the highway from St. Sylvester's Historic Mission Church where I had volunteered five or six weeks of my time one summer, painting and stuccoing with half a dozen other volunteers from the Lake Helen Reserve just down the road

One Rule to Live By

(it was their church), and I did a few stretching exercises and bounded down the highway, with the doubt of my experience of looking into the face of God fresh on my mind. "Did I really look into the Face of God?" I kept asking myself.

But as I ran, the run took over, as it always did when I got into the zone, and my mind had no time to think about anything because the run itself became its own experience, and I let everything go and just let the experience of the run wash over me; but about three miles down the highway, I spotted a small flock of Canada geese by the familiar uprooted weather-worn old pine tree on the sandy shore in the curb in the road, and I stopped to take in the spectacle; but for some reason, as I took in the huddling geese the thought came to me, "Wouldn't it be something if there were thirty birds?"

I smiled at the thought of the Sufi allegory *Conference of the Birds,* because if there were thirty birds there, looking like they had just flown from a very long journey, it would symbolically confirm that I had looked into the Face of God; and with bated breath, I began counting.

One, two, three, four, all the way to twenty-five and no more; and my heart sank. I counted again just to be sure, and to my surprise two more waddled out from behind the tangle of roots, and there were twenty-seven now, three birds short of confirmation, and my heart sank even deeper.

But ever the optimist, I jumped onto the guard rail for a better view, and I could see them all now, some waddling and the rest stationary, and I counted twenty-nine, one short of the confirmation I desperately needed, and I felt mortally wounded. But I had to be absolutely certain, so I counted again, and again, and once more hoping for a miracle; but there were definitely twenty-nine birds and no more, and I jumped off the guard rail and sprinted down the highway, dejected and disillusioned.

But not more than thirty or forty yards down the highway and it hit me like a bolt of lightning—***I'M THE THIRTIETH BIRD!***" And I had my symbolic confirmation! My doubt left my *mind, and I never again doubted my experience of looking into the Face of God.*

12 Rules for Life: An Antidote to Chaos was the good professor's naked truth, forged in the smithy of his own purpose-driven life (working three hours a day for fifteen years to write *Maps of Meaning*, plus years of lecturing on his research material and practical wisdom garnered from his clinical practice), and as incredible as some of his "connections" were *(like his lobster thesis that has become a meme for his message and has since sprouted into a cottage industry with the lobster logo printed on T-shirts, coffee cups, and other memorabilia)* that helped him resolve the puzzle of the human condition, his wisdom rang so true to me that it wrenched my heart to see that he had gone as far as his brilliant mind could take him to wholeness and completeness, but not through the eye of the needle, which was why I felt *compelled* to send him *The Pearl of Great Price* to read three years before he was even called to give his iconoclastic message of hope to the world.

"Again, the kingdom of heaven is like unto a merchant man, seeking goodly pearls. Who, when he had found one pearl of great price, went and sold all that he had, and bought it," said Jesus (Matthew 13: 45-46); but not until one has broken the code of Christ's sayings will one apprehend the wisdom that will see them through the eye of the needle; this is why I wrote my novel *Jesus Wears Dockers,* to share my "interpretation" of Christ's sayings with my readers.

But that's neither here nor there really, because there is only self-initiation into the mysteries of life, and life is fundamentally an individual journey of self-discovery; so, it doesn't really matter what Jordan Peterson says, or what I say, or what C. G. Jung or anyone says, we all have to negotiate our own way to wholeness and completeness, and if what we say resonates with the world, so be it. Which brings me back to the Jordan Peterson phenomenon and the intellectual firestorm that he has stirred up in the world with the imperative of *12 Rules for Life: An Antidote to Chaos*.

He's not yet completed his 100 city global tour, but he's caused such a stir with his refreshing, albeit shocking point of view that he's initiated a whole new conversation on moral responsibility and God and the bible and the meaning of our existence, and the world is listening, with some of his followers going back to their Christian roots because of the good professor's refreshing psychological perspective on the bible stories, and wonder-struck followers like Paul VanderKlay, pastor of a Christian Reform Church in Sacramento, California who has his own YouTube platform, discuss the effect of Peterson's message online to keep the conversation going—a phenomenon, indeed!

So, it's obvious that his message is resonating with the world; or, to be fair, with a very large sector of society that is fumbling in the dark. Like our respective hero Carl Gustav Jung, who wrote, *"the sole purpose of human existence is to kindle a light in the darkness of mere being,"* so too is professor Peterson kindling a light in the darkness of our crazy modern world by providing an answer to the angry question of my poem, *What the Hell is Going on Out There?*

Which brings me to the spiritual musing I was called to write when we got back from our little getaway up north this summer, a musing that will help open the secret door that *12 Rules for Life: An Antidote to Chaos* prepares one for, especially young men drawn to the good professor's message like lost souls to the hoopoe bird, not unlike the young poet who inspired this spiritual musing:

When the Student is Ready

There's an old joke. If you want to make God laugh, tell him your plans. This implies that we never know how our life is going to turn out, despite everything we do to make it go our way; but that's because we have free will as well as a destined purpose, and if we stray too far from our destined purpose, Providence will always intercede to bring us back to our destined purpose.

Despite science's contention that free will is an illusion, we all know that choices have consequences, and eventually *(unless we are unreasonably stubborn)* we will become more discerning in the choices we make to prevent unpleasant consequences. This is free will and not animal instinct. Which brings me to today's spiritual musing: how can we know that the choices we make will not bear unpleasant consequences?

We cannot, of course; but as we grow in our discernment, we take calculated risks and hope that the choices we make will not bear unpleasant consequences. Like the gifted young poet Micah, whom the great choreographer of life introduced me to when Penny and I went to the Lakehead on our little getaway this summer, said in the opening poem "Advice" in his second book of poetry *Above the Old Birch Trees*: "Take a chance, /dig deeper, /take more risks."

This is sage advice from a young poet who's just beginning to play the game of life (and life is a game really, with all of its rules and consequences; literally, and otherwise); but as we get older, fear has a way of dampening our spirit for risk-taking, and many of us settle into what Thoreau called a life of "quiet desperation," waiting for the day when we are called to our reckoning like Everyman was in the medieval morality play that was the inspiration for my poem *Noman* that I wrote in high school and which became the central theme of my memoir *The Summoning of Noman* that I wrote fifty years later.

Thank God for youth then when the seeds of our life are planted, giving us the potential to realize wholeness and completeness; but, life being what it is, not all seeds take root ("Ten thousand acorns fell from the oak, /five took root, /and one became a tree," from my book *Not My Circus, Not My Monkeys*), and not everyone is fortunate enough to realize their destined purpose. This is why I was so excited when the great choreographer of life introduced the young poet into my life with Penny's gift of *Above the Old Birch Trees*; and it was this delightful coincidence that inspired today's spiritual musing…

One Rule to Live By

The great choreographer of life is not a figment of my imagination; it is the Logos, the Word, the Voice of God, Providence, which in my own journey of self-discovery I came to recognize as *the omniscient guiding principle of life* that keeps us connected with our destined purpose, whether we are aware of it or not, and which has also been referred to throughout history simply as the *way*.

The *way* is everywhere to be found (Jesus called the *way* by many names, essentially all meaning a transformative process as well as a destination, and Carl Jung recognized the *way* as life itself), but not everyone finds the *way* until they are ready; this is the mystery of the human condition that the young poet is struggling to resolve. That's why he was meant to come into my life, and I into his; he, to find inspiration in my writing that will help him find the *way* and connect with his destined purpose of wholeness and completeness, and me to offer encouragement in his own journey of self-discovery, because he is the acorn that has just taken root and I am the acorn that has become a tree.

And how do I know this? Aside from his book of poetry *Above the Old Birch Trees,* which bared an anguished soul crying out to the Universe for direction and purpose, but because of what he revealed about himself in our short online chat that we had the day I sent him a friend request when I saw his post on Facebook with a photo of him and Penny's sister proudly holding his new calendar at the market of the CLE grounds in the Lakehead where he was promoting his books (two books of poetry and one youthful memoir inspired by his trip to Scotland), and his 2019 calendar adorned with photos he had taken of the area, the young poet confirmed why the great choreographer of life wanted us to connect:

O: Penny's sister gifted me your new calendar, and Penny gifted me your book of poetry *Above the Old Birch Trees.* Love the calendar, but your poetry book engaged me from the first three lines ("Take a chance, /dig deeper, /take more risks."), and I read the whole book over the weekend. You have a gift. Will be ordering your other books from Amazon. Good luck on your lifelong journey.

M: Thank you for your kind words, I hope you enjoy the other books as well.

O: Your inner journey fascinates me. Have been friends with your aunt Fiona and uncle Clifford for years. Looking forward to how your life unfolds, which I'm sure you'll be working into your poetry. Don't mind telling you, that one of your lines in your book *Above the Old Birch Trees* has to be one of the most powerful lines I've ever read: "Life fears art." But do you know why?

M: I think one reason could be that it shows us the truth of ourselves we wish didn't exist, or at least that it shows us difficult truths that most people would rather not face.

O: That's the poet's gift, to see what other people don't want, or refuse to see; but then, as the gifted New Zealand short story writer Katherine Mansfield said, "Literature is not enough," implying that the wisdom of literature is not enough to satisfy the longing in one's soul for wholeness and completeness, and so one may well ask: where does one go from here? That was my quest, which I have resolved to my satisfaction and have been writing about for years. Check out *My Writing Life*, if you have time. Keep writing, Micah. Your poetry is a birthing of your inner self.

M: I will, thank you!

O: You're welcome. Have to get back to my work-in-progress. Don't hesitate to initiate a dialogue whenever you're in the mood for a good discourse. *Ciao* for now.

Not only is this young man a gifted poet, but a gifted pianist who played at Carnegie Hall and who also won a competition in Italy and is currently studying at university for a degree in music, not to mention his passion for photography and mountain climbing; and it was obvious to me from the first poem I read in *Above the Old Birch Trees* that he was suffering from what professor Harold Bloom called an "immortal wound" that will never heal until he finds his own *way* and realizes his destined purpose to wholeness and completeness (it's not a coincidence that he called his youthful memoir *Without a Trail)*, and I simply *knew* that we were meant to connect; because, as the old saying goes, when the student is ready...

One Rule to Live By

That's why so many young people, especially alienated and disaffected young men that have been immortally wounded by the wonder of professor Peterson's message—reading his life-affirming book *12 Rules for Life: An Antidote to Chaos*, which has now hit two million in global sales, and viewing his online lectures that have millions of followers and counting—are flocking to his book tour talks that average 2500 people in every city in North America, Europe, and Australia, because there's a hole in the soul of the world that neither religion, science, nor politics can fill, and the good professor's divine imperative to help the world find its way again that it lost when science eroded religion's credibility which sick little Friedrich Nietzsche pathologized in *Thus Spoke Zarathustra* with his spiritually numbing God-is-dead philosophy, reminded me of the starfish story and Dr. Jordan Peterson's newfound sense of purpose and meaning.

The starfish story, adapted from "The Star Thrower" by Loren Eiseley, has been used by motivational speakers throughout the world to inspire dreams and noble ambitions, however foolhardy, like the good professor's *daemonic* imperative to right the world with his *12 Rules for Life: An Antidote to Chaos* and book tour talks and interviews, podcasts, and online lectures, a story that allegorizes professor Peterson's noble ambition, as the starfish story joyfully illustrates:

Once upon a time, there was an old man who used to go to the ocean to do his writing. He had a habit of walking on the beach every morning before he began his work. Early one morning, he was walking along the shore after a big storm had passed and found the vast beach littered with starfish as far as the eye could see, stretching in both directions.

Off in the distance, the old man noticed a small boy approaching. As the boy walked, he paused every so often, and as he grew close, the man could see that he was occasionally bending down to pick up an object and throw it into the sea. The boy came closer still, and the man called out, "Good morning! May I ask what you are doing?"

The young boy paused, looked up, and replied "Throwing starfish into the ocean. The tide has washed them up onto the beach and they can't return to the sea by themselves, When the sun gets high, they will die, unless I throw them back into the water."

The old man replied, "But there must be tens of thousands of starfish on the beach. I'm afraid you won't really be able to make much of a difference."

The boy bent down, picked up yet another starfish and threw it as far as he could into the ocean. Then he turned, smiled, and said, "It made a difference to that one."

No one knows how many poor souls the tides have washed upon the shoals of life only to wither and die because they could not make their way back to the ocean, but along came an impassioned U of T professor of psychology and clinical therapist who hailed from a small prairie town in northern Alberta with nothing but an obsessive dream of solving the problem of evil, emboldened by the myth-shattering Russian writer Aleksandr Solzhenitsyn and pioneering depth psychologist C. G. Jung and other great souls like Dr. Victor Frankl and Jean Piaget, who risked his career and clinical practice when he was called to stand up for free speech and help all the broken souls make their way back to the ocean so they could continue on their destined journey to wholeness and completeness, a heroic endeavor that gave the good professor a renewed sense of purpose and meaning; and all the weary souls that have taken his message to heart praise him for giving them the hope they desperately needed to reclaim their interrupted lives—*"His example gave me permission to begin thinking about what I might become in a world that has lost its bearings, even as I had lost mine,"* said one of his followers in *Esquire* magazine;

One Rule to Live By

and she is only one of the many thousands of starfish that the young boy threw back into the ocean...

36. The Brilliance of Friedrich Nietzsche

"I am Zarathustra, the godless; where do I find my equal? All those are my equals *who determine their will out of themselves, and who push all submission away from themselves,"* declared Nietzsche's hero with no less hubris than Satan in Milton's *Paradise Lost* who cut off his nose to spite his face rather than bow to God's will.

"Better to reign in Hell, than serve in Heaven," said Satan, and Nietzsche followed suite by declaring God dead rather than submit to God's imperative; but—*and this is the but that opened the gates of hell and set loose all those nasty heathen demons upon the world*—did brilliant little Friedrich Nietzsche know what God's imperative was, or did he misperceive the God of Christianity for the redemptive will of the Logos'? Why such contempt for Christianity?

That's the brilliance of Friedrich Nietzsche and the tragedy of his teaching; *by honoring man's free will in his tendentious teaching of the Superman, he dishonored God's redemptive imperative, because poor little Friedrich Nietzsche had to have his cake and eat it too...*

"I was fascinated...yet repelled at the same time. I found it difficult to discover the right attitude toward Nietzsche," wrote Rudolf Steiner in his book *Friedrich Nietzsche: Fighter for Freedom*. And after much study, Steiner concluded: "This was the picture of Nietzsche that appeared in my thought. He revealed to me the personality who did not see the spirit, but in whom unconsciously the spirit fought against the unspiritual views of his age," making of Friedrich Nietzsche a paradoxical man who drove himself insane rather than submit to the imperative of his divine nature and reconcile the dual consciousness of his *essential* and *existential* self, the *being* and *non-being* of his false and true self, futilely justifying his resistance to God's imperative like Milton's proud Satan.

I never understood my fascination with Nietzsche either when studying philosophy at university, and it wasn't until I found the answer many years later to the question that had called me to university that I learned that the Logos, *the omniscient guiding principle of life*, was responsible for the authors that changed my life, like P. D. Ouspensky, whose book *In Search of the Miraculous* introduced me to Gurdjieff's teaching that awakened me to the **secret way**, C. G. Jung, whose *Memories, Dreams, Reflections* opened me up to a psychological understanding of the individuation process that helped resolve my deep-seated issues with Christianity, Dr. Victor Frankl, whose *Man's Search for Meaning* confirmed my understanding of the gnostic way, and many more authors whose books were just what I needed at that time in my life; but never Friedrich Nietzsche, for whom I always had an instinctive antipathy and could never bring myself to study.

One can, and many have made a lifelong study of Nietzsche, whose seductive brilliance can be spellbinding (professor Peterson gave a 45 minute talk on one paragraph of Nietzsche's *Beyond Good and Evil*, which only confirmed my reason for dropping out of university), but never quite grasping why he turned on God with such *daemonic* ferocity and embracing the idea of eternal recurrence that justified his Satanic pride and trapped his soul in the recurring cycle of the same miserable life forever; but having broken the cycle of eternal recurrence, which I explored in the memoir of my parallel life in *The Summoning of Noman*, I *know* that Nietzsche was wrong in the basic premise of his teaching that there is no God and we either embrace our fate or be crushed by it, and I *know* that his whole philosophy was founded upon the monstrous lie of his false nature, a brilliant house of cards built upon the foundation of his devastating, albeit brilliant life-lie.

Nietzsche was trapped by his fate in the meaninglessness-of-life paradigm until he was granted the insight of the eternal recurrence of all life while out on a walk one day in the Swiss village of Sils Maria, and he gleefully took up the intellectual challenge of the idea of eternal recurrence and grew to love his self-imposed fate of returning to his same life forever so he could overcome the oppressive spirit of nihilism that made *(his)* life meaningless and absurd, which gave birth to his Satanic hero Zarathustra who proudly justified why he had turned on God; but was it God the Logos that proud little Nietzsche had turned on, or the God of Christianity for whom he had a pathological antipathy? Wasn't his *amor fati* just an ironic rationalization of his unhappy, miserable life? Did Nietzsche's whole philosophy grow out of a false premise, a brilliant justification of his own *non-being*, his ferociously shadow-possessed personality? A monstrous life-lie? A house of cards?

I understand why he would believe that God was dead and that we had killed him (*I also walked away from the God of Christianity, but not Christ the Logos*), which drove Nietzsche out of his mind trying to resolve the imperative of the *enantiodromiac* nature of his dual self; but the teaching that his Satanic hero Zarathustra gave to the world has led the world down the proverbial path and left the world dangerously, dangerously wanting; which brings to mind a spiritual musing that I wrote on how I resolved the issue of my own dual nature by adopting a **special attitude** to life that satisfied the longing in my soul for wholeness and completeness, and made me happy—a **special attitude** that reflects the "*correct interpretation*" of Christ's nay-saying to life that Nietzsche misunderstood with such pathological antipathy that it finally drove him into catatonic madness:

My Secret to a Happy Life

One Rule to Live By

Yesterday Penny and I made our first batch of Italian sausages in Georgian Bay, just like my parents used to make; well, not quite the same, because in this batch we did not add fennel seeds to our spices of salt, black pepper, chili pepper flakes, granular garlic, and paprika. We made the first batch without the fennel seeds, because I'm going to give some to my neighbor Tony who does not like fennel seeds in his homemade sausages; and today we're going to make the second batch with fennel seeds, and with less paprika.

After we ground the meat and mixed in the spices, Penny fried up a couple of small patties to taste the result, and we found it a little dry; so, I added a cup or so of red wine that I had made last fall with Tony and mixed it into the meat, and Penny fried up two more patties and it tasted fine; and then we spent an hour or so stuffing the meat into the casings that we slid onto the funnel attachment of our electric meat grinder.

I like fennel seeds in my Italian sausages, but there was a time when I denied myself the pleasure of eating sausages altogether because I had taken up a special way of life that was inspired by the Sufi path that Gurdjieff's teaching had introduced me to. Serendipity had introduced Gurdjieff into my life by way of Ouspensky's book *In Search of the Miraculous* in my second year of philosophy studies at university, and as I "worked" on myself with Gurdjieff's teaching I created what Gurdjieff called a "magnetic center" which attracted me to teachings of a similar nature, like Sufism and the sayings and parables of Jesus. Actually, Gurdjieff called his Fourth Way teaching "esoteric Christianity," which was inspired by the secret teachings of the Essenes that Jesus was initiated into when he was a young man.

The premise of the Sufi Path is that one must "die before dying" to become their true self, which is a very difficult teaching to understand, let alone practice; but this is what Jesus meant with his paradoxical saying: *"He that findeth his life shall lose it, and he that loseth his life for my sake shall find it."* And since I was on a quest to find my true self, I took Gurdjieff's teaching of "work on oneself" to heart, which over time pulled the **secret way** of the Sufi Path and Christ's sayings and parables into my life; and by **secret way**, I mean cultivating a **special attitude** with life that nourishes one's inner self.

This, then, is the subject of today's spiritual musing that came to me this morning while "talking" with St. Padre Pio for my book *A Sign of Things to Come,* a creative exercise in what Jung called "active imagination," not unlike Neale Donald Walsch's "conversations" with God; and as I shared yesterday's sausage making experience with my fellow countryman (Padre Pio was born in the village of Pietrelcina, not too far north from where I was born in the village of Panettieri, Calabria) I got the strongest feeling to write a spiritual musing on this **special attitude** that is essential for the growth of one's inner self, an attitude of **conscious living** which is reflected in a poem that I wrote a few years ago—

Sufi Sausages

The best sausages that I ever tasted
are made from a secret recipe that I found one day
while looking for the secret way.

I was so hungry for God that I would have eaten anything
to preserve my spiritual strength;

and I did, a cult concoction of sun and nonsense
that gave me spiritual cramps for many years.

Then I chanced upon a Sufi sausage maker who gave me
a secret recipe that changed my life forever.

"You take the casing that you have," he instructed me,
"and stuff it with the meat of the last supper."

I had no idea what he meant, until I re-read the Christian Bible;
and from the moment I caught the light that Jesus shone,

I discerned the Sufi sausage maker's wisdom,
and I began to practice the sacred art of Sufi sausage-making.

The first few batches that I made were much too spicy,
because I stuffed my casing with every esoteric meat
that I could find;

but with time, patience, and an ardent desire for God,
I learned to stuff my casing with the freshest meat of all,

the tender flesh of my own simple, daily life;
and the more I died to my mortal flesh,

the sweeter my sausages tasted, and the more strength
I gathered for my long journey back home to God.

The most difficult aspect of my quest for my true self was decoding the language of the **secret way**, which is so well hidden that only the most devout seeker will ever decode the meaning of life's purpose; but once I did, the **secret way** of the Sufi Path and Christ's sayings and parables and the simple gnostic way of life gave up their secret, and life finally began to make sense to me.

But I still had a lot more living and many years of writing before I could explain the **secret way,** until one day I realized that it all came down to a **special attitude** with life that reflected the essential truth of every spiritual teaching, and by **special attitude** I mean the secret of **conscious living** that Gurdjieff's teaching made me wise to.

Of course, we are all conscious despite what Gurdjieff said about man being asleep to life, but consciousness is relative to every person, and waking up to life is a matter of degree for everyone; but it was Gurdjieff's purpose as well as the Sufi Path and the sayings and parables of Jesus to speed up the process of self-realization and waking up to life, which in the language of the **secret way** means taking evolution into our own hands to complete what Nature cannot finish.

Nature will only evolve us so far, said Gurdjieff; and to complete what Nature cannot finish we have to take evolution into our own hands by cultivating a **special attitude** with life that speeds up the process of becoming our true self, which is the essential meaning and purpose of our existence.

It took years for me to realize why Nature cannot evolve us to our full potential, but the more I "worked" on myself (which I encoded in my poem as the sacred art of Sufi sausage-making), the more I grew in truth and understanding, and it finally dawned on me one day that the **secret way** was all about resolving the consciousness of our dual nature; or, as Jesus expressed it in the secret language of his teaching, making our two selves into one self whole and complete.

In the *Gnostic Gospel of Thomas*, Jesus was asked by someone when his kingdom would come, and he replied, ***"When the two will be one, and the outer like the inner, and the male with the female neither male nor female."*** And the two are one when we speak truth to each other and there is one soul in two bodies with no hypocrisy, as the saying is explained in *The Unknown Sayings of Jesus,* by Marvin Meyer.

This **special attitude** with life then is nothing more than learning how to live one's life with **conscious intention,** which means **karmic responsibility**; because as long as we refuse to wake up to the governing principle of life, which in *A Sign of Things to Come* St. Padre Pio called "the law of corrective measures," we remain trapped in the endless cycle of karma and reincarnation, which is why we have to take evolution into our own hands to complete what Nature cannot finish and become our true self. And if I were asked to define what I mean by this **special attitude** of the **secret way**, I'd be forced to say: simply be a good person, and let your conscience be your guide. That's my secret to a happy life.

For whatever deep-seated psychological reason Nietzsche lost his faith in God, it conflagrated at the age of 21 by his serendipitous discovery of the atheist philosopher Schopenhauer while browsing Rohm's second-hand bookstore in Leipzig one day. "As if by accident, he picked up Schopenhauer's *The World as Will and Idea,"* wrote Paul Marshall Allen in the Introduction to Rudolph Steiner's *Friedrich Nietzsche, Fighter for Freedom.* "In the book, I saw a mirror of the world; life and my own soul were reflected with dreadful faithfulness," wrote Nietzsche in his journal, which confirmed his anti-God feelings that cut him off from the spark of divine consciousness that he was born with and which prohibited him from reconciling his *existential* self with the imperative of his divine nature; and in his effort to overcome the oppressive spirit of nihilism born of the emerging scientific age of materialism and his willful denial of God's imperative to resolve the consciousness of his lower nature, he forged a teaching of "the eternal recurrence of all things" and embraced his *existential* self—over and over in a never-ending cycle of time eternal, a fate that he was forced to love by the imperative of his own brilliant, shadow-possessed egocentric logic.

"And if you should die now, O Zarathustra: behold, we know too what you would say to yourself... 'Now I die and decay...and in an instant I shall be nothingness...But the complex of causes in which I am entangled will recur—it will create me again! ...I shall return...*not* to a new life or a better life or a similar life; I shall return eternally to this identical and self-same life...to teach once more the eternal recurrence of all things, to speak once more the teaching of the great noontide of earth and man, to tell man of the Superman once more...'" wrote Nietzsche in a creative spasm of fevered imagination, staking his divine reconciliation on an idea of eternal egocentrism (*Thus Spoke Zarathustra*, Penguin Classics; translated by R.J. Hollingdale. Introduction, p. 24).

"*Alright,*" I imagined proud little Nietzsche saying to himself, after he walked away from his Christian faith—for whatever reason, we will never know; but it was enough for him to deny the existence of the God altogether (probably crystallized in his mind by the love of his life, Lou Salome, who humiliated and drove him into deep despair when she refused to marry him)— "*if this is the way it's going to be, then I'll embrace my miserable fate and be done with it!*"

And like Satan in *Paradise Lost,* who turned on God and embraced hell forever, Nietzsche's creative genius gave birth to the compensatory idea of the eternal recurrence of all life to ward off his inevitable psychosis, and in his febrile mind he made a sterile heaven out of his own miserable existence by embracing his fate like Milton's proud Satan; and he created his own stagnant heaven of eternal recurrence by giving birth to the Superman, whose sole purpose for being was to "overcome" his miserable existence over and over for time eternal. "Where I found a living creature, there I found will to power...And life told me this secret: 'Behold,' it said, 'I am that *which must overcome itself again and again,"* wrote Nietzsche in *Thus Spoke Zarathustra*, echoing Milton's proud Satan's "The mind is its own place, and in itself /Can make a Heaven of Hell, a Hell of Heaven."

"The Superman, the will to the Superman, the will to power and self-overcoming. Live dangerously! *Amor fati*, eternal recurrence, total affirmation of life. The great noontide. These are the slogans, the 'signs', by which Nietzsche surmounted his nihilism and resolved his crisis," wrote R. J. Hollingdale; but it was a tragically false resolution, because proud little Friedrich Nietzsche drove himself insane trying to satisfy the divine imperative of his inner self for wholeness and completeness by sacrificing his divine self to his *existential* self (eternally recurring or not), the absolute obverse of Jesus Christ's salvific teaching of making our two selves into one self whole and complete. I can hear poor little Nietzsche's tortured lost soul screaming, *"God, why hast thou forsaken me?"*

"He that loveth his life shall lose it; and he that hateth his life in this world shall keep it unto life eternal," said Jesus, which proud little Friedrich Nietzsche so wrongly misperceived that he violently denounced Christianity for its redemptive nay-saying to life *(self-sacrifice is the **secret way** of Christ's teaching, which Jesus symbolized with the death of his lower self on the sacred cross of human suffering)*; and that's the brilliance of Friedrich Nietzsche and the tragedy of his teaching—the same dilemma that haunts the pages of professor Jordan Peterson's *12 Rules for Life: An Antidote to Chaos*, and my inspiration for writing *One Rule to Live By: Be Good*...

37. The Call to the Inner Life

"Fate is the death we owe to Nature. Destiny is the life we owe to soul," wrote Jungian therapist Marian Woodman in her Foreword to *Bone: A Journal of Wisdom, Strength, and Healing*, an intimate chronical of her miraculous journey through uterine cancer to healing; which was why I gave this book to a neighbor who was diagnosed with cancer this summer and instantly fell into deep despair because both her mother and brother had died of cancer.

I loved Marion Woodman's book, and I especially love her title *Bone*, because it dared to "de-flesh" her life and pare it down to the bare bone of her existence, a courageous confrontation with herself that awakened her to the life-altering realization that we have a fate we owe to Nature and a destiny we owe to soul, which was the same conclusion that my own confrontation with myself had awakened me to, and the basic theme of *One Rule to Live By: Be Good*; that's why I said to our neighbour, who had just taken an early retirement to get the most out of the rest of her life, when she told me she had cancer and was terrified of dying like her mother and brother, "Everything happens for a reason, Tracy. Maybe life is trying to tell you something with your cancer?"

"This book is about living, not dying," wrote Marion Woodman. "It's about dying into life. With cancer, I discovered how much dying it takes to get here, here into my body, here onto Earth. It's about the soul work required to heal both," an extraordinary insight into that special way of **conscious living** that is necessary to transform our *existential* outer self and make us whole and complete; this is why I gave this remarkable book to my neighbor to read, it was the most precious gift that I could give her in her most desperate time of need.

But why does it take something like cancer to wake us up to our destined purpose, or whatever tragic loss that shocks us out of our comfortable paradigm and hurls us into chaos and confusion—the loss of a child by accidental drowning, marital betrayal, a stroke? Why does it take a tragedy to wake us up to our mortal nature? It is a quandary; but it was this thought that inspired a spiritual musing that I wrote last summer, long before my neighbor Tracy informed me that she had cancer and was terrified of dying like her mother and brother:

The Quandary of Our Modern World

Unquestionably, the pace of life has quickened today with the onslaught of the Internet, smart phones, and social media, with AI (artificial intelligence) snapping at our heels; but are we any closer to where we want, or ought to be?

That's the quandary of our modern world that I reflected upon as I re-read some of my Edgar Cayce literature that grabbed my attention in my basement library when I went downstairs the other day to look for a book that I couldn't find, which I took to be a sign from my oracle to re-acquaint myself with the literature on karma and reincarnation that called out to me from one of the dusty shelves of my basement library; but why? That's the subject of today's spiritual musing…

I make no pretense to the fact that I believe in karma and reincarnation, which given the abundance of documented information we have on the subject makes me wonder why society is still so resistant to what Socrates more than two thousand years ago called "a doctrine uttered in secret," reminding me of a letter that C. G. Jung wrote on his startling insight on man's "resistance to understanding" *(Letter to Hans Schmid, 6 November 1915)*, which I may refer to later as I work my way to a solution to the quandary of our modern world; but it was Jess Stearn's book *The Search for a Soul: Taylor Caldwell's Psychic Lives* that inspired a re-reading of the Edgar Cayce literature, because it gave me the perspective I needed to make sense of our modern dilemma, and by dilemma I mean the paradoxical fact that the quicker the pace of our modern world gets (and it seems to be speeding up exponentially with the advances in digital technology and artificial intelligence), the greater the distance we seem to be from where we want, or ought to be.

It's a whirlwind of activity *out there,* but where are we going?

I read an article in one of my weekend papers recently about a ritzy resort retreat that offered luxury suites at exorbitant rates because they were architecturally engineered so their clients could not access the outside world with their laptops and smart phones, thereby offering them a box of time for disconnected rest and relaxation. How ironic, that our modern world has become so self-indulgent that we can no longer say no to our obsessive need to be connected with what's going on *out there.*

I chuckled at the irony, because it's not what's going on *out there* that has our modern world in a schizophrenic frenzy, but what's going on *in here*—in the little universe of our own private world; and that's the crux of our dilemma, because what's going on *out there* can't seem to satisfy the irrepressible longing in our soul for wholeness and completeness, and we're always left wanting.

As serendipity would have it (*I just love it when the merciful law of divine synchronicity kicks in to assist me in my writing*), just to confirm my point about our modern world's obsessive need to be connected with what's going on *out there,* I just happened to inadvertently check my email and Facebook page a moment ago *(how ironic!),* and a writer friend from Texas had just posted a cartoon depicting children sitting on the front steps of a house and other children walking by on the sidewalk, all with their eyes locked onto their smart phones and a yellow caution road sign with the warning: SLOW, CHILDREN TEXTING. And the caption read: "PLAYING OUTSIDE THESE DAYS." What more proof does one need for our obsessive need to be connected with what's going on *out there*?

This is the disease of our modern world that has infected our young generation—the obsessive need to be connected with what's going on *out there,* whatever *out there* may be for each afflicted person—be it email, Facebook, Twitter, Instagram or whatever digital window on the world that one may be locked into; and time fritters by as we hungrily try to satisfy the irrepressible longing in our soul with the empty social calories of what's going on *out there*. No wonder some enterprising individual has offered exorbitantly priced weekend retreats for those who can afford to pay to get away from what's going on *out there*.

I had read *The Search for a Soul: Taylor Caldwell's Psychic Lives* many years ago, which was the inspiration for my own seven past-life regressions many years later that became the basis of my novel *Cathedral of My Past Lives*, but I was strongly nudged to read Stearn's book again, because I felt a need to re-acquaint myself with how our current life is unconsciously affected by our past lives, as Taylor Caldwell's life certainly was because her novels were drawn from those ancient times in which she had lived and where she drew her vast knowledge and information for her stories, like her historical novel *Great Lion of God*, the fascinating story of St. Paul's life and his miraculous conversion to Jesus Christ's teaching.

At her friend Jess Stearn's request, Taylor Caldwell was hypnotically regressed to some of her past lives to help her heal her grief from her husband's recent passing, and it was enlightening to see how many of the people she knew back then that she met again in her current lifetime, like her husband whose recent death had sent her into deep depression, and the vital role that they played in her life (her writer friend Jess Stearn, no less); all of which pointed to the karmic purpose of our life.

And that's what's missing in today's world, the stubborn resistance to our karmic need for spiritual growth and self-fulfillment, which is displaced by our obsessive need for egoic gratification and social attention that we crave to satisfy with what's going on *out there*.

I wrote a spiritual musing alluding to this obsessive need, which I titled "I'm On Facebook, Therefore I Am," and as ironic as I was in my musing, the point I wanted to make was that social media cannot satisfy our inherent longing for self-fulfillment; but very few people make the connection between what's going on *out there* and what's going on *in here*, and our world today suffers the tragic malaise of spiritual emptiness more than any other age in human history. And that's the irony of our modern world.

One Rule to Live By

C. G. Jung, the founder of Analytical Psychology, foresaw this in his clinical practice, and in his book of essays *Modern Man in Search of a Soul* he spells out the problem: "During the past thirty years, people from all the civilized countries of the earth have consulted me. I have treated many hundreds of patients, the larger number being Protestants, a smaller number of Jews, and not more than five or six believing Catholics. Among all of my patients in the second half of life—that is to say, over thirty-five—there has not been one whose problem in the last resort was not that of not finding a religious outlook on life. ***It is safe to say that every one of them fell ill because he had lost that which the living religions of every age have given to their followers, and none of them has really been healed who did not regain his religious outlook***" (*Modern Man in Search of a Soul*, C. G. Jung, p. 229, bold italics mine).

Jung said that most people who came to him for therapy suffered from a sense of meaninglessness, and it was his duty to help them find a sense of purpose; this is how he developed his remarkable psychology of individuation—because the more one grew in the consciousness of their own identity, the more fulfilled they would be. *"As each plant grows from a seed and becomes in the end an oak tree, so man becomes what he is meant to be. He ought to get there, but most get stuck,"* said Jung; and that's the problem of our modern world—we ought to get *there*, but we get stuck.

It appears then that modern man is stuck *out there* somewhere, and until we come to the realization that when all is said and done *out there* is not where it's really at, but *in here*, in the little universe of our own private world; and until we see this, we will never satisfy the longing in our soul to be what we are meant to be, which is why I was drawn back to the Edgar Cayce literature on karma and reincarnation.

Edgar Cayce was one of the world's most gifted psychics who went into a trance and did past-life readings, as well as health readings (which is how he got the name "the Sleeping Prophet"); and Jess Stearn helped bring Edgar Cayce to public attention with his books *Edgar Cayce: The Sleeping Prophet* and *Intimates Through Time: Edgar Cayce's Mysteries of Reincarnation,* which I read again; and then I re-read his book *Soul Mates* because I enjoyed reading again about people who found their soul mate, quite often serendipitously, to fulfill their past-life relationships—which was how I met my Penny Lynn, because we had unresolved karma from our past life together as man and wife in Genoa, Italy when I broke her heart and dishonored our family name with my flagrant relationship with my raven-haired mistress who, as incredible, as it may be to believe, came back into my current life as my past-life regressionist who tried to steal me again from my Penny Lynn. I didn't know she was my past-life lover, but it soon became apparent.

We are all born with a karmic purpose that determines our life, which is why I felt compelled to write today's spiritual musing; because the only solution that I can see to the quandary of our modern world is to embrace a philosophy that will connect us with our karmic purpose. But to do this, we have to take pause from what's going on *out there* and pay more attention to what's going on *in here*, in the little universe of our own private world, because if we don', life will do it for us through karmic suffering.

This brings me back to Carl Jung's insight into man's "resistance to understanding," which is born of man's fear of knowing himself, which I can vouchsafe because it's also been my experience that when one is made conscious of their destined purpose the responsibility is often too great to bear—*like resisting the urge to fall for my past-life mistress again that would have dishonored my love for Penny Lynn as I did in our past lifetime together in Genoa, Italy;* and one flees into the world *out there* to escape karmic accountability, an insight that was confirmed by a dream I had during my open-heart surgery.

In my dream, I was chased from one lifetime to the next by Nazi-like soldiers, which I discerned to mean my own past hunting me from one lifetime to the next until I came face to face with my own karma and took responsibility for my life, symbolizing the spiritual crisis of our modern world because our chickens are coming home to roost; and not until we connect with our karmic purpose will we ever hope of resolving the quandary of our modern world, a collective responsibility shared by every person.

That's what Marion Woodman meant by soul work, the realization that by working on ourselves we can heal our wounded soul and the soul of the world, which her cancer experience had awakened her to just as I hoped my recently diagnosed neighbor would come to see.

And that's what excited me about professor Jordan Peterson's book *12 Rules for Life: An Antidote to Chaos*, because his hierophantic message to the world was waking people up to their inner life and destined purpose, albeit with the psychological nuance of a clever therapist who, like his hero C. G. Jung, was well aware of man's "resistance to understanding," as his resentful critics continue to let him know because the light of his gnosis is much too bright for them.

And that's the irony; we all want the cure but not the medicine. But there's no other way to satisfy the longing in our soul for wholeness and completeness; and the sooner our crazy modern world realizes this, the better off we will be...

"*Why?*" Tracy asked, in teary disappointment. "*I did everything right. I don't smoke, I don't drink, I eat right, I exercise. Why me?*" she cried, when she revealed her desperate situation; and a week or so later she said to me, in a moment of distressing self-awareness, "*We've got everything. Maybe that's why. Maybe it's because we've got everything...*"

Unconscious guilt for the comfortable life at the expense of the inner life? It was not for me to say. "If there's one piece of wisdom that I can give you," I said to her, drawing upon Marion Woodman's gnostic wisdom of her own cancer experience; "it's to make friends with your cancer. It's not your enemy. It's not an alien entity come to destroy your life. It's your own body trying to tell you something. Listen to your cancer, Tracy. Keep a journal. Life's trying to tell you something about yourself that you need to know..."

Befuddled and confused, Tracy began her journey through Dr. Elisabeth Kubler-Ross's five stages of grief—*denial*, *anger, bargaining, depression, and acceptance*; but being a Type A Personality, I knew she would get stuck in the *anger* and *depression* stages before moving on to *acceptance*, and my heart went out to her. But the fates were kind to my neighbor, and although her cancer turned out to be incurable, it was manageable with medication; and her anger defused.

"*You can have all the money in the world, but it doesn't mean anything if you don't have your health,*" she confessed to me, shortly after her first treatment; and I smiled as I witnessed her connection with her inner life, knowing that one day she too would come to the same realization as Dr. Kubler-Ross, as will every soul that begins their journey to wholeness and completeness, which the good doctor reveals in her autobiography *The Wheel of Life: A Memoir of Living and Dying*: "**...all destiny leads down the same path—growth, love and service**," the same divine imperative of *12 Rules for Life: An Antidote to Chaos* that Dr. Peterson was called to give to the world...

38. My Mandala, My Mandate

"Each life has a natural built-in reason for being. Purpose is the creative spirit of life moving through you from the inside out. It is the deep mysterious dimension in each soul, which carries with it a profound sense of personal identity."

THE KEYS OF JESHUA
—Glenda Green

I was called to university to study philosophy to find an answer to the question that *compelled* me to go on a quest for my true self, *who am I?* And in my second year of studies I began to feel myself cast adrift in a sea of endless philosophical speculation, and I feared drowning; that's when my oracle came to my assistance and serendipity introduced me to Gurdjieff's teaching through Ouspensky's book *In Search of the Miraculous*, and this engendered the miraculous experience of **"my mandala, my mandate"** that I echoed in a spiritual musing that I wrote last year for *The Armchair Guru*, my fourth volume of spiritual musings, that shone the light of the Logos into my life:

The Hedgehog Knows One Big Thing

Just for fun and out of intellectual curiosity, the renowned Oxford philosopher Isaiah Berlin wrote an essay inspired by one line attributed to the ancient Greek poet Archilochus who died in 645 BC: *"The fox knows many things, but the hedgehog knows one big thing."*

Isaiah's essay, published in book form as *The Hedgehog and the Fox*, is both enlightening and entertaining; and just for the fun of it also, I'd like to explore his application of the hedgehog/fox metaphor to my own writing in today's spiritual musing…

I hadn't heard of Isaiah Berlin's book *The Hedgehog and the Fox* until a month or so ago when Colin Wilson (whose precocious book *The Outsider* influenced me in my youth) referred to it in his talk with Jeffrey Mishlove on his program *Thinking Allowed*, and I knew immediately what Colin Wilson meant when he said that he belonged to the category of hedgehog writers, because that's how I saw myself also.

"I've written the same book seventy times over," said Colin Wilson; which put him squarely in the hedgehog camp of writers, because according to Isaiah Berlin hedgehog writers focus on one all-embracing idea for understanding life. They possess "...a central vision, one system less or more coherent or articulate, in terms of which they understand, think and feel—a single, universal, organizing principle." And for Colin Wilson that one all-consuming central preoccupation was, in Jeffery Mishlove's words, *"reconciling this issue of the heights of consciousness and the depths of despair."*

Berlin made no huge claims for his hedgehog/fox metaphor, calling it a "starting-point for genuine investigation," with the added benefit of being an "enjoyable intellectual game" by which one could classify writers and thinkers into either camp, as he did by placing Plato, Dante, Pascal, Proust, Dostoevsky, Nietzsche, Ibsen, and many other classical writers into the hedgehog camp; and Aristotle, Shakespeare, Montaigne, Goethe, and Joyce among others in the fox camp of writers and thinkers, but focusing his attention mainly upon Tolstoy.

According to Berlin's application of the metaphor, fox writers pursue many ends, often unrelated, "seizing upon the essence of a vast variety of experience and objects for what they are in themselves, without, consciously or unconsciously, seeking to fit into, or exclude them from, any one unchanging, all-embracing...unitary vision."

In short, Berlin defined a hedgehog writer as someone who relates everything to a single vision, an organizing principle that seems to cover all of history, or a single dynamic of polar opposites like Colin Wilson's lifelong study of the depths and heights of human consciousness; and a fox writer, on the other hand pursues many ideas, not necessarily related, and often contradictory, like the great Russian novelist Leo Tolstoy.

Two camps, two types of writers; and according to this hedgehog/fox classification, I'm definitely a hedgehog writer because

One Rule to Live By

I have pursued one central idea my whole life; an unrelenting *idée fixe* which can be summed up by the simple question, *who am I?*

This became my organizing principle, and everything I did in my life was colored by my efforts to find the answer to this haunting question. I didn't talk about it openly, because that would have been a foolish thing to do, unless one was Shirley MacLaine who confessed in her memoir *I'm Over all That*, "No matter where I went I was always looking for myself" and always brought it up in interviews to expand the paradigm of social consciousness; but whether one talks about it or not, everyone will one day ask, *who am I?*

There were many things in my life that I longed for, and many avenues that I wanted to explore; but because of my hedgehog preoccupation, I focused my attention on what I felt would help me answer my haunting question. So, I was fox-like by inclination, because of my many interests; but I was a hedgehog by inner imperative, because I *had* to find my true self.

This caused me considerable anxiety, because I couldn't have it both ways; until I made a commitment one day and vowed to find my true self or die trying. And the more I focused on my *idée fixe*, the more laser-like attention I brought to my quest; which confirmed Isaiah Berlin's hedgehog/fox metaphor, because the hedgehog writer would be better disposed to a deeper insight into his preoccupying single interest than the fox writer who has many interests, because the hedgehog writer is by instinct a *centripetal thinker* (tending to move toward a center), and the fox writer is a *centrifugal thinker* (tending to move away from a center); but whether hedgehog or fox, both types play out life's drama of becoming who they are according to their own nature, thereby fulfilling their essential purpose in life.

Of course, this presupposes that life has an essential purpose; but it was because of my hedgehog conviction that I managed to answer the question *who am I?* which granted me an insight into life's essential purpose of realizing our true self, as I expounded upon in my most intimate memoir *The Pearl of Great Price* that tells the story of how I found the greatest treasure in the world, my true self.

But this is a personal realization, and I don't expect the world to see it; because, as Gurdjieff used to say, *"There is only self-*

initiation into the mysteries of life," and the only way to confirm that our purpose in life is to become our true self would be to initiate oneself into the sacred mystery of life's purpose. This is what the ancient alchemists meant when they said, *"Man must complete what nature has left unfinished."*

    I'm glad I was born to be a hedgehog writer, then; because it disposed me to devote my life to finding my true self and write about my journey, and as many regrets as I may have for not satisfying the longings of my many interests (I would have loved to become a Jungian analyst specializing in past-life regression therapy), I've accomplished what I came into this world to do; and I couldn't have asked for more.

―――――

    I went to university then because I was driven by an inner imperative that I had no control over. I could have gone any which way, to be sure; but I vowed to find my true self or die trying, and I felt *impelled* to study philosophy for an answer to my haunting question.

    But by the middle of my second year of studies I began to have an uneasy feeling that philosophy was not the path for me, and panic began to set in. That's when *for no apparent reason* I asked a fellow student who was going home to Toronto for Christmas to bring me back a book *of his own choosing* from his favorite little book store, and he brought me Ouspensky's book *In Search of the Miraculous* that cracked open the door to the **secret way** that was to change my life forever; but why did I ask him to bring me a book *of his own choosing*? What kind of strange request was this?

    Upon reflection these many years later, I can see there was always a kind of reckless abandon about me, which was both adventurous and foolish; and in my request of my fellow student, I abandoned to this adventurous/foolish spirit in me, which no doubt was the inspiration for my "letting go and letting God" experiment *(I tossed a coin to make up my mind for me)* that became the premise of my novel *The Golden Seed* many years later; but as attracted as I was to Gurdjieff's teaching of "work one oneself" that Ouspensky had introduced me to, I could not quite "get" it.

Gurdjieff fascinated me, mystified me, provoked me, and terrified me all at the same time; but I had the strongest feeling that his teaching *(made even more alluring by him also calling it "the way of the sly man")* was what I had gone to university for, and it got under my skin; that's when panic really set in, and I didn't know what to do.

Should I continue my philosophy studies and get a degree, or leave and find another path? What the hell was I to do? I had no idea whatsoever, and terror possessed me. And that's when it happened—**the miracle of my mandala experience**...

There's an old Zen Buddhist saying: *"Before enlightenment, chop wood, carry water. After enlightenment, chop wood, carry water."* Professor Jordan Peterson, whose own obsession to find an answer for "the general social and political insanity and evil of the world" also made him a hedgehog writer with his own *idée fixe*, brought his *Maps of Meaning* as far as the logic of his inquisitive mind could take him; not quite to the enlightened stage of passing through the eye of the needle, but to thematic resolution in *"Conclusion: The Divinity of Interest,"* with a quotation from his guiding light C. G. Jung, which explains why he was called by life to become a prophet and reformer with the imperative of his global bestseller *12 Rules for Life: An Antidote to Chaos:*

"The central ideas of Christianity are rooted in Gnostic philosophy, which, in accordance with psychological laws, simply had to grow up at a time when the classical religions had become obsolete. It was founded on the perception of symbols thrown up by the unconscious individuation process which always sets in when the collective dominants of human life fall into decay. At such a time there is bound to be a considerable number of individuals who are possessed by archetypes of a numinous nature that force their way to the surface in order to form new dominants.

"This state of possession shows itself almost without exception in the fact that **the possessed identify themselves with the archetypal contents of their unconscious, and, because they do not realize that the role which is being thrust upon them is the effect of new contents still to be understood, they exemplify these concretely in their own lives, thus becoming prophets and reformers**" (*Maps of Meaning: The Architecture of Belief*, Jordan B. Peterson, p. 456, bold italics mine).

Professor Jordan Peterson became possessed by the archetypal imperative of his own "crucifix symbol" that manifested to him in his prophetic cathedral dream one night while working on his book *Maps of Meaning: The Architecture of Belief*, which **mandated** him to resolve his dilemma by placing him in the center of Being; and that's exactly what happened to me when the unconscious process of individuation thrust upon me a holographic archetypal symbol in the "squaring of the circle" mandala that I experienced one night in the darkness of my bedroom in the house that three male friends and I rented in my second year at Lakehead University in Thunder Bay, Ontario.

The mandala symbol that the unconscious process of individuation manifested before my eyes in the "squaring of the circle" hologram possessed me with all the *daemonic* imperative of the archetypal hero whose sole purpose was to unite the opposites of my dual nature, and as Carl Jung said, I had no idea of the role that was being thrust upon me (neither did Jordan Peterson, who was called by his own unconscious imperative to answer his own haunting question); and although I did not know it then, my unconscious had just made up my mind for me: *I was* *"destined" by the symbolic imperative of my own unconscious need for wholeness and completeness to drop out of university and forge a new path for myself with Gurdjieff's teaching, which is why I came to call this miraculous experience "**my mandala, my mandate**."*

I was **mandated** by the archetypal hero's spirit to unite the opposites of my dual nature, but I had no cognitive awareness of my own dual nature until I began "working" on myself with Gurdjieff's teaching, which I did not "get" yet; and that's the irony of the hero's journey—they do not know the *way* until they find the *way*. And that was my quandary.

I began to sense that philosophy was not the path for me, and my creative unconscious confirmed this with the spontaneous manifestation of the "squaring of the circle" mandala hologram that appeared before my eyes that memorable night when out of sheer frustration with Gurdjieff's teaching I angrily threw Ouspensky's book *In Search of the Miraculous* down onto my desk and sat back in my chair and pouted in anger and deep despair.

Try as I may, I just did not "get" the gist of Gurdjieff's teaching despite how much it "spoke" to me, and it "spoke" to me so loud and clear that it got under my skin—another immortal wound that set my soul on fire with a pathological wonder that *possessed* me to read everything that I could get on Gurdjieff and his teaching when I finally summoned the courage to drop out of university in the second semester of my third year and forge a path for myself in the wooded forest of my life with his transformative system of "work" on oneself with *conscious effort* and *intentional suffering*, which awakened me to the simple truth that **to find the *way* one has to live it...**

So, there I was then, in my second year of studies when the *omniscient guiding principle of life* came to my assistance to set me free from the path of philosophy that had served its purpose in my serendipitous discovery of the **secret way** in

Gurdjieff's teaching, and it was only a matter of time before I made the conscious decision to walk away from university.

Philosophy was pulling me out into a sea of endless mentation that I feared would not promise me an answer to my haunting question, and the individuation process of my creative unconscious offered me the solution to my problem of resolving my dual nature in the symbolic squaring of the circle mandala that appeared to me one night, which was the only way I would ever answer the question that had called me to university in the first place, *who am I?*

I shut off the lights in my bedroom and flopped my body onto the bed and put my hands behind my head and stared into the darkness wallowing in my despair. I was so mad I did not know whether to scream or cry. I stared and stared, thinking and despairing; and the more I thought about my dilemma, the more I despaired. Philosophy was not giving me the answer, and Gurdjieff's teaching puzzled me; I saw no light whatsoever, and I despaired. And then it happened:

A tiny dot of blue light appeared before my eyes at the foot of my bed, just above eye level, and it rested there suspended in mid-air long enough for me to rub my eyes to see if it was real. I shut my eyes and opened them again, and it was still there; and then the tiny dot of blue light began to expand and grow into the shape of a circle until it was about three feet in diameter, and it sat in mid air like a donut of shimmering blue light. Dumbfounded, I just stared; and then a tiny dot of yellow light appeared within and at the top of the circumference of the blue circle, and it also expanded and grew, forming a perfectly straight line of bright yellow light within the circumference, and then it stopped, made a ninety degree turn, and formed another straight line, stopped again and made another ninety-degree turn and formed another straight line, and another, joining with itself to form a perfect square of bright yellow light within the circumference of shimmering blue light—which, though I did not

One Rule to Live By

know it then, was a symbolic squaring of the circle. Nonplussed, I just stared at the hologram circle of bright blue light with a square of bright yellow light within its circumference; and then, just as miraculously as it had appeared, it disappeared, and my bedroom was in darkness again!

It took many years to make sense of this miraculous experience, and had I not been called to read and study C. G. Jung and his Gnostic-inspired psychology of individuation, I would never have come to understand the meaning of my mandala experience; but I had to "work" on myself long and hard day and night for weeks and months and years to resolve the opposites of my dual nature—*what Jesus called making the two into one*—before the puzzle of my life finally fell into place for me.

To square the circle, one has to do the impossible, and the task that I had set for myself in my quest for my true self was not possible within the paradigm of my philosophy studies; but I did not know this cognitively. I sensed that philosophy wasn't the path for me, but I didn't know what to do about it, and deep anxiety possessed me. *Please God, tell me what to do,* I pleaded silently.

Then divine serendipity kicked in with Ouspensky's book *In Search of the Miraculous*, and the door to the **secret way** cracked open for me; but I had to drop out of university to forge my own path in life by "working" on myself with Gurdjieff's teaching, and my despair of not knowing what to do forced my unconscious to resolve my problem by manifesting the symbol of "squaring the circle" of blue and yellow light before my eyes, the mandala of the "impossible" quest for my true self—hence, **"my mandala, my mandate,"** the unconscious imperative of my individual *way*.

When the mandala symbolizing my successful quest for my true self *literally* manifested before my eyes that night, I didn't know what it meant; but after I did the impossible and "worked" my way through the eye of the needle and gave "birth" to my immortal self in my mother's kitchen one summer day while she was kneading bread dough on the kitchen table, I finally understood that I had unconsciously **mandated** myself to find my true self *(I did, after all, vow to find my true self or die trying)*, hence the symbolic squaring of the circle that my unconscious manifested in my bedroom when I did not know what to do to find my true self; and in my enlightened perspective today, I'm right back to where I started, "chopping wood and carrying water…"

39. Not a Prophet or Reformer, Just a Writer

A poet speaks not only of their own individuation process, they speak for the collective individuation of the whole world, and when my poem *What the Hell Is Going on Out There?* came to me unbeckoned and word perfect, I knew that it spoke for me and the collective psyche of the world; and one year later professor Jordan Peterson was called to his destiny and provided an answer to my angry question, and he became the prophet and reformer that the collective psyche of the world was calling for, giving talks around the world on his book *12 Rules for Life: An Antidote to Chaos*. "One of the most important thinkers to emerge on the world stage for many years," said *The Spectator*.

On *November 29, 2018*, Jordan Peterson was interviewed by Joe Rogan on his show, which was live-streamed on YouTube (*Joe Rogan Experience #1208-Jordan Peterson*), and when Jordan Peterson said that he had completed his 100 city global book tour (with more cities still to come), I *knew* that it was time to bring this story home.

In just two days the Rogan interview got a million and a half views, which speaks to the Jordan Peterson effect; but when I finished watching the interview, I hadn't learned anything new from professor Peterson that I hadn't heard before, despite the exciting new iteration of the same hierophantic message that his professorial gift for public speaking always brought to the table, and I called upon my muse to bring *One Rule to Live By: Be Good* to closure...

When I was called to write *One Rule to Live By: Be Good*, I never felt compelled to expound upon Jordan Peterson's hierophantic message, carefully analyzing each of his 12 rules for life and offering my understanding, one can explore this through his book, online lectures, podcasts, blog and many interviews (and if one wants to dig deeper, they can also read his *Maps of Meaning: The Architecture of Belief*); my creative directive was to offer a key to the door of the **secret way** that Jordan Peterson's message brought one to, should one be conscientious enough to take his shadow-dismantling, character-building message to heart—the same directive that *compelled* me to send Jordan Peterson four of my memoirs to read, two before he came into public prominence and two more when he was catapulted onto the world stage three years later to offer him insights and inspiration for his own courageous, and now quite challenging individuation process.

In an article that he wrote for *The Australian* while on his book tour in Australia, which was also published in *The National Post* here in Canada *(Saturday, March 2, 2019)*, professor Peterson tells us just how challenging his life is now *(he has expanded his book tour to include Southern and Eastern Europe and Southeast Asia)*; but trusting the Logos as he does, he embraces his challenge heart and soul, as he tells us in his dispatch from Australia in *The National Post*:

> "I talk directly to the audience. No notes. No scaffolding. I tell them, as individuals, what problem we are here to address. It's generally something of deep existential significance: the tyranny of society, the terror of nature, the ignorance and malevolence that too often characterizes the individual and the family. We talk about the darkness of life, and of suffering, and of betrayal and nihilism and hopelessness and the desire for revenge that all of that can produce. And then we extract some light out of the abysmal depths. There is no discussion of happiness as the goal of life. Happiness, welcome as it is, is a side-effect, an unexpected benefit, a bit of the grace of God. If it comes your way, open your arms to it, embrace it, and enjoy it. But it won't last. What we all need instead of happiness is meaning — the kind of meaning that will sustain each of us through the suffering that life entails, so that we can endure the self-betrayal and the dissolution of our intimate relationships through death and distance and the illness and aging and disappointment and death that await all of us, just and unjust alike. **And I tell my audiences something they all know, but have not been able to fully understand or articulate: the sustaining meaning in life is to be found in the responsibility of life, the load we voluntarily decide to**

bear (and the heavier the better). We must take care of ourselves, as individuals, in a manner that makes us better for our families, in a manner that sets the community right, such that the ship of state does not list too far right or left and sails forth for the destination that is true and proper. We must take stock of our multitudinous sins, attempt to atone for them, accept the adventure of our life, and try to encourage nature to shine her beneficial face upon us, keep the tyranny of our social organizations at bay, improve our characters as individuals and, most importantly, face the unknown with truth and courage so that we can discover what is new and necessary and eternally redemptive. It is in this manner that we cooperate in the creation of what has always been envisioned as the City of God, stumbling uphill towards it as we can."

Bravo Jordan! But I was being *called*, and I pondered how to bring this story home when to my surprise a spiritual musing that I wrote last summer popped into my mind, and as irrelevant as it may appear to be, it speaks directly to the central issue of *One Rule to Live By: Be Good*:

A Pouring from the Empty into the Void

The highly respected staff writer and book critic for *The New Yorker* James Wood said something to inveterate book lover Michael Silverblatt on a *Bookworm* podcast that called for a spiritual musing. I don't remember his exact words, but in essence James Wood said, '*When an apprentice gets hurt on a job, there's an old saying that the trade is entering his body,*' (upon reflection, he may have said this during a reading of his new book of essays, *The Nearest Thing to Life,* at the *Politics and Prose* Bookstore in Washington, D.C. that I also saw on YouTube), which reminded me of Leo Tolstoy's comment about writing his novels in his own blood, as illustrated by the oft-quoted line from his famous novel *Anna Karenina*: "All happy families are alike; each unhappy family is unhappy in its own way."

In effect, we pay for the gnostic wisdom of our life's path, which I can vouchsafe with the blood that I spilled learning my own trade of contract painting and drywall taping (my vocation, which cost me plenty of spilled blood as I learned my trade with no one to guide me, losing thirty thousand on a job one summer at the Lake Helen

Reserve because of my fool-hardy spirit and inexperience) and the craft of writing (I'm still bleeding from the blood I spilled with my first novel, *What Would I Say Today If I Were to Die Tomorrow?* that so upset my hometown that Penny and I had to relocate to Georgian Bay for peace of mind*)*; but as I listened to James Wood talking about literature, which for an articulate atheist like himself was the closest thing to religion, I got the same feeling that I got listening to the iconic literary critic professor Harold Bloom that literature was not enough to satisfy the longing in our soul for wholeness and completeness, and an old quandary popped into my mind— *the existential dilemma of modern life.*

    I cannot for the life of me get a read on social media, especially the daily posts on my Facebook feed that desperately cry out for attention like an Andy Warhol painting, as if the more "Likes" one gets on their posts the more relevant they will be to the cosmic scheme of things, and I cannot fathom whether society is overwhelmed with too much existential reality or too little, and I keep asking myself: are we drowning in the deep end of the pool, or the shallow? Has our life become a reality show for social media, an endless quotidian stream of daily living like the Norwegian writer Karl Ove Knausgaard's "hypnotically spellbinding" (James Wood's words) six volume autobiographical novel *My Struggle*?

    I cannot tell, and I have to explore my quandary in today's spiritual musing. But in all humility, I don't know where to begin, and I have to call upon my muse to assist me…

    I woke up this morning with a spiritually fatiguing issue on my mind, the archaic mediaeval face-covering niqab and burqa apparel issue that a minority of Muslim women here insist on wearing for "religious reasons," a politically sensitive issue that has polarized the people of Quebec, and I cannot help but feel that this is my entry into my spiritual musing that I could not resolve yesterday; but what does it mean?

    I've already written a spiritual musing on this issue ("A Tempest in a Teapot," which I've included in my book *The Armchair Guru*), and I could quote it here to make my point about our journey through life much easier; but I feel I have to explore my quandary from another angle for a greater understanding, and the only way to do this would be to revisit my feelings on the dilemma of the irreconcilable outer and inner journey of our life, the conflicted nature of our *existential* outer self and our *essential* inner self.

What I'm getting from social media is an endless stream of information on the outer journey of contemporary life, that aspect of society's preoccupation with the existential dimension of reality—politics (sexual harassment is the hot topic of the day that has exploded in the #MeToo movement), personal relationships, nostalgic memorabilia, always new selfies and endless recipes and health tips and cartoonish re-posts and other trivia, what in his creative genius the prodigious writer of his own contemporary world John Updike would have called "lower gossip," leaving one with the strongest impression that this fleeting life is all we have and we'd better make the most of it, and dread possesses everyone.

Life has sped up with digital technology, and whatever happens out there is instantly vented (and vetted) on social media, giving one the nauseous feeling that "the world is too much with us," as Wordsworth wrote in his eponymous poem while in the throes of the First Industrial Revolution two hundred years ago—another vicious terrorist attack in a house of worship or public setting and raging forest fires and more senseless bombings and freakish storms and floods and consequent social upheavals that will take years to recover from, blaming religious zealotry, identity politics, climate change, and recalcitrant karmic obtuseness; every day a new catastrophe, the world going to hell much more quickly than anyone expected, and we grasp at life a little tighter as writers like Karl Ove Knausgaard vainly try to make sense of the human condition, the outer becoming the inner and the inner the outer, a never-ending *enantiodromia* of self-individuation teleologically driven to personal wholeness and completeness but never quite getting there.

After listening to James Wood on *Bookworm* (who helped launch Knausgaard's career in America with his optimistic review of the first volume of *My Struggle*), engaging in his erudition but no less disappointing than the great professor Bloom's sublime nihilism, I listened to Silverblatt talking in another podcast with the new literary genius of *Infinite Jest* and messianic hope for literature before

Knausgaard came along with his six volumes of *My Struggle*, David Foster Wallace, who also could not find a way to reconcile his outer and inner journey and was driven to suicide at the age of 46 to end the pain of his existential dilemma and crippling depression, I shook my head and said, in Gurdjieffian jest, "It's all a pouring from the empty into the void," and I went off Facebook for a month or so to give myself a break.

And that's what has made professor Jordan Peterson "the most influential public intellectual in the Western world today," because his message is not a pouring from the empty into the void; it is a pouring of the Logos of his own gnostic wisdom into the spiritual vacuum of today's crazy world of postmodern nihilism, identity politics, and political correctness gone loony that religion, science, and politics cannot resolve, which is why hundreds of people *(mostly young men)* have gone up to him after each of his book tour lectures to thank him and shake his hand for helping them get their life together, some even thanking him for dissuading them from taking their own life and go on living with self-generating meaning through responsible living, proof positive of the redemptive power of the imperative of his *12 Rules for Life: An Antidote to Chaos*.

Nonetheless, true to the reprehensible saying that *no good deed goes unpunished*, "the most influential public intellectual in the Western world today" posed such a perilous threat to the malevolent spirit of the archetypal shadow spirit of life with his redemptive message of self-reconciliation that the offer of a two month fellowship extended to professor Peterson by Cambridge divinity school was rescinded, as he tells us in the *National Post, March 23, 2019*:

> "Now, the divinity school has decided that signalling their solidarity with the diversity-inclusivity-equity mob (CUSU, the Cambridge University Student Union) trumps that opportunity—or so I presume. You see, I don't

know yet, because (and this is particularly appalling) I was not formally notified of this decision by any representative of the divinity school. I heard about the rescinded offer through the grapevine, via a colleague and friend, and gathered what I could about the reason from social media and press coverage..."

Professor Peterson wanted to work on a series of lectures on the *Exodus* stories (he had already done a series of lectures on *Genesis*, which were so well received it astonished everyone, especially Christians, garnering millions of viewers on YouTube), and he was looking forward to working on his *Exodus* lectures at Cambridge divinity school to draw upon the university's long history of bible scholarship and learning, but his fellowship was rescinded when CUSU's social justice warriors played their offensive "diversity-inclusivity-equity" card:

"We are relieved to hear that Jordan Peterson's request for a visiting fellowship to Cambridge's faculty of divinity has been rescinded following further review. It is a political act to associate the University with an academic's work through offers which legitimize figures such as Peterson. His work and views are not representative of the student body and as such we do not see his visit as a valuable contribution to the university, but one that works in opposition to the principles of the University."

Exactly the opposite of what professor Peterson stood for! But that damn treacherous little spirit of wilful malevolence had to try once more to take him down by smearing the good professor's reputation for daring to shine the light of the Logos into the darkness of this world through the prism of one of the oldest and most reputable universities in the world. Ironically, professor Peterson had given a talk at Cambridge a few months earlier, which I had seen on YouTube and found very informative, and this talk was the second-most watched of Cambridge's 200 total videos; this is why he was puzzled that his fellowship would be rescinded, and although this pleased CUSU's "diversity-inclusivity-equity" loony left, many good people came to his defence.

But the tangent of this bizarre story is still unfolding, and from what I'm getting from social media, Cambridge is getting push-back from professor Peterson's devout followers, with some reputable people coming out in defense of free speech, leaving proud Cambridge with egg on its face like Whitcoulls bookstores in New Zealand that foolishly banned Peterson's book *12 Rules for Life* by associating him with the Christchurch mosque massacres on the strength of a photo that went viral of him with his arm around a young fan wearing an anti-Islam T-shirt at one of his book signings *(on Friday, March 15, 2019, fifty people were shot and killed and fifty injured in two Christchurch mosques by a 28 year old Australian white supremacist shortly after Peterson's book tour in New Zealand);* but Whitcoulls had to reinstate his book when social media got on its case, because Dr. Peterson was not responsible for what his fans wore when having their picture taken with him. This was just another example of false association and political correctness gone loony.

But this is not where my story is meant to go, and I'm being *called* to bring it home. Before I do however, I'm inclined to mention one more Peterson phenomenon that illustrates the message of Plato's allegory of the cave, and with an ironic twist that puts a big smile on my face.

This much anticipated year-long planned event not only illustrates the practical reality of my spiritual musing *"A Pouring from the Empty Into the Void,"* it also joyfully confirms my gut-wrenching decision to drop out of university where I had gone to study philosophy to find my true self—the much touted "debate of the century" between Dr. Jordan Peterson and Slovenian Marxist Slavoj Zizek, "who is considered to be the world's greatest philosopher," which took place at the Sony Center in Toronto, Canada on *Friday, April 19, 2019,* the topic being: *"Happiness: Marxism vs. Capitalism."*

I came across Slavoj Zizek many times on YouTube before this great debate took place, but he could never pull me into his worldview *(which is godless and pessimistic)*; not only because it proved to be another tiresome example of a pouring from the empty into the void, but because of his manner of speaking, which was so eccentric that it appeared he was suffering from an iteration of Tourette syndrome, an annoying tic of pinching his sweater and grabbing his nose which grew more rapid and intense as he got closer to making his point, like a revved-up engine running out of control. So, I was curious to see how this great philosophical thinker would fair with psychologist Jordan Peterson, whose consistent message of hope was nothing if not a practical way of living that would bring some measure of meaning and purpose to one's life, a creative distillation of all the gnostic wisdom that he had rendered from his maps of meaning into 12 simple rules to guide one's life through this crazy neo-Marxist postmodern world of nihilism, identity politics, and loony political correctness.

I watched the debate when it was streamed on YouTube (*tickets for the live event sold out, and scalpers were selling them for hundreds of dollars!*), and Slavoj Zizek fell into character with his idiosyncratic Tourette behavior, which clinical psychologist Jordan Peterson observed with wide-eyed bewilderment; and then I read all the follow-up reviews that I found online and watched four or five commentaries on YouTube and was not surprised to see that they all reflected a bias for one side or the other (*more seeming to favor Zizek on the strength of his "gotcha" moment when he asked Peterson to name one postmodern neo-Marxist and he couldn't, which missed the point of Peterson's critique because it wasn't postmodern neo-Marxists as such that he was holding up to account, but the unholy effects of the Marxist ideology that was cleverly "smuggled" into postmodernist thinking*), and I came away from the "debate of the century" happily confirmed in my gut-wrenching decision to drop my philosophy studies and leave university to forge my own path in life with Gurdjieff's teaching of "work on oneself." But because my poet's mind has a way of rendering experiences that I cannot quite put into words into symbolic images, I saw an image in my mind's eye of "the world's greatest philosopher" inside a cage in a zoo performing his antics for spectators passing by, with a sign in bold letters that read: PHILOSOPHER THINKING, and I burst into laughter.

Now, I know this short but necessary digression may blow up in my face when this story gets published, but it wasn't meant to poke fun at the person Salvoj Zizek, but at the idiosyncratic character of the mother of all disciplines which the "the world's greatest philosopher" symbolized, and it was just my ironic, albeit mischievous way of closing the circle of my quest for my true self which formally began at university with my philosophy studies that I *had* to drop because the way to one's true self cannot be found in the confined matrix of one's mind, but only by "doing" life. **"Which of you by taking thought can add one cubit to his stature?"** said Jesus (Matthew 6: 27).

One has to *live* their life to *find* their life, which Gurdjieff's teaching taught me how to do, especially his "way of the sly man," and watching "the world's greatest philosopher" thinking out loud only confirmed Gurdjieff's saying that all of that philosophical thinking was just another example of a pouring from the empty into the void, despite Slavoj Zizek's brilliance; and, in all honesty, I don't know why Jordan Peterson, whose message was all about how to live one's life responsibly, even bothered to challenge him to a debate for saying what he did about him.

But then, Slavoj Zizek did fire the first shots against Peterson during a Cambridge Union event, labelling the Canadian best-selling author of 12 *Rules for Life: An Antidote to Chaos* as his "enemy," going on to slam his ideas as "pseudo-scientific" and taking umbrage with his "obsession with cultural Marxism," which riled western boy Jordan Peterson who angrily tweeted Slavoj Zizek: *"If you wish to debate the validity of my "apparently" scientific theories—or any of my other claims—then let me know, and we'll arrange it."* And they did.

But then, that's the path that called professor Peterson to answer society's desperate need to know what the hell was going on out there, and he *had* to go where he was called to defend the integrity of his message; and this brings me back to my story...

Professor Peterson told Joe Rogan in the *November 29, 2018* interview that he never gave the same lecture twice on his global book tour talks *(which currently has grown to 150 cities, and counting)*, but that's not quite true; he always gives the same hierophantic message, but packaged in a new and refreshing iteration, always allowing for the free flow of the Logos that speaks to the needs of his respective audiences, because professor Peterson has the gift of being open to the Logos, which is why he never gets tired of delivering his Solzhenitsyn-inspired message to a world that is hungry to hear what he has to say *(he himself cannot wait to see what's going to come out of him with each new talk, for such is the excitement of being connected with one's inner self)*. But just what is his hierophantic message? Can it be reduced to a simple sentence, a single phrase, or word?

Isn't this why I was called by *the omniscient guiding principle of life* to write One Rule to Live By: Be Good? Isn't this what professor Peterson's message boils down to, just being a good person? And isn't his book *12 Rules for Life: An Antidote to Chaos* simply a pathway to being a good person? Isn't this the divine imperative of his hierophantic message, just being a good person and not a philosopher in a zoo thinking about what it means to be good?

If there's one thing that I have learned in my unbelievable quest for my true self, it's the simple truth that a personal pathway (path + *way* = path*way*) is both a process and a destination, and one has to forge their own *way* to their true self, which *12 Rules for Life* helps one do; because, in the words of my hero Socrates, *12 Rules for Life: An Antidote to Chaos* gets one into "the habit of soul gathering and collecting herself into herself," and the more one "gathers and collects" their soul (which is trapped in the ego/shadow consciousness of their personality), the more their true self they will be—true to the Matthew Principle, **much gathers more**.

This is why the core tenet of Peterson's iconoclastic message of taking responsibility *(both moral and practical)* for one's life fills the spiritual vacuum of their life and gives one meaning and purpose; and it doesn't matter how the good professor dresses this up in his lectures and interviews, it's always the same redemptive message of self-reconciliation, as he iterated yet again to a group of young men in London, England who got their life together by taking up the sport of boxing.

"Of all the things I've been talking to people about," said professor Peterson to the tightly knit boxing club community, *"probably the most useful to help people understand (is) that you need a meaning in your life to buttress the tragedy and the malevolence and betrayal, and that you find that fundamentally in the adoption of responsibility,"* a message that was confirmed the following year by the British actor Charlie Hunnam who starred in the new Netflix film *Triple Frontier*.

In a *Men's Health* article in which the actor talked about his admiration for Jordan Peterson, "a controversial psychologist who's spoken out against political correctness," he was asked what it was like working with a SEAL trainer for the movie *Triple Frontier*, and Hunnam compared the Special Forces training to Jordan Peterson's message.

"I really love the sense of seriousness with those guys—there's no sense of life being trivial," Hunnam told *Men's Health*. "There's no flippancy, no triviality to those guys. They were just very, very serious. I really enjoy that. I'm a big fan of Jordan Peterson, as are a lot of people right now—he's become quite an internet phenomenon, a card-carrying member of the intellectual dark web." And the actor went on to compare the Special Forces "mentality" to Peterson's way of thinking. "I love the message that he promotes, which is, 'Take your life seriously.' Carry as much responsibility as possible. I think in his words he says, 'Pick up the heaviest thing that you can and carry it.'"

And that, ironically, is the mystical appeal of Peterson's message: **shoulder the burden of your own existence, because the alternative is more of the same**—or, as he expresses it in *Rule 7* of his book: *"Pursue what is meaningful (not what is expedient),"* a task that requires the strength of character of a Navy SEAL and the moral fiber of Wordsworth's Happy Warrior. Which brings to mind one of my favorite Gurdjieff sayings: *"Once you shoulder a responsibility, it becomes the lightest thing in the world to carry."* So, it doesn't matter how Peterson iterates it; it's always the same message that speaks to each person's individual need for wholeness and completeness.

One of his 12 rules for life will speak to one person more than the other rules, but the more one "gathers and collects" oneself into oneself by shouldering the burden of their own existence, the more they will resonate with the other rules, which in the end makes one a good person whose only guiding principle will be their own conscience and free will; which brings to mind something that my inner guiding principle revealed to me after my traumatizing sexual experience brutally shocked my conscience awake and I fled from my comfortable life in my hometown of Nipigon, in Northwestern Ontario to set my feet upon my own path to my true self half a century ago.

I was twenty-three years old and living in Annecy, France. I was so culturally shocked and unbearably distraught that I went for a long walk one afternoon to think things through; and I came back from my freezing walk in the snow feeling so lost and lonely that I did not know what to do. With a sad and heavy heart, I sat at my desk and picked up my pen and the following words came to me, which became my guiding light in my lonely quest for my true self:

"Steadfast and courageous is he, who having overcome woe and grief remains alone and undaunted. Alone I say, for to be otherwise would hardly seem possible, for one must bear one's conscience alone. He must fight the

battle and he must win the battle, odds or no odds. He must win to establish the equilibrial tranquility of body and soul, and sooner or later he will erupt as a volcano of unlimited confidence which will purpose his life hereafter; and having given birth to such magnificence, he will no longer be alone alone, but alone in society, and he will see the mirror of his puerile grief in the eyes of his fellow man."

    I had no idea where those words came from (the word "equilibrial" isn't even in the dictionary, but it is the right word, or *le mot juste* as the literati would say); but so fraught with *gnosis* were those words that they gave me the inspiration I needed to continue my quest for my true self.

    Bursting with the sacred mandala of squaring the circle that appeared in my bedroom at university four years later, those words came to me in Annecy, France to encourage me to set my soul free from the insufferable prison of my ego/shadow personality; and now, half a century later, from the enlightened perspective of my true self, I *know* that they came from my higher self, which I acknowledge to be the Logos, my muse, my oracle, and *the omniscient guiding principle of life*, and, at the risk of being more personal than I have ever been in all the books that I have written, I've just been *told* by my guiding principle to bring One Rule to Live By: Be Good to closure with the most sacred experience of my entire life, **my call to the final surrender...**

40. My Call to the Final Surrender

> *"Behold, be grateful, and forgive that which you did not understand or control. For life is divine, it is perfect, and it naturally manifests the will of its creator."*
>
> *Love Without End, Jesus Speaks...*
> —Glenda Green

My call to *the final surrender* happened in the waiting room of the ICU of St. Michael's Hospital in Toronto this September where my Penny Lynn had just been operated on for a brain aneurysm and was, in the words of one of her doctors, "somewhere between here and there and very lucky to be here," a miracle which I attribute to St. Padre Pio; but this is a story in itself, which I hope to write one day when I have more distance from this whole experience that brutally shifted my world from comfortable order into terrifying chaos, and back again.

I'm the same person that I was before Penny's brain aneurysm and miraculous healing, but completely different; and it's from this difference that I've been called to bring closure to this story, because from my state of consciousness of *the final surrender*, the world makes infinitely much more sense to me now in all of its chaos and confusion; and when I listen to professor Peterson today, still out there crusading to save the world with his talks on *12 Rules for Life: An Antidote to Chaos*, I have to smile at his mission, because from where I stand today I can see that the world does not need to be saved, but understood. *"Each life has a natural built-in reason for being,"* said Jesus in Glenda Green's book *The Keys of Jeshua*. *"Purpose is the creative spirit of life moving through you from the inside out. It is the deep dimension in every soul, which carries with it a profound sense of personal identity."* And life after life after life, we keep coming back to learn this. This is what needs to be understood.

Ironically, this is the divine imperative of Jordan Peterson's hierophantic message of the sacred individual self that John Keats pointed to in a letter to his brother. In a moment of poetic genius, Keats caught a glimpse of the big picture; but he never realized his "unapprehended inspiration" because he died too young to fulfill his destined purpose to wholeness and completeness. But he did inform us that this life is the medium by which soul acquires its own identity (just as Jung and I realized that this life is the *way* to growth and self-fulfilment), and that's the genius of professor Peterson's message—to become whole and complete by taking moral responsibility for our life, which *12 Rules for Life: An Antidote to Chaos* helps one do; 12 carefully wrought rules that offer a personal way to realize the gifted poet's "unapprehended inspiration"—

> "I can scarcely express what I but dimly perceive—and yet I think I perceive it. That you may judge the more clearly I will put it in the most homely form possible. I will call the world a School instituted for the purpose of teaching little children to read. I will call the *human heart* the horn-book read in that school, and I will call the *Child able to read* the *Soul* made from that School and its horn-book. Do you not see how necessary a world of pains and troubles is to school and Intelligence and make it a Soul? A place where the heart must feel and suffer in a thousand diverse ways. Not merely is the Heart a horn-book, but it is the Mind's Bible, it is the Mind's experience, it is the text from which the Mind or Intelligence sucks its identity. As various as the lives of men are, so various become their Souls; and thus God makes individual beings, Souls, identical Souls, of the parts of his own essence. This appears to me a faint sketch of a system of salvation which does not offend our reason and humanity" (*The Vale of Soul Making*, John Keats).

"There is nothing but the self and God," Jesus confirmed to the gifted artist Glenda Green while painting his portrait that she called "The Lamb and the Lion" when Jesus appeared to her for almost four months between *November 1991* and *March 1992*, the sacred mystery that professor Peterson caught a glimpse of

One Rule to Live By

with his *Maps of Meaning: The Architecture of Belief* which he artfully rendered into his *12 Rules for Life: An Antidote to Chaos* that has taken the world by storm (global sales have reached three million, and he's lectured in 150 cities and not done yet, and I understand that he's working on a sequel to *12 Rules for Life* that will prompt another global book tour which may bring him and the world closer to soul's destined purpose of wholeness and completeness); but not until one has been initiated into the sacred mystery of the self (the *I Am* consciousness of God) will one understand the imperative of his hierophantic message, which, by happy coincidence, Jesus revealed in Chapter 2 of Glenda Green's book *The Keys of Jeshua*, "RECOVERING THE AUTHENTIC SELF":

> "Things were not created from nothing. Everything was created from 'Being.' The ultimate state of pure being is the totality of energy and potential, resting in stillness and peace with itself. In such a state all ideas for creation are formed, and these ideas are merely extensions of the self. Creation is the consequence of *I Am* moving into action, or life, through multiplying **ITSELF**. There was no instrument of creation outside of Divine Being. *I AM THAT I AM* is God. So too with yourself. The truth of who you are will not be found in actions or personal history, but in the simplicity of who you are within the stillness and peace of your inner being...In the beginning and forever 'I Am is the way; I Am is the word.'" (*The Keys of Jeshua*, by Glenda Green, p. 13).

This was my journey of self-discovery, and though I had already passed through the eye of the needle and realized my true self, little did I expect to be called again by the divine imperative of the *way* to fulfill a higher purpose, just as Jordan Peterson was called to his own higher purpose of delivering his hierophantic message of self-reconciliation with his *12 Rules for Life* and book tour talks, interviews, and podcasts; but I was called to *the final surrender* when my Penny Lynn suffered a ruptured brain aneurysm, and I had to let her go for her to come back to me.

That was the miracle that I prayed for. Never in my life would I have dreamt that I would be brought to my knees to pray like I did in my Roman Catholic youth, but so terrified was I of losing my Penny Lynn that I dropped to my knees and desperately prayed for a miracle.

"Please Padre, bring her back home to me safe and whole," was my constant plea to the healing saint who was the inspiration for my novel *Healing with Padre Pio*, and with Pastor Joel (the spiritual counsellor at St. Michael's ICU ward, who was there to comfort me in my desperate time of need), we prayed for Penny Lynn's recovery.

"She's not out of the woods yet," was the constant daily refrain, and every few hours they took her out of sedation to ask her: 1. What's your name? 2. Where are you? 3. Can you move the fingers on your right hand? 4. Now your left hand, and the same with her toes on her right foot and her left foot, and each time the nurse asked, my heart jumped to my throat; and then Penny contracted pneumonia and had to be put on a respirator, and the Pastor and I prayed harder; and then, out of my deepest, deepest despair of losing her, I was called to *the final surrender*:

Pastor Joel and I had just prayed for Penny's recovery, me first in my desperation praying to God that if she had to go I would understand but if was at all possible for her to come back to me, to please let it be so, and Pastor Joel praying to God in his own way for Penny's recovery, me on the left side of the bed holding Penny's hand and he on her right side holding her other hand, and we prayed heart and soul, and then we went to the waiting room of the ICU ward and sat, but so emotionally wrought was I when it suddenly dawned on me that I might lose my Penny Lynn that it all came pouring out of me in a volley of unstoppable tears, and I cried like I never cried before, and probably will ever cry again, and in stark awareness of my desperate situation, I turned to Pastor Joel, who had his hand on my shoulder to console me, and said, "I've just been called to the final surrender..."

One Rule to Live By

I hope one day to write the whole story of Penny Lynn's brain aneurysm and my call to *the final surrender*, but for reasons which only my oracle knows, this was the experience called for to bring closure to *One Rule to Live By: Be Good*; and now that I've had time to ponder why, I know that I was called to *the final surrender* to make good my karmic obligation to Penny Lynn for breaking her heart the way I did in our past life together in Genoa, Italy and to confirm God's existence for this story with her miraculous healing; *because after I surrendered my Penny Lynn to God, St. Padre Pio did bring her back home to me safe and whole,* and good professor Jordan Peterson and renowned atheist Sam Harris, who have already discoursed on God and religion and morality in Vancouver, Canada and again to a hungry audience of 8500 people in Dublin, Ireland, and once more in London, England can argue until the cows come home about God's existence or non-existence, because the sacred mystery of God will always come down to a question of self-initiation, and my call to *the final surrender* was the price that I had to pay for *divine reconciliation...*

A month after I brought Penny Lynn home from rehabilitation at Bridgepoint Hospital in Toronto, safe and whole *(still very weak, but with full presence of mind and all of her motor skills intact),* we got a call out of the blue from an old friend in Orillia.

Penny was on the living room couch resting, and I was in the sunroom reading when the phone rang. Penny answered, and to our surprise it was our friend from Orillia whom we hadn't seen in seven or eight years. She was packing books into boxes for her move to a new apartment when she got an urge to call us, and Penny told her about her brain aneurysm and miraculous recovery, and after talking for a few more minutes Penny handed the phone to me and I shared my call to *the final surrender* with her; but no sooner did I share the most sacred experience of my life, when our friend excitedly said, *"That's* when her healing started! You had to let her go for her to be healed! That was the miracle!"* And just then—as if to seal *my final surrender* with Penny Lynn's miraculous healing—*a vision appeared to her of a beam of golden light streaming down into my body from heaven!*

Our friend is gifted. When I had to have triple bypass surgery nine years ago, she called to tell me that her spiritual guide had told her to tell me to get a quartz crystal and carry it on my person before my surgery, which was cancelled twice for different reasons, which I now believe was to prolong the healing benefits of the crystal because my heart was damaged from two heart attacks and the surgeon was dubious about performing bypass surgery; but after the operation, the surgeon said to Penny, with a puzzled look on his face, that he only had to do a double bypass and not a triple, because one of the blocked arteries was almost normal, and a few years before this surprising phone call, our friend had a vision of the novel I had just written on my past lives and gave me the title that she saw on the cover in her vision, *Cathedral of My Past Lives*, and she also told me a few more things about my life that only a gifted psychic could possibly know, so I had history with her gift, and when she told me that Penny's miraculous healing started when I was called to *the final surrender*, I believed her. Penny was my whole life, and letting go of her was the most difficult thing I ever had, or will ever have to do; but it gives me comfort to know that Pastor Joel was there to witness it, or no one would believe me. *"I have to let her go, Joel,"* I said to him, convulsing with unstoppable tears. *"I've just been called to the final surrender..."*

Why else would our gifted friend call out of the blue? Why, if not to confirm the essential mystery of the *way* that Jesus symbolized with his crucifixion and revealed to Carl Jung's spiritual guide Philemon in the final words of *The Red Book* when he said, *"I bring you the beauty of suffering. That is what is needed by whoever hosts the worm,"* the sacred mystery of self-sacrifice that proud little Friedrich Nietzsche so tragically misperceived and resisted his whole miserable life, **the mystery of letting go of our final attachment to our existential self to realize the purity of the immortal I Am consciousness of our divine nature**; but, in all honesty and with trembling humility, I did not need this confirmation. My friend's call was for my readers' edification.

Again, I never cease to marvel at how *the merciful law of divine synchronicity* works in my life when I'm writing a new book, nudging my friend from Orillia to call and give me unexpected confirmation of *my final surrender* and Penny's miraculous healing for the closing chapter of this incredible but true story of only one rule to live by; and now I have to bring my story home with one final spiritual musing that answers the question of why we should be good and bring happy resolution to the divine imperative of professor Jordan Peterson's hierophantic message...

"Muse," wrote the poet Jane Hirshfield, "derives from the Latin *mussare,* meaning first, 'to carry in silence,' then 'to brood over in silence and uncertainty,' and then only finally 'to murmur or mutter, to speak in an undertone.' Musing, it seems, is a thing that happens best in the circumstances of quiet. Undogmatic and tactful before the object of attention, musing does not impose but bears witness. It quietly considers, and then, when it finally speaks, does so with the voice, respectful of other presences, that we use in a library, church, or museum— **the voice used, that is, when we feel we are in the company of something more important than ourselves**" (*Ten Windows: How Great Poems Transform the World,* by Jane Hirshfield, pp. 26-7, bold italics mine).

I carry ideas for my spiritual musings in silence, sometimes for weeks and months at a time—*even years, it seems!*—before they are given expression, and always tactfully and respectful of others; and now that I reflect upon how they are written, also in a voice that makes me feel like I'm in the company of something more important than myself, a voice that bears witness to the Logos, like my spiritual musing "Why be Good?" that I was called to write *Friday, April 17, 2015*, three years before I was called to write *One Rule to Live By: Be Good* which brings the imperative of professor Peterson's hierophantic message in *12 Rules for Life* to satisfactory resolution, I *know* now why I was called to write my spiritual musing "Why be Good?" Because, in its omniscience my oracle knew that this is what I was going to need to bring literary closure to *One Rule for Life: Be Good* that was not even conceived of yet and would not be written until professor Peterson was called by life three years later to answer the angry question of my poem, *What the Hell is Going on Out There?*

Why be Good?

When I read David Brooks' column from the *New York Times* ("Rather than building our careers, we should build inner character") in my *Friday, April 17, 2015* Life section of the *Toronto Star*, I heard my call to write a spiritual musing, **why be good?**

But for one reason or another, I put it off; and then I picked up my *Sunday, May 3, 2015 Star*, which also features *The New York Times International Weekly* and *Book Review* inserts, and as the playful spirit of synchronicity would have it, Brooks' column in the *New York Times* was titled "Goodness and Power," and the *Book Review* insert just "happened" to feature a review of David Brooks' new book *The Road to Character*; and, just to play with my mind a little more, after reading my papers yesterday afternoon the playful spirit of synchronicity nudged me to listen to the CBC *Tapestry* podcast instead of *Writer's & Company* as I had intended, and (*oh happy coincidence!*) Mary Hynes, the host of *Tapestry*, was interviewing David Brooks on his book *The Road to Character*; so here I am this morning contritely complying with the divine imperative of the omniscient guiding principle of my life to write the spiritual musing that I was called to write several weeks ago, **why be good?**

One Rule to Live By

In his review of *The Road to Character,* Pico Iyer writes: "Brooks begins with a sweeping overview of the non-intersecting worlds of moral logic and economic logic, as he has it, dividing us into an 'Adam 1,' who seeks success in the world, and an 'Adam 2,' more deeply committed to character and an inner life," and he goes on, summarizing the theme of Brooks' book: "To nurture your Adam 1 career, it makes sense to cultivate your strengths. To nurture your Adam 2 moral core, it is necessary to confront your weaknesses."

Brooks felt impelled to write *The Road to Character,* "to save my own soul," he said to Mary Hynes; and it was obvious from listening to him on *Tapestry* that he had invested way too much energy in his Adam 1 and not nearly enough energy in his Adam 2, and in the fifty-first year of his life he was making an honest effort to cultivate a better relationship with his Adam 2—his better self, if you will; and this brings me to the theme of today's spiritual musing, **why be good?**

This is a big theme, and it would certainly seem presumptuous to offer an answer to a question that has vexed some of the best minds in the world, most notable St. Augustine; but, in all humility, I bring a lifetime of gnostic wisdom to the table, which gives me the confidence to say that when all is said and done our essential purpose in life is to simply be a good person.

This presupposes a lifetime of questing for the meaning and purpose of life—a personal library of thousands of books and years of commitment to various teachings; so, my spiritual musings are nothing if not serious reflections upon the human predicament.

But to answer the question *why be good?* I have to call upon my creative unconscious to give me the proper image, because images are much more convincing than words will ever be; and in my mind's eye I see life as an elaborate maze, and man scrambling from one lifetime to the next to find his way out. And the man that I see in the maze today is *New York Times* columnist/author David Brooks.

"There is a doctrine uttered in secret that man is a prisoner who has no right to open the door of his prison and run away," said Socrates in Plato's *Phaedo,* which speaks to the perplexing nature of the human condition (the maze of life); and whether we are aware or not that we live more than one lifetime does not really matter, because

we will just keep coming back to live life over again until we are ready to look for the key that opens the door to our prison, which essentially renders reincarnation moot.

And herein lies the mystery that David Brooks yields to with his book *The Road to Character*, because Adam 1 brought him success in life but Adam 2 will open the door of his prison and set him free from the maze of the human condition. ***"Many are called, but few are chosen,"*** said Jesus; and David Brooks heard the call to save his soul by working upon his character and moral center.

Everyone will hear the call when life has made them ready, and David Brooks heard the call when he began to *notice* the distinction between Adam 1 and Adam 2 in some special people that he met serendipitously in his daily travels through life, as he tells us in his *New York Times* column:

> "About once a month, I run across a person who radiates an inner light. These people can be in any walk of life. They seem deeply good. They listen well. They make you feel funny and valued. You often catch them looking after other people and as they do so, their laugh is musical and their manner is infused with gratitude. They are not thinking about what wonderful work they are doing. They are not thinking about themselves at all.
>
> "When I meet such a person it brightens my whole day. But I confess I often have a sadder thought: It occurs to me that I've achieved a decent level of career success, but I have not achieved that. I have not achieved that generosity of spirit, or that depth of character.
>
> *"A few years ago, I realized that I wanted to be a bit more like those people. I realized that if I wanted to do that, I was going to have to work harder to save my own soul. I was going to have to have the sort of moral adventure that produces that kind of goodness. I was going to have to be better at balancing my life."*

I highlighted the last paragraph, because when life calls the voice is different; it comes from the depths of one's own tired soul, and it speaks a truth that makes one shudder. David Brooks shuddered when he heard the call, and he wrote *The Road to Character* to find the way out of his prison and bring balance to his Adam 1 and Adam 2, which speaks to the Master Key of our prison door—the liberating power of goodness.

Socrates, who believed the virtue of goodness to be the most noble virtue, said that the unexamined life was not worth living; and although that may be a bit harsh, because every life serves its destined purpose to wholeness and completeness, David Brooks examined his life and came to the realization that to have the generosity of spirit and depth of character that he needed to save his soul, he had to have *"moral adventures that produce that kind of goodness,"* and his moral adventures lay in shifting his priorities from those that were self-serving (Adam 1), to those that were more life-serving (Adam 2).

In short, David Brooks had to be less selfish and more giving, because the dynamics of the Master Key of Goodness declare that **the more you give of yourself, the more of yourself you will have to give**; and, conversely, **the less you give of yourself, the less of yourself you will have to give**. That's what Jesus meant by his paradoxical saying: *"He that loveth his life shall lose it; and he that hateth his life in this world shall keep it unto life eternal."* A deep mystery that cannot be resolved without the Master Key.

Why be good, then? Because there will come a time in one's life, whether it be in this lifetime or the next, when one will be called upon to open the door of their prison; and, like David Brooks, one will come to see that the only way to open their prison door is to simply be a good person.

And that's why we should be good!

About the Author

      Born with a spiritual restlessness that could not be tamed by my Christian faith, I became a spiritual seeker when I discovered reincarnation in Plato's Dialogues at the age of fifteen. I grew up in a small town in Northwestern Ontario, and at twenty-one I had my own pool hall and vending machine business, but my restless spirit called me away to seek out my destiny, and I sold my business and sailed to France.

      In the Alpine city of Annecy, in the Haute-Savoie region of France I had a dream that called me to my destiny. I entered into the mind of every person in the world and took every question they had ever asked and reduced them all to one question: *Why am I?* I returned to Canada and went to university to study philosophy to seek an answer to this haunting question, and by "chance" I discovered Gurdjieff, the redoubtable teacher of a system of transformative thought that he called "the Work." His Teaching excited my restless spirit and compelled me to seek out the answer to man's disquieting question in the fast, often tumultuous currents of daily living.

      Visit him at: http://ostocco.wix.com/ostocco
Spiritual Musings Blog:
http://www.spiritualmusingsbyoreststocco.blogspot.com

ALSO BY OREST STOCCO

POETRY

Not My Circus, Not My Monkeys

NOVELS

The Golden Seed
Tea with Grace
Jesus Wears Dockers
Healing with Padre Pio
Keeper of the Flame
My Unborn Child
On the Wings of Habitat
What Would I Say Today If I Were to Die Tomorrow?

NON-FICTION

A Sign of Things to Come
My Writing Life
Death, the Final Frontier
The Merciful Law of Divine Synchronicity
Gurdjieff Was Wrong But His Teaching Works
The Man of God Walks Alone
The Summoning of Noman
The Lion that Swallowed Hemingway
The Sum of All Spiritual Paths
Do We Have An Immortal Soul?
Stupidity Is Not a Gift of God
Letters to Padre Pio
Old Whore Life
Just Going with the Flow
Why Bother? The Riddle of the Good Samaritan
The Pearl of Great Price
In The Shade of the Maple Tree